NEW

Total English

INTERMEDIATE

Teacher's Book with Resource Disc

Will Moreton
with Grant Kempton

Contents

Resource Disc

     Photocopiable class activities and teaching notes

     Photocopiable video activities and answer key

     Progress tests with answer key and audio

     Achievement tests with answer key and teaching notes, audio and audioscripts

     Printable version of Class CD audioscripts and videoscripts

What's new about *New Total English*?

What makes *New Total English* different from – and better than – the first edition? Firstly, don't worry – we haven't thrown the baby out with the bathwater! We haven't changed everything. We've listened to what you said you liked about the first edition and have kept the most popular features. You'll certainly recognise the look, the format and some integral features from the first edition: the Lead-in pages, the easy-to-use lessons, the comprehensive Reference and Review and practice sections, the popular video clips. Changing to the new edition won't mean that you have to get to grips with a completely new course.

Real solutions to real needs

Some things <u>are</u> different, however. We've looked at every aspect of the course and tried to find solutions for some of your real needs. We've improved the flow of many of the lessons in the Students' Book, integrating more Can do statements and making sure that they all have clear 'outcomes'. We've also given more space to important aspects of language learning such as vocabulary, writing and listening. There's a free online Vocabulary Trainer with each level to help learners memorise new words and phrases; a complete Writing bank at the back of the Students' Book, covering different text types and writing sub-skills as well as new semi-authentic listening extracts to help students gain confidence in dealing with features such as redundancy, hesitation and ungrammatical speech. And, as you'd expect with a new edition, we've given the grammar, vocabulary and pronunciation syllabus a complete overhaul as well as updating much of the content.

New digital components

We've also included new digital components in the course package. The ActiveBook component features the Students' Book pages in digital format and includes integrated audio and video as well as interactive exercises for students to do in class or at home. The ActiveTeach component will help you get the most out of the course with its range of interactive whiteboard software tools and *MyTotalEnglishLab* will help students get better results with its range of interactive practice exercises, progress tests and automatic gradebook.

To sum up, we've kept all the best ingredients of the first edition, improved other features and added exciting new digital components to make *New Total English* an even better package. We hope you and your students will continue to enjoy using it.

The *New Total English* author team

Students' Book with ActiveBook and DVD

The *New Total English* Students' Books with ActiveBook and DVD are divided into 10–12 units that contain approximately 80–120 hours of teaching material. Each unit contains a balanced mix of grammar, vocabulary, pronunciation and skills:

- clear aims and objectives linked to the CEFR (Common European Framework of Reference)
- revised grammar, vocabulary and pronunciation syllabus
- new reading, listening and video material
- new Writing bank with model texts and focus on sub-skills
- revised and extended Pronunciation bank

ActiveBook:

- digital version of Students' Book with interactive activities and integrated audio and video
- video clips can be selected when you use the ActiveBook in your computer, or play it in a DVD player

Students' Book with ActiveBook, DVD and MyLab

Packaged with the *New Total English* Students' Book with ActiveBook and DVD, *MyTotalEnglishLab* provides students with everything they need to make real progress both in class and at home:

MyTotalEnglishLab:

- interactive exercises with feedback
- regular progress and achievement tests
- automatic marking and gradebook

Class CDs

The *New Total English* Class CDs contain all the recorded material from the Students' Books.

Workbook and Audio CD

The *New Total English* Workbooks contain further practice of language areas covered in the corresponding units of the Students' Books:

- extra grammar, vocabulary, skills and pronunciation exercises
- regular Review and Consolidation sections
- audioscripts and accompanying Audio CD
- with and without key versions available

Teacher's Book with Resource Disc

The *New Total English* Teacher's Books provide all the support teachers need to get the most out of the course:

- background notes and instructions on how to exploit each unit
- suggestions for warm-up and extension activities

Resource Disc:

- extensive bank of photocopiable and printable classroom activities
- editable and printable progress and achievement tests
- audio and video scripts

ActiveTeach and DVD

The *New Total English* Teacher's Books will be further enhanced by the ActiveTeach component which features:

- Students' Book in digital format with all the material from the ActiveBook
- all the material from the Resource Disc
- interactive whiteboard software tools
- video clips can be selected when you use the ActiveTeach in your computer, or play it in a DVD player

Vocabulary Trainer

The *New Total English* Vocabulary Trainer is a new online learning tool designed to help students revise and memorise key vocabulary from the course.
Check this exciting new component out on
www.newtotalenglish.vocabtrainer.net

Website

New Total English has its own dedicated website. In addition to background information about the course and authors, the website features teaching tips, downloadable worksheets, links to other useful websites as well as special offers and competitions. Join us online at
www.pearsonlongman.com/newtotalenglish

Each unit of the *New Total English* Students' Books has the same structure:

- **Lead-in page**
  - acts as a springboard into the topic of the unit and engages learners' interest.
  - introduces essential vocabulary related to the topic so that learners start with the same basic grounding.

- **Input lessons**
  - three input lessons, thematically linked, offering interesting angles on the unit topic. Lessons are double-page at lower levels and triple-page at Intermediate and above.
  - each input lesson leads towards a Can do learning objective in line with the CEFR Can do statements.
  - each 90-minute lesson focuses on a specific grammar area and includes vocabulary and skills work.
  - each unit usually contains at least two reading texts, a substantial listening element (including semi-authentic listenings) and pronunciation work.
  - How to... boxes develop students' competence in using language, in line with the CEFR.
  - Lifelong learning boxes offer tips and strategies for developing learners' study skills.

- **Communication page**
  - revises language taught in the previous three lessons in a freer, more communicative context.
  - each communication task practises a range of skills and has a measurable goal or outcome.

- **Vocabulary page (Intermediate and above)**
  - focuses on vocabulary systems and word-building.
  - helps learners to expand and develop their vocabulary.

- **Reference page**
  - summarises the main grammar points covered in each unit and provides a list of key vocabulary.
  - helps learners to catch up if they miss lessons and is an essential revision tool.

- **Review and practice page**
  - provides a range of exercises to consolidate key grammar and vocabulary covered in the unit.
  - can be used to check progress, enabling teachers to identify areas that need further practice.

- **Writing bank**
  - provides models and tips on how to deal with different types of writing (letters, emails and so on).
  - provides guidance on different writing sub-skills such as punctuation, spelling and paragraph construction.

- **Pronunciation bank**
  - provides a list of English phonemes, guidance on sound-spelling correspondences and weak forms.
  - summarises the pronunciation points covered in each unit of the Students' Book.

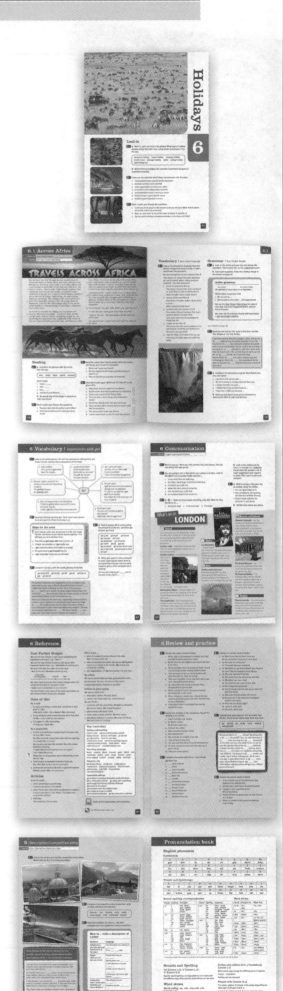

A range of support components help you get the most out of each unit:

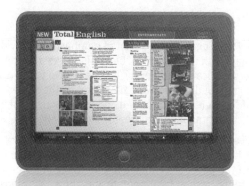

- **Students' Book with ActiveBook and DVD**
  - digital version of Students' Book with interactive activites.
  - integrated audio for Students' Book listening activities (including Reference pages and pronunciation activities).
  - wide variety of video clips (including drama, documentary and comedy) which can be selected when you use the ActiveBook in your computer, or play it in a DVD player.
  - interactive video activities.

- **Workbook with Audio CD**
  - consolidation of work covered in the Students' Book.
  - extensive practice of grammar, vocabulary and skills, including pronunciation.
  - regular Review and consolidation sections.
  - can be used in class or for self-study.

- **Students' Book with ActiveBook and MyLab**
  - interactive Workbook with instant feedback and automatic marking.
  - progress and achievement tests with automatic marking and gradebook.

- **Teacher's Book with Resource Disc**
  - provides step by step teaching notes including ideas for warmers and extension activities.
  - includes background notes and tips for dealing with particularly difficult language points.
  - Resource Disc features an extensive bank of photocopiable and printable classroom activities as well as editable and printable progress and achievement tests.

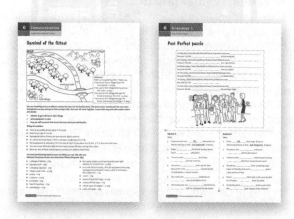

- **ActiveTeach**
  - digital version of the Students' Book to be used in class.
  - video clips that can be selected when you use the ActiveTeach in your computer, or play it in a DVD player.
  - all the material from the Teacher's Book Resource Disc.
  - a range of interactive whiteboard software tools.

- **Vocabulary Trainer**
  www.newtotalenglish.vocabtrainer.net
  - new online learning tool designed to help students revise and memorise key vocabulary from each unit of the course.

- **Website**
  www.pearsonlongman.com/newtotalenglish
  - features background information about the course and authors as well as teaching tips, downloadable worksheets and links to other useful websites.

Teaching approaches

Grammar

New Total English places a lot of emphasis on providing learners with the grammar 'building blocks' they need to communicate confidently. It aims to give learners a thorough foundation in grammar and, at the same time, provides plenty of structured and free practice. Each unit deals with grammar in a broadly similar way:

- **Clear presentation and analysis**

Each lesson has a clear grammar aim which is stated at the top of the page. Lessons are double-page at lower levels and triple-page at Intermediate and above. New language items are presented in context via reading and/or listening texts and grammar rules are then analysed and explained via the Active grammar boxes, which are a key feature of each lesson. *New Total English* takes a 'guided discovery' approach to grammar and learners are actively invited to think about grammar and work out the rules for themselves.

Active grammar

(Past Simple)   (Past Perfect Simple)

We **wanted** to remember all we **had seen** ...

Which action happened first?

1 *We saw things ...*
2 *We wanted to remember ...* (the experience)

We use the *Past Perfect*/*Past Simple* to make it clear that one event happened before another one in the past.

We make the Past Perfect Simple with *had/hadn't* + *past participle*/*infinitive*.

- **Varied, regular practice**

Once learners have grasped the important rules, all new language is then practised in a variety of different ways so that learners are able to use the grammar with confidence. Practice activities include form-based exercises designed to help learners manipulate the new structures as well as more meaningful, personalised practice. Additional grammar practice exercises can be found in the Review and practice sections at the end of each unit as well as in the Workbooks and *MyTotalEnglishLab*. This component, which features the Workbook exercises in digital format, also provides learners with extra guidance, tips and feedback. The Teacher's Book provides a lot of guidance on how to deal with tricky grammar points. It also contains a Resource Disc with an extensive bank of printable and photocopiable classroom grammar activities which are designed to practise the language in freer, more communicative contexts.

- **Easily accessible reference material**

In addition to the explanations contained in the Active grammar boxes, there is a Reference section at the end of each unit which provides a summary of the grammar rules as well as extra language notes and examples. Audio recordings of the rules and examples are available on the ActiveBook and ActiveTeach components.

Vocabulary

New Total English recognises the central role that vocabulary plays in successful communication. The emphasis is on providing learners with high-frequency, useful vocabulary which is regularly practised and revised. New vocabulary is presented and practised in a variety of different ways.

- **Lead-in pages**

Each unit starts with a Lead-in page which provides a springboard into the topic of each unit. Featuring a variety of attractive picture prompts and related exercises, the Lead-in pages are designed to help teachers elicit vocabulary that learners already know as well as pre-teach essential vocabulary for the rest of the unit.

- **Topic-based vocabulary**

Each unit focuses on useful vocabulary relating to the topic of the lessons as well as vocabulary arising from the listening and reading texts. Items are generally presented in context and practised through a variety of exercises.

Vocabulary | biographies

 Match the phrases (1–6) from the listening with the meanings (a–f).

1 a difficult start in life
2 one of the greatest ... of all times
3 against the odds
4 from an early age
5 is widely considered to be
6 is best known for

a although it seemed very unlikely
b most people agree this person is
c one of the best ... ever
d problems in childhood
e from childhood or youth
f is famous because of

Additional vocabulary practice is provided in the Review and practice sections of the Students' Book and in the practice exercises in the Workbook. Photocopiable vocabulary activities are also available on the ActiveTeach and on the Resource Disc which accompanies the Teacher's Book.

- **Vocabulary pages (Intermediate and above)**

At the lower levels there is a lot of emphasis on building learners' knowledge of high-frequency words and phrases as well as common lexical sets. Learners are introduced to collocation work at a very early stage and from intermediate level onwards, there is a greater emphasis on vocabulary systems and word-building.

- **Vocabulary Trainer**

Each level of *New Total English* is accompanied by a Vocabulary Trainer. This unique online learning tool focuses on the key vocabulary in each unit and helps learners memorise new words and phrases.

Speaking

The key aim for most learners is spoken fluency. However, most learners find it difficult to talk about topics which hold no interest for them and many cannot express themselves easily without support. *New Total English* develops spoken fluency in a number of ways – by giving learners discussion topics they want to talk about; by setting up situations where they are motivated to communicate in order to complete a specific task; by providing clear models and examples of how to structure discourse and by encouraging them, wherever possible, to express their own ideas and opinions.

• Fresh angles on familiar topics

Topics in *New Total English* have been chosen for their intrinsic interest and relevance. Obscure topics, i.e. those which are only likely to appeal to a minority audience, have been avoided and discussion questions have been deliberately chosen to encourage learners to draw on their own lives and experience. Inevitably, many of the topics have been covered in other ELT coursebooks but wherever possible, we have tried to find a fresh angle on them.

• Structured speaking activities

Many of the lessons in *New Total English* culminate in a structured final speaking activity in the form of a survey, roleplay etc. Learners are given time to prepare what they are going to say and prompts to help them. The activities often involve pair and group work to maximise learners' opportunities to speak in class. Many of the structured speaking activities are linked to the CEFR Can do statements.

• How to... boxes

There are regular How to... boxes throughout the course which focus on the words and expressions learners need to carry out specific functions. e.g ordering food in a restaurant.

How to... describe an object

Comparing it to something else	It's a kind _____ music player.
	It's similar _____ an Mp3.
	It looks like an Mp3 player.
Describing its function	It's used _____ playing music.
	It's used _____ joggers.
	It's a thing _____ playing music.
Describing its features	It's made _____ plastic.
	It's rectangular/square/circular etc.

• Communication pages

Communication pages feature at the end of each unit and engage learners in a variety of problem-solving tasks and activities. These give learners practice in a number of different skills including speaking.

• Photocopiable class activities

The photocopiable activities on the ActiveTeach and on the Resource Disc are also specifically designed to promote speaking practice.

Pronunciation

New Total English pays particular attention to pronunciation, which is integrated into lessons which present new language. The pronunciation syllabus includes word and sentence stress, weak forms, intonation and difficult sounds. The Pronunciation bank at the back of the Students' Books provides a summary of all pronunciation points in the book as well as a list of English phonemes, guidance on sound-spelling correspondences and weak forms. The ActiveTeach includes audio to accompany the Pronunciation bank. There is additional pronunciation practice in the Workbooks and Workbook Audio CD.

Listening

Listening is one of the most difficult skills to master and *New Total English* places particular emphasis on developing learners' confidence in this area. Listening texts include short scripted dialogues as well as longer, unscripted semi-authentic listenings. There is additional listening practice in the Workbooks and the video clips on the ActiveBook and ActiveTeach components further enhance learners' confidence in understanding the spoken word.

• Scripted listening activities

Scripted listening activities include short dialogues as well as longer extracts including conversations, interviews and stories. There are lots of simple 'Listen and check your answer' exercises as well as longer, more challenging extracts where learners have to listen for specific information.

• Semi-authentic listening activities

As well as the more traditional scripted listening activities, *New Total English* also includes a range of semi-authentic listening texts, i.e. recordings of one or more people speaking in an unprepared, unscripted way, although they are aware of the relevant level and therefore have adapted their own language to a certain extent accordingly. Learners benefit from listening to a semi-authentic recording because the spontaneity of spoken English means that it is full of false starts, hesitations, redundancy and 'ungrammatical' sentences. Learners need to be aware of these features and they need to develop confidence in dealing with them in order to cope with listening in the 'real world'.

• Video clips

New Total English provides a video clip to accompany each unit of the Students' Book. The videos feature a range of authentic material from a variety of different sources including short films and clips from TV documentaries and drama. The video clips expose learners to real English and are designed to motivate learners to 'raise their game' in terms of developing their listening skills.

To make the material more accessible to learners, photocopiable activities for each video clip are available on the ActiveTeach and on the Resource Disc. There are additional interactive video exercises on the ActiveBook and ActiveTeach which students can complete in class or at home.

The video clips are available on the ActiveBook which accompanies each Students' Book and on the ActiveTeach. You can select the video clips when you use the discs in your computer, or you can play them in a DVD player.

Reading

Many learners need to be able to read texts in English – for their studies, for work or simply for pleasure – and *New Total English* recognises that reading is an extremely important skill that can have a beneficial effect on all aspects of language learning including vocabulary, spelling and writing.

New Total English encourages learners to read as much as possible – in most units there are at least two substantial reading texts – and care has been taken to introduce students to as wide a range of text types as possible, from simple forms and advertisements to short texts from newspapers and magazines.

Reading texts are accompanied by a range of activities that are designed to check comprehension as well as develop key reading skills such as reading for gist, reading for specific information, guessing the meaning of words from the context and so on.

• Choice of texts

As with the listening material in *New Total English*, texts have been chosen for their intrinsic interest as well as for their usefulness in providing a vehicle for the particular grammar and vocabulary points in focus. Many of the texts have been adapted from authentic, real-life sources such as magazines and websites, and where texts have been adapted or graded, every effort has been made to remain faithful to the orignal text type in terms of content and style.

• Exploitation of texts

Each reading text in *New Total English* is accompanied by a number of exploitation exercises that have been carefully selected to develop learners' reading skills. Activities include comprehension and vocabulary work as well as practice in dealing with different reading sub-skills such as reading for gist. There are also a number of jigsaw readings where learners work together and share information.

Unit 1 Lesson 1.1 Exercise 10a

Student B

Read the text below and answer the questions.

1   How did François behave at the restaurant?
2   What did his parents-in-law think?
3   Why did he behave that way?
4   How did he feel afterwards?

Not in my culture...

The first time they met François, my parents insisted on taking him to the nicest Persian restaurant in Los Angeles. My father ordered some starters, which François ate enthusiastically while questioning my mother about the ingredients:

'Are these Persian cucumbers?'

'Is the cheese made with sheep's milk?'

Once the starters were finished, François selected the biggest dish on the menu, the *sultani*, a combination of lamb, beef, and

---

• Length and complexity

The length and complexity of the reading texts in *New Total English* get more challenging as the course progresses. At lower levels, the texts are very short and the emphasis is on training learners to read for specific information. At higher levels, learners are introduced to a a greater range and variety text types and more emphasis is placed on textual analysis.

Writing

In these days of electronic media, it is easy to forget that writing is not simply speech written down – effective writing has all sorts of conventions that differ from speech and that are necessary to learn in one's own language as well as in a foreign language.

New Total English pays particular attention to the important skill of writing. One of the most important new features of the revised edition is the Writing bank at the back of each Students' Book which contains 10–12 lessons that focus on different types of writing – emails, postcards, formal and informal letters and so on. Each lesson also provides additional advice and guidance on different writing sub-skills such as punctuation, spelling and paragraph construction.

• Model text types

Each Writing bank lesson has a Can do statement which refers to the written output that students complete at the end of the lesson. The lesson usually starts with a warmer that engages students in the topic. Learners then go on to focus on a model of the text type and in most cases, there is some comprehension work to ensure that students are familiar with the content before they start working on the format and related sub-skills. The lesson always finishes with a contextualised written output.

• Writing sub-skills

One of the most important aspects of the Writing bank is that it examines the sub-skills of writing in detail. This is important as it helps learners to build on and develop their writing skills, rather than simply providing practice in writing. Among the sub-skills covered are punctuation, grammatical cohesion, paragraphing and features such as varying the vocabulary used to both enhance interest and ensure lexical cohesion.

• How to... boxes

How to... boxes are a particular feature of the Writing bank. They usually focus on a particular sub-skill of writing and in some cases on written conventions, such as email or letter layout, appropriate formality of language for the text type or order of presentation of the content (such as in a review).

How to... use formal linkers

1 Adding an idea	*Moreover,*
	Furthermore,
	_____ ,
2 Making a contrast	*Nevertheless,*
	_____ ,
	_____ ,
	_____ ,
3 Concluding	*Overall,*
	_____ ,

Learner training

New Total English places a strong emphasis on learner training and good study habits are encouraged and developed via the Lifelong learning boxes which are featured in many lessons. The Lifelong learning boxes provide useful tips and suggestions on how to continue learning outside the classroom.

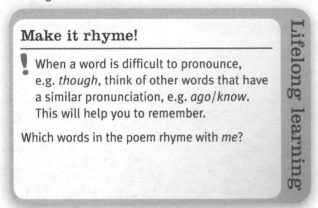

Make it rhyme!

! When a word is difficult to pronounce, e.g. *though*, think of other words that have a similar pronunciation, e.g. *ago/know*. This will help you to remember.

Which words in the poem rhyme with *me*?

Lifelong learning

Revision and testing

There are plenty of opportunities for revision in *New Total English* and language is constantly recycled throughout the course. At the end of every unit, there are special Review and practice pages which take the form of mini-progress checks, enabling learners to identify areas where they might need further practice. Interactive versions of the activities on these pages are available on the ActiveBook and ActiveTeach. The Workbook and accompanying Audio CD provide further practice in grammar, vocabulary and skills covered in the corresponding Students' Book. The Workbook is available in with key and without key versions.

For learners who are really serious about making rapid progress in English, *MyTotalEnglishLab* provides the perfect solution. This exciting component features the Workbook exercises in digital format as well as tips and feedback on common errors.

Regular progress and achievement tests are provided on the ActiveTeach, Resource Disc and *MyTotalEnglishLab*. *MyTotalEnglishLab* also includes automatic marking and a gradebook.

New Total English and exams

The table below shows how the different levels of *New Total English* relate to the University of Cambridge ESOL main suite examinations in terms of the language taught and the topics covered.

Starter	Builds foundation for KET
Elementary	Useful for KET
Pre-Intermediate	Useful for PET
Intermediate	**Useful for FCE**
Upper Intermediate	Useful for FCE
Advanced	Useful for CAE

While *New Total English* is not an examination preparation course, a student who has, for example, completed the Upper-intermediate level would have sufficient language to attempt the Cambridge ESOL FCE (First Certificate in English) examination. Many of the exercises in the *New Total English* Students' Books and other components are similar in format to those found in the Cambridge ESOL main suite examinations but specific training is required for all EFL examinations and we would strongly recommend this.

New Total English and the CEFR

New Total English is correlated to the CEFR (Common European Framework of Reference). Please see the *New Total English* website:
www.pearsonlongman.com/newtotalenglish for details of CEFR Can do statements for each level of the course.

CEFR	
A1	Starter
A2	Elementary
B1	Pre-intermediate
B1+	**Intermediate**
B2	Upper Intermediate
C1	Advanced

Students' Book Contents

13

Students' Book Contents

UNIT		Can do	Grammar
6 **Holidays** p 77–90	6.1 Across Africa	Describe a memorable photo	Past Perfect Simple
	6.2 Down under	Get around a new place	Uses of *like*
	6.3 Travellers' tales	Talk about unexpected events	Articles
	Vocabulary p 87 **Communication** p 88 **Writing bank** p 158	Expressions with *get* Suggest and respond to ideas Write a detailed description of a place **How to...** write a description of a place	
7 **Learning** p 91–104	7.1 Learning from experience	Describe a learning experience	Subject and object questions
	7.2 Great teachers	Describe a teacher from your past	*Used to* and *would*
	7.3 It's never too late	Carry out an interview	Modals of ability, past and present
	Vocabulary p 101 **Communication** p 102 **Writing bank** p 159	Learning: idioms and phrasal verbs Discuss options and make a decision Summarise a short article **How to...** write a summary	
8 **Change** p 105–118	8.1 Changing the rules	Discuss problems and suggest changes	Second Conditional
	8.2 Change the world	Express and respond to opinions	Adverbs
	8.3 Making the right decisions	Describe the effect of important decisions	Third Conditional
	Vocabulary p 115 **Communication** p 116 **Writing bank** p 160	Word building Express and respond to feelings Write about change **How to...** write a personal email	
9 **Jobs** p 119–132	9.1 Freedom at work	Ask for clarification	*Make, let, allow*
	9.2 Skills and experience	Take notes while listening	Reported speech
	9.3 New on the job	Describe job skills	Past obligation/permission
	Vocabulary p 129 **Communication** p 130 **Writing bank** p 161	UK and US English Answer interview questions Write a formal email/letter of application **How to...** write a formal email/letter of applicati	
10 **Memories** p 133–146	10.1 Childhood memories	Respond to a poem	*I wish/If only*
	10.2 Memorable people	Briefly describe a famous person	Review of past tenses
	10.3 Saying goodbye	Understand cultural differences	Phrasal verbs
	Vocabulary p 143 **Communication** p 144 **Writing bank** p 162	The senses Talking about memories Write a simple essay **How to...** write a simple essay	

Communication activities p 147–152	**Writing bank** p 153–162	**Pronunciation bank** p 163–164

14

1 Friends

Overview

CEFR Can do objectives

1.1 Encourage further conversation by expressing interest in what is said
1.2 Start a conversation with a stranger
1.3 Retell a simple narrative in your own words
Communication Describe a friend
Writing bank Write a semi-formal email, introduce yourself

CEFR Portfolio ideas

a) Write an Internet dialogue with a friend. Keep the conversation going by using echo questions.
b) In groups of four, roleplay a party situation where you are meeting and introducing new friends and record it on video.
c) Write a short story about a strange experience you have had. Try to use as many time expressions as possible.
d) Imagine you are registering your friend for a dating agency. Prepare a video introduction about your friend. Make sure you make it as positive as possible.

Lead-in

OPTIONAL WARMER

Ask Ss to write their own name in the centre of a piece of paper. They then choose a maximum of six family and friends' names. Ask Ss to write close friends or family near their name and other names further away.

1 ▶ Put Ss in pairs to tell each other if they have ever been in situations like the ones shown in the photos. Ss discuss what types of relationships the photos show. Get feedback from the class.

Answers
Main photo: old/best/close friends
Top photo: colleagues, manager and employee
Middle photo: husband, wife
Bottom photo: colleagues, friends, acquaintances

2 ▶ In pairs, Ss put the words into four groups. If there are any words the Ss don't know, encourage them to explain them to each other. Check the answers with the whole class. Practise saying any words which the Ss find difficult to pronounce.

Suggested answers
a) boss, classmate, colleague
b) father-in-law, husband, stepmother
c) acquaintance, best friend, close friend, ex-girlfriend, friend of a friend, old friend
d) stranger, team-mate

▶ Ask Ss to add any more words they know to each group. Go round and monitor to check correct spelling. Get feedback from the whole class and write Ss' words on the board.

3 ▶ Tell Ss to cover column B of the table. In pairs, they read column A of the table and discuss what the phrases in **bold** mean. Get feedback from various Ss. Ss uncover column B of the table and match the **bold** phrases from A with the definitions from B. Check the answers with the class and elicit more example sentences.

Answers

1	h	3	e	5	c	7	f
2	d	4	a	6	b	8	g

4 ▶ Ss look back at the words from the box in exercise 2. Ask them to write down four people they know and choose four adjectives for each person. Put Ss in pairs to describe their relationships with the people they chose. Monitor and assist where necessary. Write an example on the board: *I get on really well with my boss. He's really funny and outgoing.* Get feedback from the whole class and write examples on the board.

1.1 A lot in common?

In this lesson, Ss discover what they know about unusual hobbies and use phrasal verbs to find out about each other's spare-time activities. They then listen to unusual hobbies and study the use of auxiliary verbs in the listening. After practising how to pronounce echo questions, Ss complete the lesson by finding out what they have in common with their class colleagues.

Speaking and listening

1 ▶ Put students in pairs to match the hobbies (1–5) with the photos (A–E). Check the answers with the whole class. Ask if any Ss do these activities and elicit what they know about them.

> **Answers**
> 1 E   2 C   3 D   4 A   5 B

2a ▶ Focus Ss' attention on the gapped sentences 1–10. In pairs, Ss complete the gaps with the correct prepositions from the box. Let Ss compare their answers with a different partner and then check the answers with the whole class.

> **Answers**
> 1 about   4 on   8 in
> 2 for   5 about   9 to
> 3 at   6 on   10 in
> 7 about

b ▶ Divide the class into groups of three or four. In their groups, Ss choose five of the questions in exercise 2a to ask other Ss in the class. Put Ss in pairs so they are working with a partner from a different group. Ss write down what they think their partner's answers will be.

c ▶ Ss ask each other their questions and write down the answers. Get feedback from various students.

3a ▶ 🔘 1.2 Focus Ss' attention on the questions from exercise 2a. Play the recording. Ss listen and make notes of the questions that each speaker answers. Ss compare their answers in pairs. Draw a table on the board with four columns. In the first column, write the numbers of the speakers. In the second column, write the question that each speaker answers.

> **Answers**
> Dialogue 1 – question 3   Dialogue 3 – question 6
> Dialogue 2 – question 9   Dialogue 4 – question 8
>   Dialogue 5 – question 4

b ▶ Elicit the key words from the Ss and write them in the third column of the table on the board.

> **Answers**
> Dialogue 1 – juggling
> Dialogue 2 – astronomy (daughter not speaker)
> Dialogue 3 – snowkiting
> Dialogue 4 – Chinese
> Dialogue 5 – sudoku

c ▶ Play the recording again and ask Ss to take notes. Ss compare their answers in pairs. Check the answers with the whole class and complete the final column of the table.

> **Answers (Final Table on the board):**
>
> | Question | Key word | More information |
> |---|---|---|
> | 3 | juggling | can juggle with five balls; can't juggle with plates |
> | 9 | astronomy | studies stars and planets; has an expensive telescope |
> | 6 | snowkiting | kite attached to board; terrifying; does it once a year. |
> | 8 | Chinese | learning Mandarin and t'ai chi (a kind of martial art) |
> | 4 | sudoku | Japanese number puzzle; all lines and boxes must include every number between 1 and 9 |

4 ▶ Put Ss into pairs. Give Ss a few minutes to talk about any unusual hobbies or activities they have tried. Get feedback from the whole class.

> **OPTIONAL VARIATION**
> Ss individually think of an unusual hobby or activity that they have tried. Then, in pairs, Ss ask each other a maximum of twenty questions to try and guess what the activity or hobby is. Ss can only answer 'yes' or 'no'. The best examples can then be used in a class activity.

> **OPTIONAL EXTENSION**
> Ss prepare a poster presentation of an unusual hobby or activity that other Ss might not know much about.

Grammar | auxiliary verbs (do, be, have)

> **OPTIONAL WARMER**
> Tell Ss a hobby or sport that you do. Write the following two options next to each other at the bottom of the board. *1* The number of times you do the hobby/sport a week, e.g. *Two or three times a week.* *2 No, I don't.* In pairs, Ss think of questions they can ask you to give these two answers. Elicit the Ss' questions and write correct questions above each answer. Elicit/teach the difference between the two questions. (1 is a *Wh-* question and 2 is a *Yes/No* question.) Focus Ss' attention on answer 2 and explain that it is a short answer. Elicit the verb that is used from the question. Explain that it is a negative answer and elicit/teach the negative verbs used in first and third person for the Present, Past and Present Perfect. At this stage, don't discuss auxiliaries.

5a ▶ Ask Ss: *What are auxiliary verbs?* (*do, be, have*) and *Why do we use them?* (*they are used as helping verbs, e.g. in the present perfect, past perfect and, continuous tenses; in the passive form and for questions, negatives and question tags*). Ss then add auxiliary verbs to the Active grammar box.

b ▶ 🔘 1.3 Ss listen and check their answers before doing a class check. Ss then practise saying the dialogues in pairs. Draw Ss' attention to the Reference on page 19 and elicit the auxiliary verbs in the examples.

Active grammar

1	did	6	haven't
2	Does	7	don't
3	Have	8	have
4	Are	9	is
5	don't		

---

6 ▶ Ss read and correct the mistakes in the four dialogues. Let them compare with a partner and then get feedback from the whole class.

Answers

1 A: What subjects do you <u>like</u> reading about?
   A: Are you? What sports <u>do</u> you like?
2 B: I <u>don't</u> worry much. I guess sometimes I worry about money.
   A: <u>Do</u> you? I do too.
3 A: <u>Do you use</u> the Internet a lot?
   B: No, not really. I <u>don't</u> have time. Do you?
4 B: No, I <u>haven't</u>. What about you?
   A: Yes, it <u>was</u>.

OPTIONAL EXTENSION

Put Ss into pairs. Each pair chooses one dialogue from exercise 6 and personalises the information. Ss then act out their dialogues for another pair or the whole class.

Pronunciation | intonation in echo questions

7a ▶ Ss do the task individually, using part C of the Active grammar box to help them. Ss can then check in pairs, but do not do a class check.

b ▶ 🔘 1.4 Play the recording. Ss listen and check their answers. Get feedback from the whole class.

Answers

1	Do you?	5	Are you?
2	Has he?	6	Do you?
3	Are you?	7	Have they?
4	Did you?	8	Does he?

---

c ▶ Play the first question and answer again and write the echo question on the board. Elicit whether Ss think it shows interest or lack of interest (*interested*). Draw an arrow above the question and ask Ss: *Does the intonation*

go up or down at the end? (*up*). Play the remaining echo questions, using the same procedure for each one. Check that Ss have understood the difference between interested and uninterested intonation. Draw Ss' attention to the Pronunciation bank on page 164.

Answers

1	interested	5	uninterested
2	interested	6	uninterested
3	uninterested	7	interested
4	interested	8	interested

---

d ▶ Model the example with a student. Ss practise the other dialogues in pairs, adding extra information where possible. Get feedback from various pairs in the class. Explain to Ss that they shouldn't overemphasise their interest as this can mean they are being sarcastic which can have the opposite effect.

Speaking

8a ▶ Read the instructions with the Ss and check understanding. Go through the example. Give Ss a few minutes to write the two things they are looking for.

b ▶ Tell Ss they are now going to go round the class, asking questions to find people who match their sentences from part a. Encourage Ss to use the forms they studied in the Active grammar box. Model the example, then get Ss to mingle to complete the activity. Get feedback from various Ss by asking them to report back on someone who they had something in common with.

OPTIONAL EXTENSION

Tell Ss that for the next lesson, they are going to find out about an activity, hobby or skill that is unusual or different. They should find out all they can. At the beginning of the next lesson, put Ss into groups of four and select a student in each group to start. The student starts with a statement on the subject they have researched as if it is their skill, interest or hobby, e.g. *I have a snail farm at home.* The other Ss in the group should ask questions to find out as much as they can, using the forms from the Active grammar box. Tell Ss that they have to keep asking questions and getting answers for at least ninety seconds. Then change the speaker. Continue until all four Ss have presented their topic.

Reading and speaking

9 ▶ Put Ss in pairs and give them two or three minutes to discuss the questions. Get feedback from the whole class and write the typical features of the Ss' culture/ cultures on the board. Tell Ss that these features might be considered the *stereotype* for their culture. Ask Ss: *Do you think all people in your culture are like this? Do you think stereotypes are helpful?* Then, discuss the Ss' answers to the last question as a whole class.

10a ▶ Put Ss in pairs and label pairs A or B. Ss A individually read and answer the questions on page 10, whilst Ss B individually read and answer the questions on page 147. Ss then check the answers with their partner. At this stage, do not do a class check and do not give the correct answers.

> **Answers**
> A 1 He called her 'gordita' – little fatty.
>   2 She felt angry but didn't say anything.
>   3 Everyone was shocked. and she felt embarrassed.
>   4 He said that 'gordita' is something you say to people to show you love them.
> B 1 He ate as much as he could.
>   2 They were surprised by how much he ate and worried he would be sick.
>   3 He thought it would please his parents-in-law.
>   4 He needed to lie down.

b ▶ Reform pairs with one student A and one student B. Tell Ss to tell their partners the story they read in their own words. Encourage Ss to do this with their books closed, only opening them if they really get stuck. In the class check, ask Ss B to tell you about Ss A's story and vice-versa. Then check the answers for exercise 10a with the whole class.

c ▶ Ask Ss in pairs to discuss any possible cultural misunderstandings they have had. In the class check, discuss some of these and ask Ss what could have been done to avoid the misunderstanding.

> **OPTIONAL EXTENSION**
> Ss think of a possible cultural misunderstanding to act out. Other Ss have to guess what the misunderstanding is and what could be done to avoid it.

1.2 How many friends?

In this lesson, Ss listen to someone talking about their friends. Through this context they study vocabulary for describing personality and practise pronunciation of 'ea'. They also use different strategies for making friends with a stranger. Ss read about the importance of having lots of friends which provides the stimulus for revision of the Present Simple and Present Continuous tenses.

Listening

> Cricket is one of the national sports of England and is played in many countries of the old British Empire (e.g. England, Australia, New Zealand, India, Pakistan, Bangladesh, Sri Lanka, South Africa, West Indies). It is played by two teams of eleven players with a bat and ball and a target called a *wicket*. The game is considered to be about four hundred years old and in recent years has expanded across the world so that it is now the second most widely played team sport in the world.

1a ▶ Ss discuss the questions in pairs. Change pairs and let Ss discuss again. Get feedback from various Ss, who report what their partners told them.

b ▶ 🔘 1.5 Play the recording, ask Ss to compare answers in pairs, then get feedback from the class. Ask Ss: *What is different about this friendship? (There are eighteen years between them.) Do you think you could be friends with Rob? Why/Why not?*

> **Answers**
> 1 Rob
> 2 They met about three years ago while working at the same school.
> 3 Rob seems younger than he is; he's sincere, funny and kind. They have a lot in common and have the same sense of humour.
> 4 Rob likes cricket.

Vocabulary | personality

2a ▶ Divide the class into pairs and ask the Ss to do the activity. Pairs then form groups of four to check their answers. Before doing a class check, elicit which adjectives are positive and negative and then let them check again.

> **Answers**
> 1 pleasant   6 upbeat
> 2 kind-hearted   7 encouraging
> 3 dependable   8 sulky
> 4 jealous   9 selfish
> 5 generous   10 mean

> **OPTIONAL EXTENSION**
> Ss act out a person with one of the characteristics and the other Ss have to guess which adjective is being is shown.

b ▶ In pairs, Ss discuss the question and give reasons for their answer. Then have a class discussion.

> **OPTIONAL VARIATION**
>
> 1) This can be done as a pyramid activity. Ss start in pairs and try and agree on the three most important adjectives. Then repeat the task with two pairs per group and then again with four pairs. Get feedback from the whole class.
> 2) With stronger classes, after the pairwork, one student comes to the board and argues why one adjective is important. Then other Ss in the class must give reasons why they disagree. If the Ss cannot defend one of the objections, then the student who made the objection comes to the board and the process starts again. At the end of the time allocated, the adjective being defended is the winner.

c ▶ Ss do the activity in pairs. Get feedback from various Ss.

Pronunciation | sounds and spelling: 'ea'

3a ▶ 🔘 1.6 Ss listen to the words and put them in the correct column.

> **Answers**
> /iː/ upbeat, mean /ɪə/ fearful
> /e/ pleasant, jealous /aː/ kind-hearted

b ▶ 🔘 1.7 Play the recording and get Ss to repeat the sounds as they are played. Do a whole class check and then an individual check.

c ▶ Give Ss a minute to add more words to each column and another minute to check in pairs. Then ask Ss to read out their words with the correct pronunciation. Ss can refer to the Pronunciation Bank on page 163 for more examples.

Speaking

> **OPTIONAL WARMER**
>
> Write the following on the board:
>
> '*Strangers are just friends waiting to happen.*'
> – Rod McKuen (American poet, composer and singer)
>
> Check that Ss understand the meaning of the quote. Ask Ss: *Do you agree with this quote? Why/Why not?*

4a ▶ Ss discuss the questions in pairs and then compare with another pair. Get feedback from the whole class.

b ▶ Ss study the How to... box and put the headings in the correct place. Ask Ss to point out the key words that helped them choose the correct answer. Then drill the conversation starters as a whole class.

> **Answers**
> A at a bus stop B on public transport
>   C at a party

> **OPTIONAL EXTENSION**
>
> With stronger classes, you might brainstorm more conversational starters using a variety of situations, e.g. on a beach, in a class.

c ▶ Do this as a whole class activity. To begin with, read out one of the conversation starters and ask one of the Ss to respond. Then check if people think this is a good response (make sure Ss understand that they have to provide stimulus for further conversation, rather than answering '*yes*' or '*no*'). The S who answered now chooses another conversation starter and chooses another student to respond. Continue with this for a few minutes until the conversation starters have been used a few times. Decide with the rest of the class on the best responses.

d ▶ Ss do the activity in pairs. The pairs then give their script to another pair to act out.

> **OPTIONAL EXTENSION**
>
> This should be done like musical chairs. Agree with the Ss on a situation, e.g. a party. Ss then mingle trying to start a conversation with a 'stranger'. If two people can have a conversation which involves more than two turns, they can sit back down. e.g. *A: Have you tried the chicken? It's delicious. B: No I haven' t. Is there any left? A: Yes there is, would you like some? B: Yes, please.* The last two people left standing are out and have to write a script for the situation. You can then decide on another situation and start again. The last pair left in the game are the winners. The losing pairs can then act out their scripts in front of the class. The winning pair can also model their conversation. In classes of more than ten students you could divide the class into two separate teams.

Reading

> Social networking sites such as Facebook or Twitter are becoming increasing popular with people of all ages. They allow you to create a profile of yourself, contact friends or people you knew in the past and, indeed, make new friends. People can upload photos, make comments on each other's news and photos and chat to each other in real time through a messenger service. Facebook always implies a two-way relationship as you cannot follow another person's life unless they accept you as a friend. With Twitter, however, the relationship can be one way and you can follow the life of people who don't even know you exist. MSN is a messenger service where people can communicate in real time and it's also a search engine. Ebay is a website where people buy and sell things.

5a ▶ Ss discuss the statements in pairs. Elicit feedback, but do not give the correct answers. If Ss think an answer is false, ask them to provide the correct answer.

b ▶ Ss read and check their answers. Give them no more than three minutes to do this. Let them check their answers in pairs before doing a class check. If the answer is false, elicit the correct answer. Check how many of their predictions from exercise 5a Ss got right.

> **Answers**
> 1 T
> 2 T (but they are not all close friends)
> 3 F (130 is the average)
> 4 F (about five)

6 ▶ Give Ss about four minutes to do this activity before letting them check in pairs. Get feedback from the whole class. Ask Ss: *Which answers are you surprised by? Why? Do you agree with the article? Why/Why not? Can you name five 'true friends'?*

> **Answers**
> 1 two percent of salary
> 2 because people with better social skills do better in the workplace
> 3 100
> 4 more than 300 million
> 5 although we may know more people, we will still have the same number of close friends

7 ▶ Ss read the different comments in pairs and decide which opinions they agree or disagree with. Then get feedback from the whole class, making sure Ss can justify their answers.

8 ▶ Ss discuss the questions in pairs. Get feedback from the whole class and elicit reasons for their answers.

Grammar | Present Simple and Present Continuous

> **OPTIONAL GRAMMAR LEAD-IN**
> Write the following sentences on the board:
> *1 I am a teacher. 2 I'm wearing _____* (complete this sentence with something you are wearing that day).
> In pairs, Ss discuss the difference between the two sentences.
> Elicit/explain that the first sentence describes a general state and that the second sentence is something which is true at that moment. Ask Ss what the names of these two grammatical structures are (Present Simple and Present Continuous). Ss write two similar sentences about themselves, one using the Present Simple and one using the Present Continuous. Ss read their sentences to their partner. Check the sentences as a whole class.

9a ▶ Ss read sentences (1–5) in the Active grammar box and match them with the rules (A–E).

> **Active grammar**
> 1 B   3 E   5 D
> 2 C   4 A

b ▶ Write *I hate cheese* and *I'm hating cheese* on the board. Ask Ss if they think both sentences are correct. Elicit which one is incorrect (*I'm hating cheese*). Elicit that some verbs, especially those that refer to a state and not an action, can only be used in the simple form. Ss then complete the task individually and check in pairs. Get feedback from the whole class. Refer Ss to Reference page 19. Ask Ss: *What structure do we use for habits/ routines, things that are true/permanent or describing a state? (Present Simple). Do we use the Present Continuous for describing things that are happening now? (Yes.) Do we use the Present Simple for temporary situations that are happening around now? (No, we use the Present Continuous.)*

> **Answers**
> Action verbs: go, do, eat, play
> State verbs: believe, like, need, want, understand
> Both: live, think, have

10 ▶ In pairs, Ss complete sentences 1–10 using the correct Present Simple or Present Continuous form of the verbs in brackets.

> **Answers**
> 1 Are you reading   6 are you living
> 2 doesn't work   7 Do you understand
> 3 need   8 are you thinking
> 4 Do you want   9 don't want, hate
> 5 don't have   10 'm staying

11 ▶ Write the prompt from number 1 on the board: *What/you/do?* and ask Ss students to make a question about a job. (*What do you do?*) Write the full question on the board. In pairs, Ss make questions from the other prompts (2–10). Ss compare their answers with another pair. Check answers with the whole class.

> **Answers**
> 1 What do you do?
> 2 What are you doing at work/school at the moment?
> 3 How often do you go out with friends?
> 4 What do you like doing?
> 5 What films do you like watching?
> 6 What do you usually do at the weekends?
> 7 Are you reading a good book at the moment?
> 8 Are you playing/watching any sports these days?
> 9 Why are you studying English this year?
> 10 Are you doing any other courses at the moment?

12 ▶ Ss ask their partners the questions from exercise 11 and note down the answers. Get feedback from the whole class.

1.3 Brotherly love?

In this lesson, Ss listen to people talking about someone they fell out with. They then read about the Dassler brothers and through this text, look at the grammar of the Present Perfect Simple and the Past Simple.

Listening and speaking

> **OPTIONAL WARMER**
>
> Write these words on the board: *fight, argue, discuss, fall out with*. In pairs, Ss talk about the meaning of these words/phrases and decide which word is the odd one out. (Answer: *discuss* is the odd one out as it does not necessarily imply a disagreement.)

1a ▶ ● 1.8 Focus Ss' attention on the photos. In pairs, Ss decide what the relationship is between the people in each photo. Get feedback from the whole class. Play the recording. Ss listen and match each speaker with a photo. Ss compare their answers in pairs before checking with the class.

Answers			
1 B		2 A	3 C

b ▶ Ss listen again and complete the notes in the table. Pause between each speaker for Ss to write their answers.

c ▶ Ss check their answers in pairs.

Answers

Speaker	1	2	3
Who do they talk about?	father	Romina – best friend	Sarah – a colleague
How long have they known/ did they know each other?	all his life	twelve years	one year
Why/When did they fall out?	Aged fifteen; he came home at five in the morning and didn't call to say he'd be late.	They had an argument over money while they were on holiday last year.	Sarah was unfriendly and said bad things about her. She said she was lazy and a bad worker.
How is their relationship now?	Fine – he has always been very kind to him.	They haven't seen each other since then.	There is no relationship. She doesn't know what Sarah is doing now.

Vocabulary | arguing

2 ▶ Check that Ss understand the meaning of *argument*. Put Ss in pairs to guess the missing words. Then play the recording for Ss to listen and check their ideas, before checking with the whole class.

Answers	
get angry	have an argument
lose your temper	have a (huge) row
see red	fall out over something

3 ▶ Ss discuss the questions in pairs or small groups. Monitor and note down errors. Write the errors on the board and encourage Ss to self-correct.

Reading

Adidas and Puma are two of the leading brands of sports equipment and in particular sports shoes. The companies were founded by two brothers, Adolph and Rudolph Dassler, who fell out with each other and became rivals. Adidas has generally been the more successful company, reflected in their deal with football star David Beckham to wear their sports clothes. This deal was reputedly worth $150,000,000 to Beckham. The photo shows a statue of Adi Dassler in the brothers' hometown in Germany, with Argentinian footballer Lionel Messi who also endorses Adidas boots.

Run DMC was an American hip-hop band, particularly popular in the 1980s. They were ranked forty-eighth by *Rolling Stone* magazine in their list of the greatest musical acts of all time.

Mohammad Ali (1942–) is considered to be the greatest boxer of all time. Born Cassius Clay, this American boxer won the Heavyweight world title three times. He only lost five fights in a career of sixty-one fights. In 1999, he was crowned sports personality of the century by BBC television.

4a ▶ Focus Ss on the words in the box. In pairs, Ss try and predict what the story will be about. Get feedback from the whole class and write some ideas on the board. At this stage, don't confirm any answers.

b ▶ Ss read the text to find the correct answers. Get feedback from the whole class, comparing the answers with their predictions.

Answers

an argument: The Dassler brothers argued, which led them to found separate companies, Adidas and Puma.
a business: The brothers formed a shoe company together
a nickname: Adolph Dassler's nickname was Adi, which later became part of his company's name.
a shoemaker: The Dasslers' father was a shoemaker.
a wild cat: Puma was named after a wild cat.
the 1932 Olympic Games: The Dassler brothers' first company provided the shoes for Germany's athletes at the 1932 Olympic Games.

5 ▶ Ss read the text again and mark the sentences true (T) or false (F). Encourage Ss to correct the false sentences. Check the answers with the whole class.

Answers
1 F (He was a shoemaker.)
2 T
3 F (They probably argued about money or women.)
4 T
5 F (Adidas is more successful than Puma.)
6 F (Some of the Adidas and Puma employees still don't talk to each other.)

6 ▶ Ask Ss: *What do you do when you find an unknown word in a text? Do you (a) Look it up in a dictionary? (b) Ignore it? (c) Try and work out its meaning?* Ask Ss to discuss this in pairs and give reasons for their answers. Get feedback from the whole class. Explain that always looking up words in a dictionary can make reading very slow and boring, while sometimes ignoring words means you might miss something important. Read through the Lifelong learning box with the Ss and check understanding. Focus Ss on the definitions 1–4. Brainstorm any synonyms for the words that the class might know before putting Ss in pairs to find the words in the text.

Answers
1 supplied
2 founded
3 relocated
4 market leaders

OPTIONAL EXTENSION

Ss make short paragraphs or sentences using words they know but think their colleagues don't know. Then pass the sentences to other Ss to try and guess the meaning from the context.

7 ▶ In pairs, Ss take turns to retell the story. Remind Ss to use the phrases from exercise 2 and the verbs from exercise 6.

Grammar | Present Perfect Simple and Past Simple

OPTIONAL GRAMMAR LEAD-IN

Write the following sentences on the board.
1 I lived here since 2001. 2 I have seen him yesterday.
Tell Ss that the sentences are not correct. In pairs, Ss correct the sentences. Get feedback and write the corrections on the board, underlining the verbs: *1 I have lived here since 2001. 2 I saw him yesterday.*
Elicit the names of these structures: *1 Present Perfect Simple. 2 Past Simple.* In pairs, Ss discuss why we use these structures. Get feedback from the class.

8a ▶ Ss read the sentences and decide individually if they are examples of the Present Perfect Simple or the Past Simple. Ss check in pairs and try to create a rule for the difference between the two structures. Get feedback from the whole class.

Active grammar
1 Present Perfect   5 Past Simple
2 Present Perfect   6 Past Simple
3 Past Simple   7 Present Perfect
4 Present Perfect   8 Present Perfect

b ▶ Focus Ss on the Active grammar box. They choose the correct options individually, then compare answers in pairs. Check the answers with the whole class. Then refer Ss to the Reference on page 19.

Answers
1 Past Simple
2 ago, for
3 Present Perfect Simple
4 period, point
5 Present Perfect Simple
6 not yet, already

OPTIONAL EXTENSION

Get Ss to look back at the sentences from exercise 8a. Using the Active grammar box, elicit why the Present Perfect Simple or Past Simple is used in each sentence.

9 ▶ Ss read the three short texts and choose the correct answers individually before checking in pairs. Check answers with the whole class and encourage Ss to give reasons for their choices.

Answers
1 have played   3 played
2 starred   4 has had
                   5 hasn't learnt

10 ▶ Focus Ss' attention on the words in the box. Ss do the task individually and then compare answers in pairs. Get feedback from the whole class. Elicit rules as to where these words normally appear in the sentence.

Answers
1 since   3 already   5 for
2 ago   4 yet   6 just

Speaking

11 ▶ Put Ss into pairs to discuss the question for a few minutes. Encourage Ss to think of at least two advantages and two disadvantages. Then put Ss in groups of four to share their information and come to an agreement. Get each group to report back their decision. Perhaps Ss in your class have worked in a family company. Encourage them to share their experiences.

1 Vocabulary | phrasal verbs

In this lesson, Ss look at phrasal verbs connected to the theme of families and relationships. Ss then use these phrasal verbs to talk about their childhood and family.

OPTIONAL WARMER

Write the following phrasal verbs on the board: *look after*, *get on with*, *carry on*, *grow*. Ask Ss which is the odd one out and why. Answer: *grow* because it is not a phrasal verb. Explain that phrasal verbs are formed with a verb and a preposition, a verb and two prepositions, or a verb and an adverb.

1a ▶ Ss read the text and answer the questions. Check the answers with the whole class.

Answers
1 English and French because she was brought up in France, but her parents were English.
2 English because the English student should have been practising her French.
3 Because she wanted to be like the English student. She wasn't successful because she wasn't really artistic.

b ▶ Get Ss to find *brought up* in the text. Elicit again what the difference is between a normal verb and a phrasal verb. Ss work in pairs to find the other phrasal verbs.

Answers
grew up, looked after, told off, carried on, got on, looked up to, took after

2 ▶ Ss discuss the meaning of the phrasal verbs from exercise 1 and write a definition for each one. Get feedback from the whole class. Ss match the phrasal verbs from column A with the definitions in column B, referring to the text from exercise 1. Check answers with the whole class.

Answers
1 c   4 g   7 a
2 h   5 d   8 b
3 e   6 f

3 ▶ Ss do the activity individually and then check their answers in pairs. Remind them to change the form when necessary. Get feedback from the whole class.

Answers
1 take after
2 get on
3 grew up
4 carried on
5 told me off
6 brought up
7 look up to
8 looked after

4 ▶ Put Ss in small groups to read the questions. Ss answer the questions in their groups. Get feedback by getting various Ss in each group to tell the class one interesting thing about another member of their group.

5 ▶ Think of an example of something you have learned recently and tell the class how you learned it, including whether you used any techniques to remember things. Ask Ss how they record and remember new vocabulary and brainstorm ideas on the board. Read through the Lifelong learning box with the Ss. Ask them to write one (or more) of their answers from exercise 4, using a phrasal verb, on a clean piece of paper. Then put Ss back into their groups of three and four. One person collects the papers, shuffles them and hands them out. Each student reads out their sentence(s) and the other Ss guess whose it was.

1 Communication

Online dating is one of the fastest growing services on the Internet. In a world where more people have full-time jobs and less time for social activities, finding a date online is becoming increasingly popular, especially amongst the 'babyboomer' generation (people born between 1946 and 1964). As well as online dating agencies which charge a fee, there are free sites, too. You can also date in virtual reality or using Skype or other video-enhanced services. You can also meet partners thought social networking sites.

In this lesson, Ss talk about meeting a new partner. They find out more about Internet dating through the listening and how people describe themselves on these sites. They study phrases that can be used to describe someone's qualities and finish by writing their own profiles.

1a ▶ Put Ss into small groups to discuss the different ways of meeting a new partner. Get feedback from the whole class. Elicit any other good places to meet a new partner.

b ▶ 🔘 1.9 Read through the questions and elicit possible answers for question 1. Write some ideas on the board. Ss listen to the recording and compare answers in pairs. Check the answers with the whole class. If necessary, play the recording again before giving the answers.

Answers
1 seven million
2 sites for: readers of particular newspapers, animal lovers, classical music fans and beautiful people
3 rather than writing your own profile, a friend describes you

OPTIONAL EXTENSION

Ask Ss about Internet dating sites. Ask Ss: *What sort of people use them? Would you think of using them? Why/Why not? Do you think they are good idea for a business? Why/Why not?*

2 ▶ Ss do the activity individually and then check in pairs. Get feedback from the whole class. Ask Ss what they think of the descriptions. Are they reliable? Why/Why not?

Answers
1 Nadia and Richard went to school together.
  Sam and Jenna shared a house at university.
2 Nadia: genuine, loyal and honest, thoughtful and caring, funny, lively
  Sam: great sense of humour, never dull, has an opinion on everything, good listener, kind and fun, sporty
3 Nadia: fabulous cook, famous for her dinner parties, enjoys socialising
  Sam: sporty, likes mountain climbing and surfing

OPTIONAL VARIATION

Ss do the activity in pairs. One student reads about Nadia and finds the answers while the other student reads about Sam. Ss then share their answers before doing a class check.

3 ▶ Read through the qualities with the Ss. Elicit which phrase includes a phrasal verb (*get on with*) and its meaning. Also elicit the meaning of the following: *sense of humour, fun to be around, life and soul of the party, never a dull moment*. Ss think about which five qualities they would choose. Ss compare their answers in pairs and then with another pair. Finally, get feedback from various groups.

4 ▶ Read through the instructions. Use Sam's profile and ask Ss to underline where the four points are covered in his profile. Check with the whole class. Then give Ss ten minutes to write their friend's profile. Encourage them to use at least two of the phrases from exercise 3.

OPTIONAL EXTENSION

Collect the profiles in and shuffle them up. Then put Ss into small groups. Give each group three or four profiles. Groups should check and correct the profiles and then decide on the profile that is most likely to succeed. These should then be presented to the rest of the class for other Ss to comment on.

Review and practice

1 ▶

Answers					
1	is	4	Have	7	has
2	Has	5	don't	8	Doesn't
3	are	6	Are	9	Haven't

2 ▶

Answers

1 A: Do
B: are
2 A: Do
B: don't
3 A: Are
B: don't
4 A: Do
B: don't, have

5 A: Do
B: are
6 A: Have
B: haven't
7 A: are
B: 'm/am
8 A: Have
B: have

3 ▶

Answers

1 don't feel
2 don't know
3 'm/am working
4 'm/am helping out
5 'm/am enjoying
6 like

7 Are you doing
8 'm/am dealing
9 think
10 get up
11 'm/am getting up
12 hate

4 ▶

Answers

1 left
2 've/have done
3 've/have been
4 got

5 worked
6 came
7 've/have bought
8 've/have been

5 ▶

Answers

1 stranger
2 in common
3 fluent in
4 saw red
5 generous

6 sympathetic
7 looks up to
8 carried on
9 keen on
10 lost touch

Writing bank

See page 153 in the Students' Book

1 ▶ Ss read the emails and make notes in the table.

Answers		
	Tomas	Margarita
Job	works in an office	teacher
Interests	snowboarding, skiing, music	walking, cycling, watching films
Family	–	husband and two children.

2 ▶ Ss read the emails again and answer the questions.

Answers
Tomas's email is informal.
Margarita's email is semi-formal.

3a ▶ Ss look at the 'informal' features in the How to... box and find an example of each in email A.

Answers
1 I LOVE it!!!
2 Also listen to a lot of music. Can't wait to find out all about you!
3 What bands do you like? I love Lady GaGa. Cool.
4 :)
5 I LOVE it !!!
6 Hi there,
7 Cheers

b ▶ Ss complete the How to... box with words from email B.

Answers
2 Using
3 longer
4 Not using
5 Not using many
6 *Dear*
7 *Best wishes*

4a ▶ Ss make notes about their job, studies, family and interests.

b ▶ Ss write a reply to Margarita, using a semi-formal email style.

Overview

Lead-in	**Vocabulary:** Types of media
2.1	**Can do:** Give opinions and agree/disagree
	Grammar: Defining relative clauses
	Speaking and Pronunciation: **How to...** give opinions and agree/disagree
	Reading: *Man on Wire*
	Listening: Dubbing or subtitling in foreign language films
2.2	**Can do:** Describe an object
	Grammar: The passive
	Vocabulary: Television
	Speaking and Pronunciation: **How to...** describe an object /n/ and /ŋ/
	Reading: Completely reliable ... and built to last
	Listening: Eco-gadgets
2.3	**Can do:** Describe an important event from your life
	Grammar: Past Simple and Past Continuous
	Speaking and Pronunciation: Word stress on word endings
	Reading: News stories
	Listening: The news
Vocabulary	In the news
Communication	Describe a film
Writing bank	Write a description of an event
	How to... sequence a narrative
Extra resources	ActiveTeach and ActiveBook

CEFR Can do objectives
2.1 Give opinions and agree/disagree
2.2 Describe an object
2.3 Describe an important event from your life
Communication Describe a film
Writing bank Write a description of an event

CEFR Portfolio ideas
a) With a friend, imagine you are going to take part in a radio debate discussing plans for your town or city. First, on your own, decide what you want to do. Then record your radio programme to try and agree on three priorities for the city. Make sure you use phrases to show agreement and disagreement.
b) You lost a very valuable item when you went to a restaurant last week. Write an email to the restaurant, describing the item and asking if they have found it.
c) You have been asked to write an article for an online newspaper entitled 'An event that changed the world'. Write a short article describing the event. Use the How to... box on page 154 to help you.
d) With a friend, video yourselves making a film review programme. Choose three or four films you have seen recently and discuss what you thought about them. Share the video with the rest of the class and get their feedback.

Lead-in

Documentaries are usually serious programmes which investigate certain real-life issues. Docu-dramas, however, do the same thing but use actors to recreate real situations, rather than using real-life film. This is particularly common with events where there is no pictorial record.

OPTIONAL WARMER
Write *media* on the board. Explain that there are different forms of media, e.g. the TV, radio and Internet. In pairs, Ss brainstorm words related to the media. Get feedback from the whole class and write the words on the board. Leave the words on the board (in a mind map) to facilitate discussions.

1 ▶ Ss discuss the questions in pairs, using the photos. Get feedback through a class discussion.

2 ▶ Put Ss in pairs to read the text and underline the key sentences and phrases related to media habits. Check this as a whole class (*spend more time on the Internet than watching TV; average person does five other things at the same time as watching TV, including going online to look at websites or to IM their friends; television ... popular ... particularly reality TV shows and soaps; less likely to watch documentaries or chat shows, tend to get their news online; if read a newspaper ... favourite sections are sports pages, gossip and human interest stories; film ... popular, particularly comedies and horror films; docu-drama ... has also become fashionable*). In pairs, Ss compare their own habits with those described in the article. Get feedback from the whole class

3a ▶ Ss find vocabulary in the article and complete the table. Let them check in pairs before getting feedback from the whole class. Check that Ss understand all the vocabulary.

Answers
Computers: online, website, IM (instant messaging)
Television: TV, reality show, soap, documentary, chat show
Film: comedy, horror, docu-drama
Newspapers: sports page, gossip, human interest story, current affairs, business section

b ▶ Ss brainstorm extra words to add to the table and compare their ideas in pairs or small groups. Get feedback from the whole class. You can recreate the table on the board and add all the words (or get your Ss to write them up) and compare them with the words from the warmer activity.

EXTEND THE LEAD-IN
This can be done in groups or as a whole class, depending on class size. Tell Ss to look at the words on the board. Each student will have at least thirty seconds to talk and try and use as many of the words on the board as correctly as possible in their speech. The winner is the student who uses the most words correctly in a coherent speech.

2.1 Silver screen

In this lesson, Ss read about a documentary film of a man walking a high wire between the twin towers of the World Trade Center. The text also provides examples for the grammar focus on defining relative clauses, which Ss use to talk about a film they have seen. They then listen to people talking about foreign language films, which provides the context for studying how to give opinions and agree/disagree. They also think about how to interact with people outside the classroom.

OPTIONAL WARMER

Write *silver screen* on the board. Tell Ss that this phrase describes one type of media. Elicit which media and then why they think it describes films. Write *action* below *silver screen*. Tell Ss that this is one type/genre of film. Elicit other types of films. Make sure *documentary* and *drama* are covered and suggest *docu-drama*. In pairs, Ss write down two films that they think are typical films for each type/genre. Go through each type. Encourage Ss to think of adjectives they could use to describe films. While doing this, check Ss understand the meaning of *gripping, poignant, fascinating* and *inspiring*.

Speaking and reading

The 'twin towers' were part of a complex of seven buildings which made up the World Trade Center in New York. The two towers were 110 metres tall. The buildings were destroyed on 9 September 2001.

As well as walking a tightrope between the twin towers, Philippe Petit has also walked a tightrope from the Eiffel Tower to a nearby building, across Broadway in New York and at the Plaza Mikado in Tokyo.

1 ▶ Ss do the activity in pairs. Get feedback from the whole class.

2a ▶ Ss read the text to answer the first three questions. Put Ss in pairs to compare their answers and discuss question 4. Get feedback from the whole class. For questions 1 and 3, ask Ss which information in the text helped them to decide.

Answers
1 docu-drama
2 how Petit planned and carried out a tightrope walk between the twin towers in New York
3 Yes, he/she thought it was fascinating and inspiring

b ▶ Ss do the task individually and then in pairs, before doing a class check. Check the answers with the whole class, asking Ss to correct the answers, where possible.

Answers
1 F (it was going to be built)
2 T (1974)
3 T (Notre Dame and Sydney Harbour Bridge)
4 F (they had to forge documents and get past security guards)
5 T
6 F (only photos)
7 F (he stayed there for 45 minutes)

Grammar | defining relative clauses

OPTIONAL GRAMMAR LEAD-IN

Tell Ss you are going to check their knowledge of the media. Ask them to write down the following:
a) The name of the person who invented the TV. (John Logie Baird)
b) The country whose film industry is nicknamed Bollywood. (India)
c) The country where the programme *Who wants to be a millionaire?* started. (the UK)
d) The year when the first 'ad' was made. (1941)
e) The search engine which is used by most people. (Google)
f) The reality TV show that has been broadcast in over twenty countries. (Big Brother)
Check the answers with the class and copy them onto the board. Ask the Ss who John Logie Baird was. If the Ss can't give you '*He was the person who invented the TV*', write it on the board. Ss write similar clauses for b–f. Write these clauses on the board. Underline the defining relative clauses. Elicit the name of the structure, then ask Ss to read the notes on page 33.

3a ▶ Focus Ss' attention on sentences 1–6. Ss use the words from the box to complete the sentences. Check the answers with the whole class.

Answers
1 that/which
2 who
3 when
4 where
5 that/which
6 whose

b ▶ Ss complete the rules in the Active grammar box using the words from exercise 3a. Check the answers with the whole class. Explain to Ss that these clauses give extra information that is necessary to understand the noun. Draw three houses on the board and write: *The house was sold. Do we know which house was sold?* (No) Draw a tree in front of one of the houses. Change the sentence so it reads: *The house which has the tree in front of it was sold. Do we know which house was sold?* (Yes) Ask Ss to identify the relative pronoun in the sentence (which). Tell Ss that there is a full explanation on Reference page 33 and give them time to read it.

4 ▶ In pairs, Ss add a relative pronoun to each sentence. Check the answers with the whole class.

Answers
1   That's the studio <u>where</u> the last Bond film was made.
2   Goldeneye is the name of the house <u>where</u> Ian Fleming wrote the original stories.
3   *Dr No* is the first Bond book <u>which</u> was made into a film.
4   George Lazenby is the man <u>who</u> only played Bond once.
5   Daniel Craig is another actor <u>who</u> took the role.
6   Derby County is the football team <u>which</u> Bond actor Timothy Dalton supports.

5 ▶ Ss do the activity individually and then check as a whole class. Make sure Ss can explain why the change was necessary/unnecessary and why they chose the relative pronoun.

Answers
1   2001 is the year when the first Harry Potter film was made.
2   Joanne Rowling is the author whose books were turned into the Harry Potter films.
3   Scotland is the country where most of the outdoor scenes were filmed.
4   Warner Brothers is the company which produced the films.
5   Richard Harris and Michael Gambon are the actors who have taken the role of Dumbledore.
6   $1.3 billion is the amount of money which the first three films made.

Speaking

6 ▶ Read through the instructions with the Ss. Give Ss a few minutes to prepare what they are going to say and then put them in pairs to describe their films. Change the pairs and repeat the activity. Get feedback from the whole class and decide which of the films described sounded the most interesting.

OPTIONAL VARIATION

This can be done as a 'guess the film' activity. Model this by giving a description of a film, using only the four points given and ask the Ss to guess the film. Then give Ss no more than five minutes to do the same activity themselves. Put Ss in pairs to guess each other's films. You can swap the pairs around a few times and finish by watching some examples as a whole class.

OPTIONAL EXTENSION

Ss write short film reviews of a film they have seen. They can take pictures from the Internet and then put them up on the wall. The films should be ones that are preferably on at the cinema now. You can then decide as a class which film is the best to go and see.

Speaking and listening

Le Herisson (The Hedgehog) (2009) is a French comedy drama about an eleven-year-old girl who is bored and decides to kill herself on her twelfth birthday.

Red Cliff (2008 and 2009) is a two-part Chinese epic war film, set in the third century AD. It is the most expensive Asian film and broke box office records in China. It was directed by John Woo.

OPTIONAL WARMER

Ask Ss to look back at the photos from *Man on Wire*. Ask Ss: *Were they appealing? Why/Why not? How effective are film posters? Have you been directly affected by a film poster?* Ss look at the two film posters on page 24. Ask Ss: *Which film looks the most appealing? Why?*

7 ▶ Ask Ss to look at the posters and elicit what makes these films different from Hollywood blockbusters. Then put Ss into pairs to discuss the questions and get feedback from the whole class.

8a ▶ Discuss the questions quickly with the whole class. Write the most popular answers on the board.

b ▶ ⬤ 1.10 Play the recording and ask Ss to take notes. Get feedback from the whole class.

Answers
Sue: subtitling
Ekaterina: subtitling
Ben: dubbing (because he thinks it's hard to watch a film and read subtitles at the same time)

c ▶ Ss read through the questions. Check understanding and play the recording again. Ss answer the questions and then check in pairs. Check the answers with the whole class.

Answers
1	Sue	4	Ben
2	Ben	5	Sue
3	Ekaterina	6	Ekaterina

9 ▶ Put Ss in pairs to read through the How to... box. Ss match the headings from the box with the correct example phrases. Check the answers with the whole class.

Answers

A Giving an opinion
B Asking for an opinion
C Agreeing
D Disagreeing
E Saying it may change (according to what happens)

10a ▶ ● 1.11 Tell Ss they are going to listen to some statements which they will agree or disagree with. Ss write numbers 1–5 in their books. Play the recording. Ss tick the statements they agree with and cross the statements they disagree with. Refer to the audioscript on page 166 if necessary.

b ▶ Play the recording again, pausing after each statement while Ss write their responses. Remind them to use the phrases from the How to… box.

c ▶ Put Ss in pairs to discuss their responses. Encourage them to use expressions from the How to… box in their discussions. Get feedback from the whole class.

OPTIONAL EXTENSION:

Put Ss in pairs (A and B). Tell Ss to write down the names of five famous people who are often in the public eye. Ss share the names they have written with a partner. S A has one minute to talk about one of the famous people, using expressions from the How to… box. S B listens and can either agree or disagree with S A. When responding, Student B should use expressions from the How to… box. After one minute, Ss change roles. Get Ss to tick the expressions from the How to… box each time they use them. Continue until the Ss have discussed all the famous people. Monitor and give feedback at the end.

---

11 ▶ Individually, Ss think of the last time they used English outside class, then compare answers in pairs. Focus Ss on the Lifelong learning box. Ss write a list of the different ways they interact with English outside class. Ss compare their lists in pairs. Get feedback from various pairs and explain how important it is for Ss to have contact with English outside class. For homework, Ss find short English language articles from the Internet, a magazine or a newspaper and bring them to the next lesson. Ss read each other's articles.

OPTIONAL VARIATION

For homework, ask Ss to find a website in English which they find interesting. Tell Ss they will give a short presentation to the rest of the class in the next lesson. Encourage Ss to use as much of the language covered in Lesson 2.1 as possible. Ss describe the website to the class and talk about what they found interesting. Ss can then look at the sites they heard about and can investigate either in class or for their next homework. Ask Ss to give feedback on the new websites.

2.2 Built to last

In this lesson, Ss talk about gadgets and, in particular, the television. Ss begin by listening to a discussion of eco-gadgets, which provides the context for the language of how to describe an object. They are then introduced to the vocabulary of television and adjectives that could be used to describe TV programmes. This leads to some pronunciation work on /n/ and /ŋ/. The reading text on television also provides the context for studying passive structures.

OPTIONAL WARMER

Write the word *gadget* on the board and elicit a definition. If necessary, read out the following three definitions and ask them to guess which one is correct: (a) *a machine that is used to keep the house clean* (b) *a mechanical or electronic device with a practical use* (c) *something that is different or unusual.* Elicit examples of gadgets from Ss and then ask them to decide which they think is the most important gadget in use today. Get Ss to explain their reasons. Finally, ask them if they think the TV is an important gadget. Can we live without it?

Listening

1a ▶ Put Ss in pairs to guess what the gadgets are and what they have in common. Get feedback from the whole class, but don't confirm any answers.

b ▶ ● 1.12 Play the recording. Ss match the gadgets from exercise 1a with the speakers and then compare their answers in pairs. Check the answers with the whole class. Elicit the words that helped them choose their answers.

Answers

1	A	3	B
2	D	4	C

c ▶ Elicit the answer from the whole class, without listening again.

Answer

They are all environmentally friendly or 'eco-gadgets'.

2 ▶ Play the recording again. Ss note down the good and bad points of each gadget. They then compare notes with a partner and compare again with another pair. Get feedback from the whole class.

Answers

A Good – fast and easy cycling
   Bad – powered by petrol
B Good – worked well, looks nicer than plastic one
   Bad – doesn't look professional
C Good – easy to wind up
   Bad – solar panel didn't work well
D Good – clear sound, cheap
   Bad – doesn't look very good

3 ▶ Put Ss in pairs to discuss the gadgets. Refer Ss back to the How to... box on page 24 and encourage them to use the language of agreeing and disagreeing. Get feedback from the whole class. Elicit any other eco-gadgets Ss might know of.

Speaking

4 ▶ Ss complete the activity individually. Check the answers with the whole class, making sure Ss are clear which form follows the preposition. Elicit other possible words that could follow the prepositions.

> **Answers**
> It's a kind of music player.
> It's similar to an Mp3.
> It's used for playing music.
> It's used by joggers.
> It's a thing for playing music.
> It's made of plastic.

> **OPTIONAL EXTENSION**
> Ss make example sentences using the How to... box to describe the gadgets on page 25.

5a ▶ Ss think about a gadget they own (or someone they know owns) and write their descriptions. Check that no two Ss have the same gadget and that the gadgets are not too obvious.

b ▶ Ss describe their gadget to a partner, who will try and guess what the object is. Choose Ss to demonstrate the activity for the class.

Vocabulary | television

> Guineas were originally gold coins that were used in the UK between 1663 and 1813. They were originally worth one pound sterling but later increased in price because of the cost of gold. It later became a colloquial term for *pound*.
>
> The Coronation is the ceremony at which someone is officially made king or queen, usually at Westminster Abbey.
>
> The London Olympic Games in 1948 were the first Summer Olympic Games to be held after the Second World War. It was the cheapest Olympic Games because of the financial situation after the war.

> **OPTIONAL LEAD-IN**
> Write the word *television* on the board. Elicit a description of a television, using the phrases from the How to... box on page 25. Brainstorm words that Ss associate with *television*. Write these words on the board and check Ss understand the meaning of all of them.

6a ▶ Write *television* on the board. Ask Ss: *Does the word 'colour' go before or after 'television'?* (before). Tell Ss that this is an example of a collocation and check

they understand the meaning of *collocation*. Ss identify which words from the box go before *television* and which go after. Ss then compare their answers with a partner. Get feedback from the whole class.

> **Answers**
> television channel, television commercials, digital television, live television, on (the) television, television presenter, television producer, television programme, satellite television, television screen, television set, television viewers

b ▶ Ss put the words in brackets in the correct place and then complete the sentences in their own words. Put Ss in pairs to read their sentences to each other.

> **OPTIONAL VARIATION**
> Once Ss have completed their individual sentences, number Ss from 1–5. Ss have to find out what the most popular response is for their numbered sentence. Get feedback from the whole class to find out the results of the survey.

c ▶ Ss decide which adjectives in the box are positive or negative and then compare their answers in pairs. Check the answers with the whole class and check understanding of the adjectives.

> **Answers**
> Positive: entertaining, exciting, gripping, incredible, inspiring, moving
> Negative: annoying, boring, nauseating, nonsense, unrealistic, unwatchable

Pronunciation | /n/ and /ŋ/

7a ▶ ⏺ 1.13 Write the word *entertaining* on the board and elicit the pronunciation from the class. Play the recording. Ss decide how the last 'n' is pronounced. Put Ss in groups to practise the last /ŋ/ sound at the end of the word and then the whole word.

b ▶ Ss look back at the adjectives in exercise 6c. Ask them to underline all the 'n's and decide how they are pronounced. Ss check their answers in pairs. Don't ask for feedback at this point.

> **Answers**
> /n/ an̲noying, e̲ntertaini̲ng, i̲ncredible, i̲nspiring, nauseati̲ng, no̲nsense, u̲nrealistic, u̲nwatchable
> /ŋ/ annoyi̲ng, bori̲ng, entertaini̲ng, exciti̲ng, grippi̲ng, inspiri̲ng, movi̲ng, nauseati̲ng

c ▶ ⏺ 1.14 Play the recording for Ss to check their answers. Get feedback from the whole class. Ss then listen again and repeat the words as a whole class and then individually.

d ▶ Ss work in pairs to think of programmes they have seen which could be described using the adjectives from exercise 6c. Remind Ss to use the example phrases. Get feedback from the whole class and ask Ss to report what their partners said about a programme. Elicit other Ss' opinions about the same programme. Again, encourage Ss to use the adjectives from exercise 6c in their responses.

OPTIONAL EXTENSION

Prepare a table for each student with four adjectives from exercise 6c used as column headings. Each table should use different adjectives. Hand out one table to each student who should write at least one TV programme or film in each column and then write their names on the top. Collect the tables and then hand them out again, making sure no student gets their own table. Ss then make sentences using the table they have and Ss can guess who they think wrote it, e.g. *This person thinks 'Warehouse 13' is entertaining but thinks 'Bones' is boring. Who is it?* They can also discuss whether they agree with the sentences.

Reading

8 ▶ Start by eliciting descriptions of the photos from the whole class. Then put Ss in pairs to discuss the two questions. Get feedback from various Ss.

9 ▶ Ss read the article and find out what the numbers refer to. Let Ss compare their answers in pairs before checking answers with the whole class.

Answers
1948: the date of the first London Olympic Games
3,000: the number of TVs lost in London bombings
1936: when the Marconiphone was made
11,000: the equivalent of 60 guineas in pounds today
12: the size of the screen in inches

---

10 ▶ Elicit from Ss that they should (a) read the questions first and underline the key words in the questions; (b) look for the key words or synonyms of the key words in the text to find where the answer is. Make sure Ss understand they should not read the whole text. Ss underline the key words. Check what they have underlined with the whole class. Ss then answer the questions. Check the answers with the whole class, making sure Ss give reasons for their answers.

Answers
1 T
2 NG
3 T
4 F (ten years)
5 T
6 F (his grandfather was)
7 NG
8 T

Grammar | the passive

OPTIONAL GRAMMAR LEAD-IN

Write the following words on the board:
John Logie Baird   invent   TV

In pairs, Ss make a correct sentence using the words in this order. Tell Ss to change the form of the verb if necessary. (John Logie Baird invented the TV.) Now write the words on the board in the following order:
TV   invent   John Logie Baird

In pairs, Ss make a correct sentence using the words in this order. Tell Ss to change the form of the verb and add extra words if necessary. (The TV was invented by John Logie Baird.) Ask Ss what the name of this grammatical structure is (the passive).

In pairs, Ss write more sentences using the passive about famous films, books and songs. Check Ss' answers.

---

11 ▶ Ss look back at the text and complete the sentences in the Active grammar box. Copy the sentences on the board and elicit the answers to fill the gaps. Ss then read rules A–C and match them with sentences 1–3. Get feedback from the whole class. Ask Ss to identify verb forms used in the passive (*to be* + past participle) and write this on the board. Refer Ss to Reference page 33 and give them time to read the notes. Ask Ss: *What happens to the object of an active sentence when it is changed into a passive sentence?* (It becomes the subject.) *What is the main focus of a passive sentence?* (The person or thing affected by the action.) *What preposition do we use if we want to include the person who did the action in a passive sentence?* (by)

Active grammar

It <u>is</u> thought to be Britain's oldest working set.
It <u>was</u> made over seven decades ago.
The set <u>has been</u> converted from analogue to digital.
It can <u>be</u> used for many years to come.

A 2
B 3
C 1

---

12 ▶ Do the first question with the whole class. Look at the first sentence. Ask Ss: *Is the sentence active or passive?* (active). *What verb(s) need to be used?* (could receive) Then elicit the second sentence. Ss do the rest of the activity individually and then compare their answers in pairs. Get feedback from the whole class.

Answers
1 could be received
2 owned
3 is replaced
4 made
5 are made
6 could be watched

13a ▶ Write sentence 1 on the board and elicit one extra word to make the sentence correct. In pairs, Ss add one word to sentences 2–8. Don't ask for feedback at this point.

b ▶ 🔘 1.15 Play the recording for Ss to check their answers. Get feedback from the whole class.

Answers

1   A father and son who made millions of pounds from fake DVDs have <u>been</u> jailed for six years.
2   Hundreds of thousands of DVDs were produced <u>by</u> workers hired by the gang.
3   The DVDs <u>were</u> sold cheaply in pubs and markets.
4   It is estimated <u>by</u> the police that the criminals made around £43,000 a day from the operation.
5   The gang members lived a life of luxury until they <u>were</u> caught.
6   However, police believe that most of the money the gang made <u>has</u> been taken out of the country.
7   <u>It</u> is estimated that criminal gangs in the UK make about £300 million a year from fake DVDs.
8   Police dogs have now <u>been</u> trained to find hidden DVDs.

OPTIONAL EXTENSION

Put Ss into small groups. Ss write the introduction to a news programme, including at least five headlines using the passive tense. Ss then act out their news introduction for the rest of the class.

2.3 Stories in the news

Some newspapers in the UK, known as tabloids, have a reputation for not always being accurate in their reporting. They also often include strange stories which are hard to believe.

In this lesson, Ss read some strange newspaper stories and, through this context, analyse the grammar of the Past Simple and Past Continuous. They then talk about events in their lives using the Past Simple and Past Continuous.

OPTIONAL WARMER

Write *newspaper* on the board. Put Ss in pairs and give them one minute to write as many words as they can think of related to newspapers. Ask Ss how many words they have written. The pair with the most words read out their words. Write them on the board. If the other Ss have any different words, write them on the board. In pairs, Ss put the words on the board into groups using their chosen categories. Get feedback from the class.

Speaking and listening

1a ▶ Put Ss in pairs to discuss the first question. Get feedback from the class. Then focus on the opinions and discuss the second question with the whole class.

b ▶ 🔘 1.16 Play the recording. Ss identify the various opinions. Get feedback from the whole class.

Answers

Different newspapers report the same story in different ways. *both*
Newspapers sometimes try to make news stories sound worse than they are. *Eben*
Newspapers have to make stories sound exciting in order to sell. *both*

2a ▶ Check Ss understand all the words in the box. Ss complete the sentences with words from the box. Check the answers with the whole class.

Answers

1   delivers
2   takes
3   escapes
4   saves
5   survives
6   inherits

---

b ▶ In pairs, Ss match the headlines with the pictures and describe what they think happened in each situation. Get feedback from the whole class.

Answers

1	D	4	B	
2	C	5	F	
3	E	6	A	

Reading

3a ▶ Ss read quickly through each text and choose a headline for each story. Tell them not to worry about any words they don't understand at this stage. Let Ss check their answers in pairs before getting feedback from the whole class.

Answers

A	2	D	3	
B	4	E	5	
C	6	F	1	

b ▶ Explain that some of the stories cover similar topics. For example, both stories B and D mention restaurants. In pairs, ask Ss to find other similarities between stories B and D. Get feedback from the whole class. Individually, Ss look at the list of topics 1–7 and write the number of the stories beside the topics.

c ▶ Ss compare their answers in pairs. Check the answers with the whole class.

Answers

2	A, E	5	A, B, D, E, F
3	B, C, D, E	6	C, F
4	A, E	7	B, E

4 ▶ Ss read the text again slowly and answer the questions in pairs. Check the answers with the whole class. Check if there are any words or expressions that Ss don't understand in the text.

Answers

1. a Calais, France
   b She was too embarrassed.
2. a He couldn't cook 'such a fine creature'.
   b He sent an employee to set him free.
3. Mrs Barese's neighbours
4. Lala caused €10,000 of damage: dropped a vase, threw paper towels, flooded the restaurant.
5. seagulls and a turtle
6. a first aid and helping mothers give birth
   b his passenger was having a baby

5a ▶ Ss do the activity in pairs. Check the answers with the whole class.

Answers

1	take; f	5	return; c
2	get; e	6	give; d
3	move; b	7	take; a
4	cause; g		

b ▶ Ss cover the texts. In pairs, Ss take turns to retell the stories, using the phrases from exercise 5a to help them. Monitor closely and note errors. Write the errors on the board and encourage Ss to self-correct.

c ▶ Ss discuss the questions in pairs. Get feedback from the whole class.

Pronunciation | word stress on word endings

6a ▶ Ss look through the news stories (A–E) and complete the table with words that use each ending. Let Ss compare answers in pairs before getting feedback from the whole class.

Answers

-ee	-eer	-ese	-ette
employee	career	Vietnamese	cigarette
escapee			
refugee			
coffee			

b ▶ 🔵 1.17 Check Ss understand the meaning of *stress pattern*. Play the recording and pause after each word for Ss to note the stress pattern. Elicit the exception. Refer Ss to the Pronunciation bank on page 163 to read the rule.

Answers

The stress is on the last syllable in all the words except *coffee*.

c ▶ With the whole class, brainstorm other words to add to each column of the table .

Grammar | Past Simple and Past Continuous

7a ▶ Ask Ss to look at the Active grammar box and tell them to answer question 1 in pairs. Elicit the answer.

Active grammar

The <u>underlined</u> verbs describe something temporary and in progress.

b ▶ Ss read rules A and B, then find more examples of the Past Continuous in the texts on pages 28–29 and underline them. Ask various Ss to read them aloud. Tell Ss that the Past Continuous is used in the following cases: to describe something temporary and in progress, to say that something happened in the middle of a longer action and to set the scene at the beginning of a story. In pairs, Ss then discuss question 2. Elicit the answer. Tell Ss to look at Reference page 33 and give them a few minutes to read through the notes. Ask Ss: *Which tense do we use for complete, finished actions in the past?* (Past Simple) *Which tense is used for the action which interrupts the Past Continuous?* (Past Simple) *Do we use the Past Simple for temporary actions and situations?* (No) *Do we use the Past Continuous for longer or permanent situations?* (No) Focus on the pronunciation of the weak forms of *was* /wəz/ and *were* /wə/. Ss practise saying the sentences from the Reference section on page 33.

Active grammar

State verbs are not normally used in the continuous form, e.g. *like, love, hate, want, need, prefer, know, understand, believe, remember.*

8 ▶ Ss complete the sentences individually and then compare answers in pairs. Check the answers with the whole class.

Answers
1   was working, met
2   was, liked
3   arrived, was cooking
4   knew, met
5   didn't break, was playing, fell
6   checked, were sleeping
7   was listening, didn't hear
8   saw, Were you wearing

9 ▶ Ss complete the activity individually. Check the answers with the whole class.

Answers
I remember when my little sister was born. I was ten years old, and I was staying in London with my parents. I knew my mother <u>was expecting</u> a baby, but I <u>didn't know</u> how soon it would arrive. I was really <u>hoping</u> for a girl. It happened when I <u>was</u> at a friend's house. It was her birthday and so she <u>was having</u> a party. My grandmother came to collect me, but when she told me the news I was so excited that I <u>ran</u> down the stairs, and I <u>fell</u> and broke my arm. I <u>visited</u> my mother and sister in hospital, and I had to spend the night there with my arm in plaster, too.

Speaking and writing

10 ▶ Before looking at the book, ask Ss what they think the basic ingredients of a story are. Then go through the four stages on page 30 before Ss identify the stages in the story from exercise 9. Check the answers with the whole class.

Answers
1   I remember when my little sister was born. I was ten years old, and I was staying in London with my parents. I knew my mother was having a baby, but I didn't know how soon it would arrive. I was really hoping for a girl.
2   It happened when I was at a friend's house. It was her birthday and so she was having a party. My grandmother came to collect me,
3   but when she told me the news I was so excited that I ran down the stairs, and I fell and broke my arm.
4   I visited my mother and sister in hospital, and I had to spend the night there with my arm in plaster, too.

11a ▶ Ss choose one of the events and make notes. Explain that they do not have to write full sentences.

b ▶ Give Ss a few minutes to go organise their notes, making sure they have information on all four stages from exercise 10.

c ▶ Put Ss in groups to tell each other about their events. Get feedback from various Ss, who should report one of the stories they heard.

2 Vocabulary | In the news

In this lesson, Ss look at different verb + noun collocations and their use in the context of newspaper articles. Ss then write their own newspaper report using these collocations.

> **OPTIONAL WARMER**
>
> Write *take a ___* on the board. In pairs, Ss think of different ways of completing the phrase. Get feedback from the class, and write the Ss' ideas on the board. Explain that some verbs are often followed by certain nouns and that this is called collocation.

1a ▶ In pairs, Ss look at sentences 1–9 and decide which noun does not collocate with the verb. Check the answers with the whole class and check understanding of the collocations.

> **Answers**
>
> | | | | |
> |---|---|---|---|
> | 1 | a | 6 | b |
> | 2 | c | 7 | a |
> | 3 | a | 8 | c |
> | 4 | b | 9 | a |
> | 5 | a | | |

b ▶ Focus Ss' attention on the photos and put them in pairs to do the activity. Get feedback from various Ss.

2 ▶ Do this as a whole class activity with books closed. Draw the table on the board and appoint two monitors, one to fill in the 'a/an' column and one to fill in the 'no article' column. The rest of the class then work to fill in the table.

3 ▶ Focus the Ss' attention on the different newspaper pages in the box. Put Ss in pairs to discuss which of these sections of a newspaper they would normally read and why/why not. The pairs then decide on which pages they would find the collocations from exercise 1a.

> **Suggested answers**
>
> Arts section: come into fashion, perform a song, perform a play
> Business section: make a profit, come into money
> Current affairs: commit a crime, cause trouble, cause an accident, break a record
> News and gossip: come into fashion, come into money, commit a crime, commit suicide, have a baby, have plastic surgery
> Science section: make a discovery, develop an idea, develop a product
> Sports pages: win a race, win a match, break a record

4 ▶ Ss do the activity individually. Remind them that they may have to change the tense of the verb to fit the context of the sentence. Check the answers with the whole class.

> **Answers**
>
> 1 performed a/the song
> 2 came into
> 3 made a discovery
> 4 develops a product
> 5 have plastic surgery
> 6 commit a crime
> 7 caused an accident

5a ▶ Ss try to do the activity individually at this stage. Monitor and help Ss with ideas if necessary.

b ▶ Ss compare their list with a partner. Get feedback from the whole class.

> **OPTIONAL VARIATION**
>
> Ss write the list of famous people in a different order from exercise 5a. Ss show their lists to a partner who guesses who each person is, using a collocation from exercise 1, e.g. *I think Lady GaGa performs songs on TV.*

6a ▶ Check the meaning of the word *gossip*. Give Ss a few minutes to discuss the questions in groups of three or four, then continue the discussion quickly with the whole class. Ask Ss: *Where do you find most gossip? Which magazines/TV programmes focus on gossip?*

b ▶ Read through the instructions and practise saying the opinions as a whole class. Put Ss in small groups and give them some time to think. Ss then tell each other their celebrity gossip and give their own opinion.

c ▶ Elicit phrases for giving opinions and then compare the Ss ideas with the How to... box on page 24. In the same groups, Ss tell their gossip again and the other Ss in the group should give their opinions. Then do the same as a whole class, allowing the whole class to comment.

> **OPTIONAL VARIATION**
>
> When you have read the instructions and practised the opinions in exercise 6a, tell Ss they should try and make notes on two pieces of celebrity gossip, one true and one made-up. Then for exercise 6c, Ss in the group have to decide which gossip they think is true and which is false, and give their reasons.

2 Communication

The Orphanage (2007) is a Spanish horror film about a woman who returns to her old home to open a school for disabled children. Then her son starts talking to an invisible friend. The film opened at the Cannes Film festival and was very successful. It won seven Goyas (Spanish film awards).

Did you hear about the Morgans? (2009) is an American comedy about a city couple who see a murder and have to enter the witness protection programme. This means having to get used to living outside the city. The film was not very successful and Sarah Jessica Parker won a Golden Raspberry for being the worst actress of 2009.

Transformers, Revenge of the Fallen (2009) is a science fiction film and is the second Transformers film, after the first was a huge box office hit. The second film, however, was not as successful. Although it made a lot of money, it got mostly negative reviews from film critics. It won the Razzle award for worst picture of 2009 but also became the twenty-third highest grossing film of all time.

In this lesson, Ss talk about films. They listen to a description of a film and then practise how to talk about them.

OPTIONAL WARMER

Put a number of film titles on the board (preferably films that the Ss have probably seen). Ask Ss which ones they have seen. Then elicit what Ss know about the film and construct a rough description on the board. This should give Ss something to compare with when they have finished the lesson.

1 ▶ Ss work in pairs to discuss the questions. Remind Ss to give reasons for their answers. Get feedback from the whole class.

2a ▶ 🔘 1.18 Draw Ss' attention to the three posters and elicit descriptions of the poster and film. You could revise film genres at this point. (You may also want to check if anyone has seen these films and encourage those people to let the other students speak.) Play the recording. Elicit the answer and encourage Ss to give reasons for their answer.

> **Answers**
> A   *The Orphanage*

b ▶ Focus Ss on the table. In pairs, Ss to try to complete the sentences from memory. Play the recording again and then check the answers with the whole class.

> **Answers**
> It's a <u>horror</u> film.
> It's about <u>a woman</u> who buys the house where <u>she used to live</u> as a child. Her son starts to see <u>the ghosts of children</u> in the house and then he suddenly <u>disappears</u>.
> The main characters are <u>the woman and her husband</u>. There is also a rather spooky <u>old woman</u>.

3 ▶ 🔘 1.19 Tell the Ss they are now going to hear more about the film and should take notes. Play the recording. Ss compare their notes in pairs and make extra sentences to go into the table. Write the table on the board (or have a slide prepared on a projector) and then complete the extra information with the whole class.

4a ▶ Ss work in pairs and choose a film that they have both seen. Ask each pair to make a table like the one from exercise 2 and complete it with notes for their film.

b ▶ Put pairs into groups of four (two pairs or four members from different pairs). Ss describe their film plots without revealing the name of the film and the rest of the group tries to guess the film. The best or most challenging examples can then be done as a class activity.

OPTIONAL EXTENSION

(1) Ss write a review of the film they described, using the notes they made. This can then be pinned on the wall and Ss can read the reviews and discuss whether they agree or disagree.

(2) Ss imagine they are trying to sell the film to a producer. They meet him in a lift and have one minute to get his attention and sell the film. Give Ss a few minutes to prepare. Play the producer yourself. Ss listen to the different pitches and choose the best one.

Review and practice

1 ▶

Answers
1 have been killed
2 started
3 has been announced
4 has been discovered
5 announced
6 has sold
7 called
8 found
9 has been found
10 is selling/will sell

2 ▶

Answers
1 whose
2 when
3 which
4 where
5 when
6 who
7 whose
8 who
9 which
10 where
11 where
12 who
that can be used in 3, 6, 8, 9, 12

3 ▶

Answers
1 was, started
2 were watching, heard
3 were you doing, was reading
4 saw, was looking
5 crashed, was going
6 Were they winning, were losing
7 was studying, found
8 Did you see, was wearing, Didn't you notice
9 were you doing, was just looking
10 studied

4 ▶

Answers
1 arts
2 documentary
3 plastic surgery
4 sections
5 profit
6 accidents
7 record
8 article
9 come into
10 perform
11 screen
12 presenter

Writing bank

See page 154 of the Students' Book

1a ▶ Ss look at the photos and discuss the question in pairs. Get feedback from whole class, but don't confirm any answers.

b ▶ Ss read the article and check their ideas from exercise 1a. Check the answers with the whole class

Answers
The connection is the Olympic Games. Brazilians are sitting on the beach, hearing that they have won the bid to get the Olympics in 2016.

2 ▶ Ss read the How to... box and tick the phrases used in each paragraph of the article.

Answers
1 I remember when
2 after that
3 Suddenly
4 In the end, It was one of the best days of my life.

3a ▶ Ss make notes about the event they have chosen using the paragraph structure given.

b ▶ Ss write about their event using phrases from the How to... box.

Overview

Lead-in	**Vocabulary:** Home
3.1	**Can do:** Make a complaint **Grammar:** Future plans **Speaking and Pronunciation:** **How to...** complain politely **Reading:** Your home – My home **Listening:** A home exchange Problems with the home exchange
3.2	**Can do:** Compare cities **Grammar:** Comparatives and superlatives **Vocabulary:** Adjectives describing places **Reading:** *City I love*, Why not move to ... ? **Listening:** Kyoto, Japan
3.3	**Can do:** Take notes while listening **Grammar:** Future possibility **Vocabulary:** Compound nouns **Speaking and Pronunciation:** Word stress in compound nouns **Reading:** What does the future hold? **Listening:** Future predictions
Vocabulary	Prefixes and suffixes
Communication	Describe hopes, dreams and ambitions
Writing bank	Write an email of complaint **How to...** complain
Extra resources	ActiveTeach and ActiveBook

CEFR Can do objectives
3.1 Make a complaint
3.2 Compare cities
3.3 Take notes while listening
Communication Describe hopes, dreams and ambitions
Writing bank Write an email of complaint

CEFR Portfolio ideas
a) You work in the complaints office of your local council. You are tired of reading silly complaints. Write to your boss and complain, giving examples of the silly complaints you have received.
b) Write an article for an online magazine, describing a well-known town or city in your country and comparing it with a town or city which is less well known. Try to promote the less well-known place.
c) Interview a few friends and family members about their dreams, hopes and ambitions. Video the interviews and show them to the class.

Lead-in

OPTIONAL WARMER

Tell Ss that you are going to tell them about your home. Ss work in pairs and think of questions to ask you. Monitor and check Ss' questions, correcting where necessary. Ss take turns to ask you their questions. Answer them, giving as much information as you like. Encourage Ss to ask follow-up questions if they want to find out more.

1a ▶ Focus Ss' attention on the question. Give Ss a few minutes to think about the meaning of *home* and then write notes about the prompts.

b ▶ Put Ss in groups to compare their ideas. Get feedback from the whole class.

2a ▶ Put Ss in small groups. Ask Ss to look at the table and check they understand the words and expressions. If there is any vocabulary Ss don't know, encourage them to consult their dictionaries or ask you. Ss match the words from the box with the categories in the table. Check answers with the whole class. Draw the table with the column headings and existing words on the board and then complete it with the answers. Make sure to leave space for exercise 2b.

Answers
A: an apartment, a studio flat
B: a cellar, a fireplace, a garden, a garage, a gate
C: the suburbs
D: a park and a playground, a commercial district

b ▶ In pairs, Ss think of words to add to the table. Elicit ideas from the whole class and write them on the board in the relevant column. Check the meaning of the new words with the whole class and clarify any vocabulary Ss do not understand. Elicit example sentences to check Ss can use the vocabulary in context and are using the correct pronunciation. Encourage Ss to correct each other before doing so yourself.

3a ▶ Ss do the activity in pairs. Encourage them to use words and expressions from exercise 2.

b ▶ Ss describe the place where they live. Encourage them to ask follow-up questions to find out more information. Monitor and assist where necessary. Then put Ss in different pairs to repeat their descriptions. Get feedback from the class by asking Ss to tell you something about their first and second partner's house or flat.

OPTIONAL EXTENSION

Focus Ss on the photos. Ss discuss the photos in pairs and rank the houses in order from 1–4 (1 = the place they would like to live the most, 4 = the place they would least like to live). Ss report their rankings to the rest of the class, giving reasons for their decisions.

3.1 Your place or mine?

In this lesson, Ss look at a website that offers home exchanges. They read descriptions and then listen to two families planning an international home exchange. The listening provides examples for the grammar focus on future plans, which they then practise. Ss talk about things they would need if they went to live abroad. This leads to a listening on the problems families faced on an international home exchange which provides the context for studying how to complain politely.

> **OPTIONAL WARMER**
>
> Ask Ss to look at the photos and brainstorm things they can see that are relevant to houses, e.g. outside: *walls, window, balcony*; inside: *vase, lamp*.

Reading and speaking

> There are organisations which offer house swapping holidays where families exchange their homes with other families in another country for the holidays. The advantage for the families is a saving on the cost of accommodation.

1 ▶ Give Ss a few minutes to discuss the questions in pairs. Get feedback, but don't give the correct answers at this point.

2 ▶ Write *Yourhome – Myhome* on the board. In pairs, Ss discuss what they think the title is about. Ss read the texts quickly to match the descriptions with the photos individually. Tell them not to worry about any words they don't understand at this stage. Ss check their answers in pairs. Get feedback from the whole class and ask Ss to give reasons for their answers.

Answers
Property 1: photos A and 2
Property 2: photos B and 1

> **OPTIONAL VARIATION**
>
> Divide Ss into pairs (A and B). Ss A read about Property 1 and Ss B read about Property 2. Ss then exchange property information and match the texts with the photos.

3a ▶ Ss read the texts more carefully and answer questions. Check the answers with the whole class and elicit the part of the text which gave them each answer. Ask Ss if there are any words or phrases in the text that they don't understand. Encourage Ss to answer each others' questions before asking you.

Answers			
1	Property 1	5	Property 2
2	Property 2	6	Property 1
3	Property 2	7	Property 1
4	Property 2		

b ▶ Ss discuss the question in pairs. Get feedback from the whole class.

Listening

4a ▶ 🔘 1.20 Give Ss time to read through the activities and then play the recording. Ss write *D* for the Dos Santos family and *A* for the Armitage family. Check the answers with the whole class.

Answers					
1	D	3	A	5	D
2	A	4	D	6	A

b ▶ Give Ss time to read the extracts from the listening. Then Ss work in pairs and predict the answers. Play the recording again for Ss to check their ideas. Check the answers with the whole class.

Answers			
1	're spending	4	're going
2	going to do	5	going to try
3	'll give	6	won't

Grammar | future plans

> **OPTIONAL GRAMMAR LEAD-IN**
>
> Write the following sentence halves on the board.
> 1 <u>I'm going to</u>   buy a new car.
> 2 <u>I think I'll</u>   the owner tomorrow evening.
> 3 <u>I'm meeting</u>   buy my own house one day.
>
> Ask Ss to match the sentence halves (1 buy a new car, 2 buy my own house one day, 3 the owner tomorrow evening). Ss then make their own sentences using the underlined forms. Let Ss compare ideas in pairs.

5 ▶ Give Ss a few minutes to read the Active grammar box. In pairs, Ss find examples of each structure in exercise 4b. Check the answers with the whole class. Refer Ss to the Reference on page 47 and give them time to read through the notes. Ask Ss: *What structure do we use if we want to talk about intentions or plans in the future?* (be going to) *What structure do we use for fixed arrangements in the future?* (Present Continuous) *What structure do we use for decisions made at the time of speaking?* (will) *What structures do we use for making general predictions about the future?* 'be going to or will' Focus Ss' attention on the contracted forms of *will* and *will not* ('ll and won't)

Answers					
A	2, 4, 5	B	3, 6	C	1

6 ▶ In pairs, Ss complete the texts with the words and phrases from the box. Check the answers with the whole class.

> **Answers**
> 1 'm starting   5 's moving
> 2 're going to   6 is going to
> 3 're going to   7 'll
> 4 'll   8 is going to

Speaking

7a ▶ Read through the instructions and examples with the class. Ask Ss to decide on a list of ten items.

b ▶ Now put the Ss in pairs to guess each other's lists by asking yes/no questions. Read through the example to make sure Ss understand the task.

c ▶ Ss then compare lists and help each other to get the missing items. You may want to model this first with a student. Get feedback from the whole class. Ask Ss to read out a few examples of what they are going to do.

> **OPTIONAL EXTENSION**
> Give Ss a few minutes to write as many of the things from their lists as they can on the board. Then have a class discussion, choosing the ten most necessary items. Ss should give reasons for their opinions.

8a ▶ In pairs, Ss write three or four questions to ask other students about their plans for the topics given. Monitor Ss' work and help where necessary.

b ▶ Put Ss in groups of four. Ss take turns to ask their questions. Encourage them to ask follow-up questions. Monitor and take note of errors which can be looked at with the whole class at the end of the activity.

Listening

9 ▶ Focus Ss on the pictures of the two families during their home exchange. In pairs, Ss predict what the problems were. Get feedback from various Ss and write their predictions on the board.

10a ▶ ● 1.21 Play the recording for Ss check their ideas using the predictions on the board.

> **Suggested answers**
> Top left picture: The house was old and dark.
> Top right picture: The shower didn't work.
> Bottom left picture: The flat was too small so they had big arguments.
> Bottom right picture: There was a bar downstairs which played loud music until 4:00 a.m.

b ▶ Play the recording again. Ss take notes and then compare their answers in pairs. Get feedback from the whole class.

> **Answers**
> Miriam: the house was in the middle of nowhere, it was old and dark, nothing worked properly: the heating didn't work and there was no hot water
> Jeremy: the flat was too small, it was too hot (no fan), mosquitoes stopped them sleeping, a bar downstairs played music all night

c ▶ ● 1.22 Give Ss time to read through the questions. Then play the recording and check the answers with the whole class.

> **Answers**
> 1 over two hours
> 2 disgusting (dirty) and small
> 3 the cleaner was ill
> 4 sheets and towels because there weren't any clean ones
> 5 switched off
> 6 £100

11 ▶ Play the recording again and ask Ss to mark the phrases *M* or *R*. Get feedback from the whole class. Drill the phrases, checking for pronunciation and intonation.

> **OPTIONAL EXTENSION**
> 1) Tell Ss that you have an electrical/DIY shop. Tell Ss that they have bought something from your shop and it is broken. Encourage Ss to complain to you. Go through the four stages of complaining from the How to... box.
> 2) Give Ss a few minutes to think of a problem that they had (or someone they knew had) while on holiday. Put Ss into small groups to describe the problems. Encourage Ss who are listening to ask follow-up questions about the problem. When all the Ss have talked about their problems, Ss agree on the worst problem. Get feedback from the groups.

Speaking

12a ▶ Give Ss time to read their notes from exercise 10b. Then brainstorm different forms of compensation with the whole class and put them on the board. Let the whole class discuss the ideas, eliminating any that are impractical or irrelevant.

b ▶ Put Ss in pairs and check they understand their roles. Remind them to use the phrases from the How to... box and then Ss perform their roleplays. Change the pairs and start again. You can do this as many times as you think is necessary. Monitor and take notes of any errors. Review the errors with the whole class.

3.2 City life

In this lesson, Ss talk about cities and read a poem about city life. This leads to some work on adjectives describing places. A listening and a reading text are provided to give information about different cities around the world. The reading text also provides examples for the grammar focus on comparatives and superlatives.

Reading

1a ▶ ◉ 1.23 Draw Ss' attention to the words in the box. Then play the recording and ask Ss to tick the sounds they hear. Elicit the answers and check Ss understand the words/phrases in the box.

> **Answers**
> car horns
> car engines
> police sirens
> people talking

b ▶ Give Ss time to note down all the sounds that they can hear where they live.

c ▶ Let Ss compare their answers in pairs. Then get feedback from the whole class and ask Ss how they feel about the sounds.

2a ▶ ◉ 1.24 Focus Ss' attention on the photos and brainstorm words that Ss associate with the photos. Check the meaning of the word *verse*. Then play the recording and ask Ss to match verses in the poem with the photos. Get feedback from the whole class and ask Ss to give reasons for their answers. Don't give vocabulary or check the glossary at this stage.

> **Answers**
> 1   B   3   A
> 2   D   4   C

b ▶ Draw Ss' attention to the glossary but don't go through the words at this stage. Give Ss a few minutes to read the verses and answer the questions before comparing their answers in pairs. Check the answers with the whole class and then, finally, check Ss have understood the glossary by asking Ss for example sentences using the words.

> **Answers**
> 1   road sweepers
> 2   people hurrying, footsteps, faces
> 3   shimmering lights, stars
> 4   dreams
> The poet enjoys all the sounds and sights of the city.

3a ▶ Check the meaning of the word *rhyme* by writing the word *be* on the board and eliciting rhyming words. If Ss are having problems, write *bee* and *see* on the board before eliciting again. Look at the example and check the meaning. Ss then work in pairs to find rhymes. Get feedback from the whole class.

> **Answers**
> hurrying, scurrying
> race, face, pace, place
> nights, lights, heights
> creep, sleep

b ▶ Read through the first sentence of the instructions with the Ss. Get Ss to say the example words aloud and notice that they sound like the sound they describe. Elicit other words like this, e.g. *hiss* for the sound of a snake. Write the word *onomatopoeia* on the board. Explain that this is what we call words that sound like the sound they describe. Look at the example and then put Ss in pairs to find other onomatopoeic words in the poem. Get feedback from the whole class.

> **Answers**
> swash
> swoosh
> sputter

c ▶ Write *phone* and *fun* on the board. Elicit what these two words have in common (they start with same sound). Emphasise the first sound if necessary to help Ss. Point out that we are talking about first sounds and not first letters. Ask Ss to think of other pairs of words like this and write them on the board. Then draw Ss' attention to the examples. Tell Ss that these are examples of *alliteration*. In pairs, Ss now look for ither examples in the poem. Check the answers with the whole class.

> **Answers**
> sweepers – swooshing
> pacing – places
> city – senses – sleep

4 ▶ Ss do the activity in pairs. Get feedback from the whole class. Ask Ss: *Do you agree with the feelings in the poem? Why/Why not? After reading this poem, how do you feel about city life? Have your feelings changed?*

> **OPTIONAL EXTENSION**
>
> Put Ss into small groups. Ss write a short poem about either country or city life. Tell Ss they should have at least one example of a rhyme, one example of onomatopoeia and one example of alliteration. The groups then read out their poems and the other Ss guess whether they are talking about the town or the country.

Vocabulary | adjectives describing places

OPTIONAL LEAD-IN

Refer Ss back to exercise 4 on page 39. Elicit adjectives that were used by Ss to describe city life. Brainstorm and write the adjectives on the board and check understanding. Ask Ss to justify why they would use them. You can also brainstorm any other adjectives they think they could use to describe a city.

5a ▶ Check Ss understand the meaning of *adjective* and *opposite*. Ss do the task individually and then compare answers in pairs. Don't confirm any answers at this point.

> **Answers**
> bustling – quiet
> clean – polluted
> dull – lively
> enormous – tiny
> friendly – unwelcoming
> modern – traditional
> picturesque – ugly

b ▶ In pairs, ask Ss to think of a town or city that matches each adjective and make sentences. Write an example on the board: *London is dirty because of the amount of rubbish everywhere, but Zurich is very clean.* Get feedback from the whole class with Ss using their sentences to show they have understood the adjectives. Finally, elicit the answers to exercise 5a.

> **OPTIONAL EXTENSION**
>
> In pairs, Ss look back at the adjectives from exercise 5a. They then choose a town or city to describe using at least five adjectives. Ss present their descriptions to the class and the other Ss decide if they agree or not.

Listening

> **OPTIONAL LEAD-IN**
>
> Ask the whole class: *What do you know about Japan? Do you know the names of any Japanese cities? What can you tell me about these cities?*

6a ▶ ● 1.25 Refer Ss back to the adjectives in exercise 5a. Ask Ss to predict which adjectives they might hear in a description of Kyoto and why. Play the recording and then check the answers with the whole class.

> **Answers**
> lively, bustling, traditional, quiet, modern, friendly

b ▶ Check the meaning of *temples* and *climate*. Ask Ss what they think they heard about these words. Play the recording again and then check the answers with the whole

class. Try to elicit details of what Heather says about each place.

> **Answers**
> liked: old buildings, people, shops, restaurants, temples, nightlife
> didn't like: climate

7a ▶ Ss do the task individually and then choose at least one city that fits their criteria.

b ▶ Ss then compare their ideas in pairs. Get feedback from the whole class and find out if everyone agrees and the reasons for their opinions.

> **OPTIONAL VARIATION**
>
> 1) In pairs, Ss consider what makes a city good or bad and choose a city that fits the criteria. Then tell Ss that they are going to present an award to the best city in the world (or the country). Ss prepare and present their presentation to the rest of the class who then vote for the best city.
> 2) Ss write down the names of their cities and their criteria. Collect the names of the cities and write them on the board. Ss then read out their descriptions and the rest of the class guess which city they are referring to.

Reading

> **OPTIONAL LEAD-IN**
>
> Before starting this activity, with weaker classes, you might like to check what Ss understand by the following words: *setting, circled, life expectancy, efficient, liveable, lifespan, preserved, medieval.*

8 ▶ Ss look through the text quickly to find the names of cities mentioned in the text. Get feedback from the whole class and compare the answers with the cities Ss mentioned in exercise 7.

9 ▶ Read through the questions with the Ss quickly, making sure Ss understand *subway* and *polluted*. Ss do the task individually. Get feedback from the whole class.

> **Answers**
> 1 Krakow
> 2 Santiago, Vancouver
> 3 Santiago
> 4 Sydney
> 5 Santiago
> 6 Krakow
> 7 Santiago, Sydney

10 ▶ In pairs, Ss re-read the texts and decide on the advantages and disadvantages of each city. Get feedback from the whole class and find out which is the most popular city.

Grammar | comparatives and superlatives

Bigos is Poland's national dish. Otherwise known as *Hunter's stew,* there is no single recipe for this dish but it must include cabbage and meat. Sauerkraut (sour cabbage), puréed tomatoes and mushrooms are also common ingredients.

OPTIONAL GRAMMAR LEAD-IN

Write the following gapped sentences on the board:
1 _____ is taller than _____ .
2 _____ is the tallest person in the class.
Ask a student to complete the spaces on the board with names of Ss in the class. Ss then discuss the endings of the adjectives and when to use them.

11 ▶ Give Ss time to read through the Active grammar box. Then put Ss in pairs to look back at the underlined sections of the text. Ss focus on the examples of comparatives and superlatives and match them with the rules in the Active grammar box. Check the answers with the whole class.

Answers
A life expectancy is higher than the global average
B Vancouver has a reputation for being more relaxed than other cities.
C It is also sunnier than you might imagine.
D you won't find anywhere better to live than Sydney
E Although the weather is not as good as in some cities, it's at least very mild.
F it isn't one of the world's cleanest cities
G It is the world's fifteenth most expensive city.
H Krakow is one of Europe's leafiest cities.
I one of the best preserved medieval city centres in Europe

12 ▶ In pairs, Ss complete the text with the comparative or superlative form of the words in brackets. Remind Ss to add *than* if necessary. Check the answers with the whole class and write the answers on the board.

Answers
1	the biggest	5	friendlier than
2	the most interesting	6	as cold as
3	more comfortable	7	the most delicious
4	better than	8	the oldest

13a ▶ Model this activity first. Choose a city that all the Ss know (it could be the town or city you are in now) and write sentences 1, 2 and 3 on the board, including the gaps. Then elicit what Ss think should be added to complete the sentences, checking that they understand the structures and the meaning of the sentences. Ss then do the activity individually. Put Ss in pairs to read out their sentences and discuss whether they agree with them. Monitor and note down any problems. Get feedback from the whole class.

b ▶ Ss write their five sentences individually. Then, in pairs, Ss read out their sentences and discuss whether they agree with them. Get feedback from the whole class.

OPTIONAL VARIATION

Ss do the activity individually as above but give three possible answers, e.g. *It's probably the oldest city in Europe. a) Prague b) Bonn c) Manchester.* Put Ss into pairs. Ss read out their sentences and the three options. Their partner has to guess which city they are referring to. Ss can then decide if they agree or not.

Speaking

14a ▶ Put Ss in small groups. Ss choose three places in their own country which they think are the best places to live. Give the groups some time to prepare short presentations for the rest of the class. Remind Ss to give reasons for their choices.

b ▶ Groups read out their presentations and then Ss vote for the best one.

OPTIONAL VARIATION

As above, but Ss prepare at least three reasons why they have chosen each of their three best places. Ask for nominations for the third best place in the country. Each group nominates their candidate and gives their reasons. Give an extra minute for groups to give extra reasons or for other groups to give reasons why they think one of the nominations should not be considered. Ss then vote but cannot vote for their own nomination. Do this again for the second and first place in the country.

3.3 Eco-homes

In this lesson Ss look at the issue of life in the future, specifically with reference to being more eco-friendly. Ss read an article about a professor's predictions for the future and listen to people commenting on those predictions. The article provides examples for the grammar focus on future possibility. Ss look at different ways of expressing future possibility and practise these forms. Ss look at compound nouns and practise how to pronounce them.

> **OPTIONAL WARMER**
>
> Write *Life in the future* on the board. Below it, write *homes* and ask Ss to predict what houses will be like in thirty years' time. Then write *technology* and elicit predictions. Finally, write *resources* (give the example of *water*) and then elicit whether Ss believe resources will be the same or different in thirty years' time. Write *eco-friendly* on the board and ask Ss to read the definition on page 42. Ask Ss if they want to change any of their predictions when considering the environment.

Reading

Note – It is advisable to have dictionaries available for this section.

1 ▶ Put Ss in pairs to discuss the questions. Then get feedback from the whole class.

2a ▶ Give Ss a moment to read the title and introduction to the article and then get feedback. Focus Ss on the words in the box. Elicit the meanings from Ss and practise the pronunciation of each word/phrase individually and as a whole class. In pairs, ask Ss to decide what relevance each word has to an eco-friendly future and therefore why it might be significant in the article. Get feedback from the whole class. Put the best ideas on the board.

> **OPTIONAL VARIATION**
>
> With weaker classes, give Ss two or three minutes to check the meanings of the words and phrases in the box with a dictionary before continuing with the rest of the activity.

b ▶ Ss read the text to check if any of their predictions from exercise 2a were true. Check the answers with the whole class, referring to the ideas you wrote on the board earlier.

3a ▶ Ss do the activity individually. Check the answers with the whole class. With stronger classes, try to get Ss to give answers in their own words whenever possible.

> **Answers**
> 1   by bodyheat
> 2   space can be arranged in different ways
> 3   they will provide oxygen
> 4   to run a car
> 5   because water will be more expensive
> 6   tell us when food is about to go out of date and provide recipes

b ▶ Check that Ss have identified all the predictions in the article by eliciting them and writing them on the board. Ss discuss the predictions in pairs. Then put two pairs together to make groups of four to discuss again. As Ss discuss their predictions, walk around and monitor answers to review in the class check.

Listening

4 ▶ 🔘 1.26 Read through the instructions with the Ss. Play the recording and then let Ss compare their answers in pairs. Play the recording again for Ss to find reasons for their answers before getting feedback from the whole class.

> **Answers**
>
> | | Tracy | Stig |
> |---|---|---|
> | Homes will be smaller. | ✓ a good idea – we don't need as much space as we think we do | ✗ rich people will always be able to have big houses |
> | People will stop using cars. | ✗ doesn't think it will happen unless people are forced to do it | ✗ new fuels will have to be developed |
> | People will keep fish to eat. | ✗ hard to imagine and won't grow quickly enough | ✗ |
> | Fridges will be intelligent. | ✓ thinks it's already happening | ——— |
> | Robots will be more common. | ✗ hard to imagine (but you never know) | ✓ there are already some robots and this will be developed further |

Grammar | future possibility

> **OPTIONAL GRAMMAR LEAD-IN**
>
> Write the following sentence prompts on the board:
> 1   *Astronauts/travel to Mars*
> 2   *Scientists/find a cure for AIDS*
> 3   *My country/win the World Cup*
> 4   *Spanish/become the most important language in the world*
> 5   *I/speak English perfectly*
>
> Ss work in pairs and decide how likely it is that these things will occur in the next ten years. Go around the class, taking note of how Ss express future possibility. Get feedback and write some of the Ss' ideas on the board.

5 ▶ Ss look back at the underlined sections of the text and complete the sentences in the Active grammar box. Check the answers with the whole class. Then refer Ss to Reference page 47 and give them time to read through it. Focus Ss on the use of *will* before the adverb in affirmative

sentences and the use of *won't* after the adverb in
negative sentences. Also draw Ss' attention to the use of
the infinitive without *to* after *may/might/could*. Finally, put
Ss in pairs to answer questions 1 and 2.

Active grammar

Our houses <u>will definitely</u>/certainly have to become much
    better insulated.
Fuel <u>will probably</u> become much more expensive.
Homes <u>probably won't</u> be as big.
The climate <u>may</u>/might/could change significantly.
We <u>may</u>/<u>might not</u> all have cars.

1   The adverb comes after *will* in positive/affirmative
    sentences and before *won't* in negative sentences.
2   *could*

6 ▶ Ss do the activity individually and then compare their
answers in pairs. Check the answers with the whole class.

Answers			
1	will probably	3	probably won't
2	will definitely	4	might not

7 ▶ Read through the instructions and the example
with the Ss. Discuss whether Ss agree with the example
sentence and if not ask them to think of other sentences.
Ss do the task individually and then compare their answers
in pairs. Get feedback from the whole class.

8a ▶ Tell Ss they are going to make predictions about
other Ss in the class. Give Ss time to think and write
seven predictions without writing the Ss' names. While
writing the predictions, encourage Ss to use the ways of
expressing future possibility from the Active grammar box.
Monitor what Ss are writing and help them with vocabulary
as necessary.

b ▶ In pairs, Ss exchange their predictions. Partners try
to guess who the predictions are about. Change the pairs
and repeat the activity. Monitor the conversations and note
down any errors.

Vocabulary | compound nouns

OPTIONAL LEAD-IN

Focus Ss' attention on the four photos. Elicit what all the
photos are examples of and then elicit descriptions of
each photo. Ask Ss: *Which one looks like the best place
to live? Why?*

9 ▶ Ss read the descriptions and match them with the
photos individually. Let Ss compare answers in pairs
before getting feedback from the whole class. Elicit the
information which helped them to make their choices, but
do not focus on vocabulary at this stage.

Answers			
1	C	3	D
2	A	4	B

10a ▶ Write *motorhome* on the board. Explain that
this is an example of a compound noun and elicit what a
compound noun is (a noun made from two smaller words
put together). Ss then look for more compound nouns
in the descriptions from exercise 9. Check the answers
with the whole class. Check meaning as well as correctly
identifying the compound nouns.

Answers
treehouse, staircase, bedroom, bathroom, fireplace,
hillside, skylight, solar panels, bunk beds, sofabed

b ▶ Ss do the task individually and then compare answers
in pairs. Check the answers with the whole class and
confirm that Ss understand the meaning of the compound
nouns and where they can be used.

Answers
washing machine	mobile phone
central heating	air conditioning
sofa bed	fish tank
wall cabinets	swimming pool
computer screen	bunk bed
DVD player	

Pronunciation | word stress in compound nouns

11a ▶ Check first that Ss remember the difference
between a noun and an adjective. Then do this as a whole
class activity.

Answers
They are all noun + noun except *central heating* and
mobile phone which are adjective + noun.

b ▶ 🔘 1.27 Read through the instructions and check
that Ss understand the meaning of stress. Use the word
compound noun as an example. Write it on the board
and elicit which word is stressed. You could show Ss how
to mark this on the word, e.g. compound noun. Play the
recording. Ss listen and mark the stress. Then check the
answers with the whole class. Ss can then listen again and
repeat as a whole class and individually.

Answers
Only *central heating* and *mobile phone* have the stress on
the second word.

c ▶ Ask Ss to look back at the words that have the stress
on the second word. Ask Ss: *Are these two compound
nouns the same as the other compound nouns? How
are they different? What rule does this illustrate?* Do this
activity with the whole class.

Answers
Adjective + noun compound nouns usually have the stress on the second word.

OPTIONAL EXTENSION

Ss brainstorm as many compound nouns as they know. Write the two parts of the words all over the board. Then, with the whole class, put the compound nouns back together (checking meaning at the same time). You can also check that Ss can correctly stress the new compound nouns. You can then start a story snake. Start a story including a compound noun. Then a student continues the story until they use another compound noun. This continues round the class.

Speaking

12 ▶ Read through the instructions then put Ss in pairs to discuss the questions. Change the pairs and repeat the activity as Ss will be more confident the second time around. Monitor this activity, noting the correct use of compound nouns and future possibility. Get feedback from the whole class. Give Ss the opportunity to report back on what they heard from other students and ask the rest of the class to comment.

3 Vocabulary | prefixes and suffixes

In this lesson, Ss look at uses of prefixes and suffixes and how they are used to modify words. Ss will need dictionaries for this part of the lesson.

1a ▶ Put Ss in pairs to answer the questions. Check the answers with the whole class and elicit that prefixes go at the start of the word they are modifying and suffixes go at the end.

Answers
prefixes: un (not)
suffixes: ful (with) less (without)

b ▶ In pairs, Ss read the table and add more examples to the right-hand column. If Ss need help, encourage them to use dictionaries or tell them to ask you.

2a ▶ Focus Ss on the table. Discuss how adding suffixes to a word can change the word type. Ask Ss to identify which adjectives were formed from nouns and which from verbs. Get feedback from the whole class.

Answers
create/creation, attract/attraction
dirt, friend
care (verb and noun), help (verb and noun)
use (verb and noun), care (verb and noun)
enjoy/enjoyment, comprehend/comprehension

b ▶ In pairs, Ss add their own examples to the right-hand column. Check the examples with the whole class.

3 ▶ Ss read the Lifelong learning box and then work in pairs to discuss how they could organise their notebooks to note the different word forms. Get feedback from the whole class. Again with the whole class, brainstorm other words that Ss have learned recently and write them on the board. In pairs, Ss use dictionaries to find all the other word forms or suffixes and prefixes related to the new vocabulary.

4 ▶ Give Ss time to read through the advertisements. Then Ss work in pairs to complete the advertisements by changing the form of the base words in bold. Check the answers with the whole class.

Answers
Flat to rent: peaceful, Friendly, Weekly
Home needed: Lovely, homeless, responsible, sunny
Flatmate wanted: careful, expensive, breakable, messy

5 ▶ In pairs, Ss write a short advert for one of the three options given. Encourage Ss to include at least three words with prefixes or suffixes. Stick the adverts on the classroom wall. Let Ss walk around and read the adverts.

OPTIONAL EXTENSION

Tell Ss they must respond to one of the adverts and write an answer in an email which could be written for homework.

3 Communication

In this lesson, Ss read and discuss an advertisement for a TV programme. Ss then listen to two people who want to appear in the TV programme and do a roleplay explaining why they should be selected.

> **OPTIONAL WARMER**
>
> In small groups, Ss discuss if they have ever been on a TV programme or wanted to be on TV. Get feedback and ask what type of competitions Ss have entered or wanted to enter.

1 ▶ Focus Ss' attention on the photos of the houses. In pairs, Ss describe the houses and discuss which one they prefer. Ss read the advertisement for the competition and answer the questions in pairs. Check the answers with the whole class.

> **Answers**
> Ian Brown and Chiara Woods help people find their dream home and let them try out their new lifestyle.
> To apply, you should prepare a short speech explaining why you want to move and what you want to do.

2a ▶ 🔵 1.28 Focus Ss on the table and give them time to read it carefully. Check Ss understand the vocabulary in the table and then play the recording. Ss complete the notes and compare answers in pairs

b ▶ Play the recording again for Ss to check their answers. Check the answers with the whole class.

> **Answers**
>
> | | Speaker 1 | Speaker 2 |
> |---|---|---|
> | Where do you live now? | In the suburbs of the city. | In a <u>small town</u>. |
> | What type of lifestyle do you have? | It's very <u>busy and stressful</u>. | It's quite healthy but a bit dull. |
> | Why do you want to move? | I hope to <u>become completely self-sufficient</u>. | My dream is to <u>live right in the middle of a big city</u>. |
> | What are your plans for your new home? | I'm going to <u>take a course in farming</u>. I'll probably <u>get some bees</u>. I might <u>get rid of the television</u>. | I'm going to <u>find a job</u>. I'll definitely <u>go clubbing a lot</u>. I could <u>learn a new language</u>. |

c ▶ Put Ss in small groups to discuss whether Speaker 1 or Speaker 2 should be chosen for the programme. Get feedback from the whole class and make sure Ss give reasons for their decisions.

3 ▶ Focus Ss' attention on the How to... box. Tell Ss that the phrases shown here are all ways of talking about dreams, hopes and ambitions. Practise saying the phrases with the Ss and give some examples. Then Ss prepare their own sentences. In pairs, Ss tell each other their sentences. Choose a few examples to listen to and check with the whole class.

4a ▶ Tell the Ss that they are now going to apply to appear on the TV programme. Give them time to prepare what they are going to say and to make notes. Monitor and help Ss as necessary.

b ▶ Put Ss in groups of four. In each group there should be two speakers and two judges. Give the speakers a limited time to make a speech explaining why they should be on the TV programme (using their notes from exercise 4a). The judges listen and ask questions to find out more information. Monitor and note down any errors. After listening to both speeches, the judges decide who should be chosen for the programme.

c ▶ Ss swap roles so the speakers become judges and the judges become speakers. The judges again decide who should appear on the programme. Get feedback from the whole class. Ask Ss to tell you who was successful and why. Go through any errors you heard while Ss were talking. Discuss the errors with the class and write the correct forms on the board.

Review and practice

1 ▶

Answers
1   'm thinking
2   Are you going
3   is working
4   'll go.
5   are
6   'm playing
7   'll do
8   are you doing

2 ▶

Answers
1   I'll probably go and look at flats tomorrow.
2   I probably won't be able to afford one right in the centre.
3   But I might (be able to) find one in the outskirts of town.
4   I don't have a lot of time, so I might not be able to see very many flats tomorrow.
5   But I'll probably find one if I keep looking.
6   I could find a flatmate to help with the bills.

3 ▶

Answers
1   taller than
2   the biggest room
3   more beautiful than
4   as comfortable as
5   of the warmest

4 ▶

Answers
1   quieter
2   more crowded than
3   further
4   more old-fashioned than
5   colder, than
6   more picturesque
7   more polluted than
8   easier, than

5 ▶

Answers
1   polluted
2   ugly
3   touristy
4   tiny
5   bustling
6   dull
7   friendly

Writing bank

See page 155 in the Students' Book

1 ▶ Ss discuss the questions in pairs. Get feedback from the whole class.

2a ▶ Ss read the emails and check their answers in pairs.

Answers
1   because they haven't received a rental DVD (two weeks after the original email) and are still paying a subscription fee
2   because they missed an online delivery which was three hours late, but they were still charged

b ▶ Ss read the emails again and match the topics with the paragraphs.

Answers
(For both emails)
1   B
2   A
3   C

3 ▶ Ss complete the How to... box with words from the two emails in exercise 2.

Answers
I have still not <u>received</u> this DVD/the item.
Your company has still <u>charged</u> me for the groceries/the items.
I am very <u>disappointed</u> with the service.
I consider this to be completely <u>unacceptable</u>.
I would like an immediate <u>refund</u>.
I look forward to your <u>reply</u>.

4a ▶ Ss make notes on the situation by answering questions 1–4.

b ▶ Ss write their letter of complaint, using phrases from the How to... box.

4 Wealth

Overview

Lead-in	Vocabulary: Time and money
4.1	**Can do:** Use intonation to check and confirm information
	Grammar: Question tags
	Vocabulary: Phrasal verbs
	Speaking and Pronunciation: Intonation in question tags
	Reading: The true story of a real fake
	Listening: Frank Abagnale, The Ghosh test
4.2	**Can do:** Carry out a survey and present results
	Grammar: Modal verbs of obligation and prohibition
	Vocabulary: Personal qualities (1), Shopping
	Speaking and Pronunciation: Connected speech
	How to... report survey results
	Reading: Duncan Bannatyne, Good with money
	Listening: A seminar on entrepreneurial qualities
4.3	**Can do:** Ask for and give clarification
	Grammar: Zero and First Conditionals with *if/when/unless/as soon as*
	Speaking and Pronunciation:
	How to... ask for clarification
	Reading: How you are persuaded to buy more
	Listening: Behavioural advertising
Vocabulary	Confusing words
Communication	Give reasons for opinions
Writing bank	Write a report on factual information
	How to... use formal linkers
Extra resources	ActiveTeach and ActiveBook

> **CEFR Can do objectives**
> 4.1 Use intonation to check and confirm information
> 4.2 Carry out a survey and present results
> 4.3 Ask for and give clarification
> **Communication** Give reasons for opinions
> **Writing bank** Write a report on factual information

> **CEFR Portfolio ideas**
> a) Prepare a short educational video for other Ss explaining how intonation is different when you are checking information and when you are confirming information. Use at least five different examples in your video.
> b) You have been asked to write a report on how people's interests have changed over the last few years. Ask at least ten people about their favourite music, food, colours, clothes, etc. from five years ago and today and take note of how much their opinions have changed. Then write a report about your findings, using the formal linkers from the How to... box on page 156.

Lead-in

> **OPTIONAL WARMER**
> Focus Ss' attention on the photos. In pairs, Ss describe the photos and decide what the connection is between them (wealth/money). Ask Ss to discuss the advantages and disadvantages of having money.

1a ▶ In pairs, Ss discuss the questions and make decisions. Get feedback from the whole class.

b ▶ Discuss this question with the whole class. Ask Ss: *Which is more important: money or happiness? Can you buy happiness?*

> **OPTIONAL EXTENSION**
> Write the following quotations on the board.
> *'Time is money.'*
> *'Money can't buy friends.'*
> *'A fool and his money are easily parted.'*
> Elicit the meaning of the quotations and ask Ss to provide examples of situations where they might be true. Ask Ss whether they agree or disagree and why.

2a ▶ Focus Ss on the verbs and phrases in the box. Ss do the activity in pairs. If there are any expressions they are not sure of, encourage them to answer each others' questions. Check the answers with the whole class.

> **Answers**
> Money: earn, good value for, inherit, lend, steal
> Money and time: have got ... to spare, invest ... in, it's not worth the, make, not have enough, run out of, save, spend, use your ... wisely, waste

b ▶ Ss add other words and phrases they know to the table. Get feedback from the whole class and write correct expressions on the board.

3a ▶ Check that Ss understand the vocabulary in the prompts 1–6. Then Ss write one answer for each prompt.

b ▶ Put Ss in groups to discuss their ideas. Encourage Ss to ask follow-up questions. Get feedback from the whole class.

> **OPTIONAL EXTENSION**
> Ss write their answers in a different order to the prompts. Ss swap notebooks with a partner and then ask questions to match the answers with the prompts. *Do you think clothes are a waste of money? No, clothes are something I spend a lot of money on.* Encourage Ss to expand each topic by explaining their answers: *No, clothes are something I spend a lot of money on because I want to look good.*

4.1 Catch me if you can

In this lesson, Ss read the story of Frank Abagnale. They read and listen to the story of his life and exploits. The reading provides the context for studying phrasal verbs. Ss then listen and discuss the Ghosh test: a test that judges accepted normal standards. The listening provides the context for Ss work on question tags. Ss also practise the intonation patterns of question tags.

> Frank Abagnale was a famous American trickster who was played by Leonardo Di Caprio in the 2002 film *Catch me if you can* directed by Steven Spielberg. In the 1960s, Abagnale ran away to Manhattan when his parents separated. He supported himself by posing as an airline pilot, a doctor and a lawyer and by the age of twenty-one had earned $2.5 million dollars through his cheating. Abagnale cashed false cheques in over twenty-six countries before he was eventually caught in France by FBI man Joseph Shea, played in the film by Tom Hanks.

OPTIONAL WARMER

Ss work in pairs and discuss any films they know of, or have seen, which are based on a true story. Get feedback from the whole class and ask a few pairs to tell the class about the films they have seen.

Reading and listening

1a ▶ In pairs, Ss describe what they can see in the photos. Ss discuss if they know why the character played by Leonardo Di Caprio became famous. Get feedback from the whole class. If any of the Ss have seen the film, they can tell the rest of the class about the plot.

b ▶ Ss work in pairs and try to predict what the article is about using the words from the box. If there are any words Ss don't understand, encourage Ss to explain them to each other. Get feedback from the whole class and decide as a group whose prediction sounds the most likely.

c ▶ Ss read the text quickly and match the headings with the paragraphs. Tell Ss not to worry about any words they don't understand at this point. Let Ss compare their answers in pairs before checking with the whole class.

Answers
1	C	4	D
2	E	5	A
3	B		

2a ▶ Ss read the text more carefully and answer the questions. Ss compare their answers in pairs. Then get feedback from the whole class.

Answers
1. He was sixteen.
2. He was good-looking with greying hair and he dressed well.
3. He used magnetic ink to change bank code numbers and stole bank customers' money.
4. He said his uniform was lost at the dry cleaners and that he had an urgent flight.
5. He was the FBI man who arrested Frank and later became his friend. He was probably very determined, but fair/open-minded.
6. Frank is a successful security consultant.
7. He thinks he was egotistical and self-centred.

OPTIONAL VARIATION

Ss read the first paragraph of the text. Ask Ss: *What did Frank Abagnale pretend to be?* (a pilot, a doctor and a lawyer) *How much money did Frank Abagnale earn from his cheating?* ($2.5 million) In small groups, each student now reads one of the paragraphs (B–E) and matches it with a heading. Without looking at the text again, each student reports back to the group. Ss then read the other three paragraphs to check the information and which heading matches each paragraph. Check the answers with the whole class. Ss then answer questions 1–7. Ss compare their answers in pairs before checking with the whole class again.

b ▶ ● 1.29 Read through the instructions with the Ss and make sure they close their books. Play the recording. Ss find seven differences between the text and the summary. Check the answers with the whole class. If Ss had difficulty hearing the answers, play the recording again.

Answers
1. Frank Abagnale wasn't English. He was American.
2. He tricked and cheated his way to $2.5 million, not $250 million.
3. He was wanted in twenty-six countries, not cities.
4. His mother was French, not German.
5. He said his uniform was lost, not stolen.
6. He didn't pretend to be a footballer. He pretended to be a doctor.
7. He went to prison in France.
8. He advises companies on security, not on how to cheat their customers.

3 ▶ Ss discuss the questions in pairs. Monitor and take note of errors. Get feedback from the whole class then write the errors on the board. Encourage Ss to self-correct.

Vocabulary | phrasal verbs

4 ▶ Write *phrasal verb* on the board and ask Ss what a phrasal verb is (verb + particle(s)). In pairs, Ss make a list of the phrasal verbs they know. Get feedback from Ss and write correct phrasal verbs on the board and discuss their meaning. Focus Ss on the text again and tell them to underline any phrasal verbs they can see. Ss then write the phrasal verbs in the mind maps, matching them with the correct definitions. Elicit the answers from various pairs.

> **Answers**
>
> Up:
> a pick up
> b make up
> c end up
> d catch up with
> e break up
> f grow up
>
> Out:
> a work out
> b run out
> c drop out

5 ▶ Write the example sentence on the board with the three possible endings. In pairs, Ss decide which of the endings is not possible. Cross out *his exams* and elicit the meaning of the verb *drop out*. Ss cross out the wrong endings in sentences 1–7. Let Ss compare their answers in pairs before checking with the whole class. Explain the meaning of any verbs Ss do not know.

> **Answers**
>
> 1 b
> 2 c
> 3 c
> 4 c
> 5 a
> 6 b
> 7 b

Speaking

6 ▶ In pairs, Ss retell the story of Frank Abagnale using the phrases to help them. Monitor and note down any errors to be covered during the class feedback.

> **OPTIONAL EXTENSION**
>
> Ss look back at the mind maps and choose four phrasal verbs. Ss write a sentence for each phrasal verb, but leave a space where the phrasal verb goes in the sentence. Monitor and check the Ss' sentences. Ss swap their sentences with a partner. Their partner tries to complete the gaps with the correct phrasal verb. Ss show the phrasal verbs they have included in the sentences to their partner and check answers. Get feedback from the whole class.

Listening and speaking

> Juries are a group of twelve people, chosen at random, who watch a criminal trial and decide whether the accused is innocent or guilty. During the trial, the jury is kept separate from other people and will not have access to news that could in any way prejudice their decisions. Generally, anyone who is able to vote in an election is expected to sit on a jury at least once in their lives.

7a ▶ Write *Ghosh test* on the board. Ask Ss if anyone knows what this is. Elicit possible answers. Then give Ss one minute to read the text and answer the questions. Check the answers with the whole class and elicit Ss' opinions of the Ghosh test.

> **Answers**
>
> 1 to judge what the standards of reasonable and honest people are
> 2 a famous law case
> 3 No, because people do not always agree about what is wrong.

b ▶ Read through the instructions with the Ss and check understanding. Then put Ss in small groups to discuss and rank the situations. In the class check, find out if all the Ss in each group agreed or disagreed and why.

c ▶ ◉ 1.30 Play the recording. Ss write down the friends' opinions of the situations from exercise 7b. Check the answers with the whole class. Ss compare what they heard with their own decisions.

> **Answers**
>
> Most dishonest: switching price labels in a shop so you pay less
> Followed by: copying a piece of work from the Internet
> Quite dishonest: lying about your age on an Internet dating site
> Taking the odd bit of stationery and copying CDs aren't seen as very dishonest.
> Buying a dress, wearing it and returning it isn't discussed.

Grammar | question tags

> **OPTIONAL GRAMMAR LEAD-IN**
>
> Write the following sentences on the board.
> *1 I think you work in fashion.*
> *2 You work in fashion, ____ ____ ?*
> In pairs, Ss decide how they could complete sentence 2 so that it has the same meaning as sentence 1. Get feedback from the whole class and write the correct words in the gaps (don't you). Elicit/explain that sentence tags are used to confirm information in a sentence. Write the names of famous people, e.g. Stephanie Meyer. Ss have to try and remember facts about them. Stephanie Meyer wrote *Twilight*, didn't she? Monitor carefully and take notes of where Ss have difficulties so you can explain them fully after looking at the Active grammar box. Then get feedback from the whole class.

8a ▶ ◉ 1.31 In pairs, Ss read the extracts and try to add the missing words. Play the recording for Ss to check their predictions. Get feedback from the whole class and write the correct question tags on the board.

Active grammar

A: OK, so which of these do you think is the most dishonest thing to do?

B: Right, well, I think it would have to be copying work from the Internet, <u>don't you?</u>

A: I guess so. What about copying a CD from a friend. I do that a lot, <u>don't you?</u>

B: Er, yes, I suppose I shouldn't really, <u>should I?</u> What about taking stationery home from work?

A: I think that depends what it is. I don't think the odd pen is a problem, <u>is it?</u>

b ▶ Discuss this questions with the whole class. Ask Ss: *Why do you think we use these missing words?* (because it sounds more natural) *Do you have phrases like this in your mother tongue? If so, why do you use them?* Then refer Ss to the last two paragraphs of the reference section on page 61. Play the recording again. Ss decide which of the missing words express agreement and which are really asking a question.

c ▶ 🌐 1.32 Play the recording. Let Ss compare their answers in pairs. Play the recording again and get feedback from the whole class.

Answers
1 Right, well, I think it would have to be copying work from the Internet, don't you? – agreement
2 I guess so. What about copying a CD from a friend? I do that a lot, don't you? – question
3 I don't think the odd pen is a problem, is it? – agreement
4 No, but you haven't taken anything bigger, have you? – question
5 That's a bit different, isn't it? – agreement
6 If I had, I wouldn't tell you, would I? – agreement
7 I think that's pretty dishonest, actually, but people do it all the time, don't they? – agreement
When we ask a question the intonation goes up, if we expect agreement then the intonation goes down.

9 ▶ Give Ss a few minutes to read through the Active grammar box. Ss choose the correct answers individually and then compare their answers in pairs. Check the answers with the whole class. Refer Ss to Reference page 61 and give them time to read through the notes. Ask Ss: *What answer do you expect if you use a negative tag?* (Yes) *What answer do you expect if you use a positive tag?* (No) *What verb do we use in a question tag if there is no auxiliary verb?* (do, does, did and their negatives). *If you want to give a short answer, do you need to use the main verb?* (No, only the auxiliary verb.)

Answers
To make question tags, we repeat the <u>auxiliary verb</u>.
If the question is positive, the question tag is <u>negative</u>.
If the question is negative, the question tag is <u>positive</u>.
If there is no auxiliary verb, the question tag uses <u>do, does</u> or <u>did</u>.

10 ▶ Ss do the activity in pairs. Check the answers with the whole class and write the question tags on the board.

Answers
1	isn't it	5	do you
2	did you	6	aren't you
3	isn't it	7	won't you
4	have you	8	would I

Pronunciation | intonation in question tags

11a ▶ 🌐 1.32 Play the recording. Ss check which intonation pattern is used in each extract. After checking, Ss listen and repeat each extract as a whole class and individually.

Answers
1	a	2	a

b ▶ In pairs, Ss practise the questions from exercise 10 and identify whether they are expecting an agreement or asking a real question.

12 ▶ Read through the instructions with the Ss. Put Ss in pairs to discuss the topics. Remind them to use question tags when appropriate. Monitor and take notes. Get feedback from the whole class and identify any incorrect usage or poor intonation of question tags.

OPTIONAL EXTENSION

Tell Ss to think about any information that they know about other Ss in the class. Individually, Ss write five or six questions, using question tags, which they can use to confirm this information. Go round and check the Ss' questions. Ss stand up, mingle and ask their questions. Get feedback from various Ss and find out if they have learned anything new about their classmates.

4.2 Getting rich quick

Dragons' Den is a very successful reality TV show. In the show, people with new ideas, products or companies present their venture to four successful, rich entrepreneurs. These entrepreneurs then decide whether to invest in the venture or not. It is one of the most popular programmes on British television and some of the ventures have gone on to become great business successes.

In this lesson, Ss look at vocabulary connected with being an entrepreneur and read about the life of one. They then analyse the grammar of modals of obligation and prohibition and the necessary pronunciation. Ss then read an article about spending money and practise the vocabulary of shopping. Finally, they do a class survey and practise reporting survey results.

OPTIONAL WARMER

On the board, write the following ways of making money: *gambling*, *the stock market*, *investing in property*, *starting a business*, *getting a job*. In pairs, Ss rank these ways of making money from 1–5; 1 being the best way of making money and 5 being the worst. Get feedback from the whole class.

Speaking

1a ▶ Put Ss in pairs to discuss their ideas. They then compare their ideas with another pair. Get feedback from the whole class.

Suggested Answers
win the lottery, rob a bank, write a bestseller, invent something

b ▶ In pairs, Ss brainstorm some famous millionaires and answer the questions. Help with ideas if necessary, e.g. JK Rowling, Bill Gates, Madonna. Get feedback from the whole class.

Vocabulary | personal qualities (1)

2a ▶ Focus Ss' attention on the expressions in the box. In pairs, Ss check the meanings of the expressions. Ask for volunteers to explain each expression by providing example sentences.

b ▶ Put Ss in pairs to discuss questions 1 and 2 and then elicit feedback from various Ss. Write the word *entrepreneur* on the board and elicit meanings without looking at the book. Then check the definition in the book and ask Ss to discuss question 3. Get feedback from the whole class.

Reading

OPTIONAL LEAD-IN

Ask Ss to look at the photo, read the introductory paragraph and then close their books. In groups, ask Ss to make predictions about the life of Duncan Bannatyne. Ask Ss: *How do you think he got to the place where he is today? What did he do as a child? How did he make money? Did he go to university?* etc. Get feedback from the whole class and put the most interesting points on the board. These can then be checked at the end of exercise 3b.

3a ▶ Ss read the text and answer the question. Make sure Ss understand that they have to give their opinion about the qualities which Duncan Bannatyne might have. Ss compare their ideas in pairs. Then get feedback from the whole class and encourage Ss to give reasons for their answers.

Suggested Answers
be ambitious, be confident, be determined, be good with figures, know your strengths and weaknesses, work long hours

b ▶ Ss do the activity individually, correcting any false answers. Check the answers with the whole class.

Answers
1 F (it was Maths)
2 T
3 F (because he could see that the kids there had better toys)
4 F (the navy was first)
5 T

c ▶ Ss discuss the questions in pairs. Elicit feedback and ask Ss to give reasons for their answers.

OPTIONAL EXTENSION

1) Ss find out about other entrepreneurs using the Internet, magazines, etc. and give a short presentation about why they are good examples of entrepreneurs.
2) Ss look for more information about *Dragons' Den*. You could download a clip from the Internet and show it in class. Ss can then perform their own version of the programme.

Listening

4a ▶ ⬤ 1.33 Check that Ss understand *seminar*. Play the recording and get feedback from the whole class.

Answers
The seminar is for young entrepreneurs.
The topic is how to get rich.

b ▶ 🌐 1.34 Refer Ss back to the list of qualities from exercise 2a on page 53. Play the recording for Ss to take notes. Let Ss check their answers in pairs before getting feedback from the whole class. If necessary, play the recording again before confirming the answers.

Answers

be mean	be confident
don't be too generous	work long hours
don't be too extravagant	be ambitious

OPTIONAL EXTENSION

Elicit from Ss whether they agree with these points and why. Brainstorm any other qualities that might be necessary if you want to become rich.

---

c ▶ This exercise can be used as a warmer for the grammar section. Play the recording again and ask Ss to complete the notes. Get feedback from the whole class and elicit why the words are in bold. Elicit more possible answers for gaps 1, 3 and 4.

Answers

1	be too generous	4	look good
2	early	5	believe
3	waste	6	hard

Grammar | modals of obligation and prohibition

OPTIONAL GRAMMAR LEAD-IN

Write the following advice on the board.
1 You <u>have to</u> do your homework.
2 You <u>should</u> write new vocabulary in your notebook.
3 You <u>must</u> study before the exam.
4 You <u>don't have to</u> use English outside class.
Tell Ss that one of the sentences is not true. In pairs, Ss decide which sentence is false and how they could change it to make it true. (Sentence 4 should read: You <u>should</u> try to use English outside class.) Elicit the difference in meaning between the four sentences.

---

5 ▶ Give Ss time to read the meanings (A–E) in the Active grammar box. Put Ss in pairs to match the meanings with the modal verbs from exercise 4c. In the same pairs, Ss answer the question in the Active grammar box. Get feedback from the whole class. Then refer Ss to Reference page 61. Give Ss time to read through the notes. Ask Ss: *What modal is often used for rules and regulations?* (have to) *What modal do we use when the obligation comes from the speaker?* (must) *Is it correct to say* must to *or* should to*?* (No, *must* and *should* are never followed by *to*.) *What is the negative form of should?* (shouldn't)

Active grammar

1	must	1	O
2	have to		A
3	should	2	O
4	mustn't		A
5	shouldn't	3	A
6	don't have to		O

---

6 ▶ Read through the instructions and make sure Ss understand the context. Do the first question as an example with the whole class. Write it on the board and then elicit all the possible modal answers. Elicit the meaning of the sentence with each modal and decide on the best answer. Ss then do the rest of the activity individually before checking their answers in pairs and then with the whole class.

Suggested Answers

1	must	4	shouldn't
2	has to	5	mustn't
3	should	6	don't have to

OPTIONAL EXTENSION

In pairs, Ss think of more advice for people setting up their own business, using modal verbs. Get feedback from the whole class and agree on the top ten business tips (including the ones from the exercise).

7a ▶ Read through the instructions and write question 1 on the board. Ask Ss: *Which is the key word that needs to be changed in the first sentence?* (essential) Check Ss understand the meaning of this word and then elicit the modals that have the same meaning (must, have to). Ask Ss: *Is the sentence positive or negative?* (negative) and then elicit the missing word. Ss do the rest of the activity in pairs. Check the answers with the whole class.

Answers

1	mustn't	4	mustn't
2	don't have to	5	should
3	must/has to	6	must/have to

---

b ▶ Ss decide with a partner whether the sentences in ex. 7a are giving advice or taking about obligation or prohibition. Check answers with the whole class.

Answers

1	A	3	O	5	A
2	O	4	O	6	A

Pronunciation | connected speech

8a ▶ 🌐 1.35 Write the first two sentences on the board without the brackets and ask selected Ss to read them out. Ask Ss if any letters are not pronounced when we say them. Then Ss open their books. Play the recording. Get feedback from the whole class.

Answers
These sounds disappear or are elided.

b ► Check Ss understand the meaning of *vowel sound* and *consonant sound*. Ss look back at the examples from exercise 8a and choose the correct answer. Check the answer with the whole class and refer them to page 164 to read the rule.

Answers
3

c ► Play the recording again. Ss repeat the sentences individually and as a whole class.

OPTIONAL EXTENSION

Ss prepare their own sentences, showing the elision of /t/ and /d/ which they then give to other Ss to try and pronounce properly. They can also try to make it difficult by including as many examples of the elision as possible in one sentence.

Reading

9a ► Ss discuss the question in pairs. Get feedback from the whole class and write the ideas on the board. Then practise giving the advice on the board using the modals of obligation from the Active grammar box on page 54.

b ► Ss read the article to find out if any of their ideas are mentioned. Get feedback from the whole class.

10a ► Ss re-read the article and answer the questions individually. Let Ss compare their answers in pairs before getting feedback from the whole class. Make sure Ss read out complete sentences to make them passively aware of the construction being introduced here.

Answers
1 If you see a bargain in the sales you should <u>wait a day</u>.
2 You should never go food shopping without <u>a shopping list</u>.
3 You should only buy high fashion if <u>you buy it cheaply</u>.
4 If you are buying something expensive, make sure you <u>shop around</u>/<u>get the best deal</u>/<u>keep the receipt</u>.

b ► Discuss this question with the whole class and make sure Ss give reasons for their answers.

OPTIONAL EXTENSION

Brainstorm other pieces of advice for shoppers using the structures from exercise 10a.

Vocabulary | shopping

11a ► Ss look through the article to find words and phrases connected with shopping and add them to the table. Ss compare their answers in pairs.

b ► Ss compare their lists with the answers on page 147. Get feedback from the whole class. Encourage Ss to make sentences with the words to show they have understood the meaning.

Answers

Verbs	Nouns	Adjectives
spend	money	cheap(er)
afford	impulse buy	reduced
buy ...cheaply	the sales	
pay (hundreds of pounds)	(what a) bargain	
shop around	checkout	
get the best deal	(make a) shopping list	
	big ticket item	
	price comparison websites	
	an expensive mistake	
	receipt	
	refund	

Speaking

12a ► Read through the instructions with the Ss and check understanding. Put Ss into small groups. Each group writes four more sample yes/no questions. Tell them to make sure they include at least one word or phrase from exercise 11b in each question. Monitor and check that the questions are correct.

b ► Put Ss in pairs, making sure the Ss haven't already worked together. Ss interview each other using their questions from exercise 12a. Remind Ss to write down responses.

c ► Ss reform their groups from exercise 12a and collate their answers. Ss can show their results using graphs or charts.

d ► Read through the How to... box with the Ss. Supply example endings to show how the sentences work and elicit more examples from the class. Then ask groups to present their findings to each other using the phrases from the How to... box. Give Ss time to practise first. Then pair up the groups. Groups take turns to present their findings. Monitor and note down any issues to review in the class check.

OPTIONAL EXTENSION

Make a list of all the groups' questions used on the board. Ss then choose their favourite six questions. Tell Ss that they are now expected to survey at least ten people outside the class and then write a report of their findings. These can either be put up on the wall or presented in the next class. Ss can then compare their results outside the class with results inside the class.

4.3 Spend more!

In this lesson, Ss discuss advertising, supermarkets and salespeople. Ss then go on to read a text about one of these areas and exchange information about the texts. Ss look at the grammar of the Zero and First Conditionals with *if/when/unless/as soon as*. They then listen to an interview about behavioural advertising, where different ways of asking for clarification are introduced.

OPTIONAL WARMER

Elicit from Ss something they have bought for themselves recently. Ask Ss: *Why did you buy this item? How did you hear about it?* Write different ways of finding out about a product on the board, e.g. from an advert, a recommendation, etc. Discuss which factors influence their buying decision the most.

Reading and speaking

1 ▶ Focus Ss on the three photos then put Ss in pairs to discuss the questions. Monitor the conversations and note down any errors. Get feedback from the whole class. Go through any errors and encourage Ss to self-correct.

2 ▶ In pairs, Ss look at the sentences about supermarkets, salespeople and advertisements and predict what information completes the sentences. Tell them to look carefully at each sentence, particularly at the words immediately before and after each gap to help them. Get feedback from the whole class and write Ss' ideas on the board.

3 ▶ Put Ss in groups of three: A, B and C. Refer Ss A to the text on page 56, Ss B to the text on page 147, and Ss C to the text on page 151. Ss read the texts and find the sentences from exercise 2. If there are any words or expressions they don't understand, encourage them to ask you.

4 ▶ In their groups of three, Ss swap information to check their predictions from exercise 2 and discuss whether any information in the texts surprised them. Get feedback from the whole class and discuss why some information was surprising.

Answers
1 anything, anybody, anytime
2 hobbies, family, lifestyle
3 body language
4 seventy-five
5 play music
6 shopping baskets
7 celebrities
8 funny
9 mouth water

---

5 ▶ Ss work in the same groups to discuss the questions. Monitor and take note of errors. Ask each group to report what they have talked about to the rest of the class. Finally, write the errors on the board and discuss them with the class before giving feedback.

OPTIONAL EXTENSION

In pairs, Ss write their own slogan for an English school. Ss then share their slogans with the rest of the class. With the whole class, choose the best slogan to advertise a language school. If time, Ss can then discuss how they would use this slogan to advertise the school.

Grammar | Zero and First Conditionals with *if/when/unless/as soon as*

OPTIONAL GRAMMAR LEAD-IN

Write the following sentence on the board. *If you read English outside class, you'll improve more quickly.* Ask Ss if they know the name of this structure in English. (First Conditional) Elicit the structure of the First Conditional: *if* + Present Simple + *will* + infinitive without *to*. In pairs, Ss write more sentences about studying English which include the First Conditional. Ss read out their sentences to the class. Then do the same with Zero Conditional using: *If people read more, they learn more.* Highlight the difference in meaning between the two forms.

6a ▶ Focus on the Active grammar box. Read through rules A and B and check understanding. Ss then match the rules with the sentences (1–6). Check the answers with the whole class and make sure Ss give reasons for their answers.

Active grammar

1	B		4	A
2	B		5	A
3	A		6	B

---

b ▶ Ss complete the rules in section C with the words from the box. Remind Ss to use sentences 1–6 to help them. Check the answers with the whole class and make sure Ss have understood the meaning of the words in the box.

Answers

1	when		3	as soon as
2	when		4	unless

---

c ▶ Tell Ss to underline six more examples of the First Conditional in the three articles from exercise 3. Check the sentences with the whole class. Refer Ss to Reference page 61. Give Ss time to read the notes about the First Conditional and then ask Ss: *What words do we use to form the First Conditional?* (*if* + Present Simple + *will*) *Is it possible to use other verbs instead of will?* (*Yes*, modals like *can*, *should* and *may* can be used.) Focus Ss on the use of contractions for *will* ('*ll*) and *will not* (*won't*). Then do the same for Zero Conditional, emphasising the difference in meaning.

7 ▶ Ss cover column B of the table. In pairs, Ss think of ways of completing the sentence beginnings in column A using the First Conditional. Get feedback from the whole class and write correct sentences on the board. In the same pairs, Ss uncover column B and match the sentence beginnings with the endings. Check the answers with the whole class.

> Answers
> 1 c
> 2 f
> 3 a
> 4 d
> 5 e
> 6 b

8a ▶ Ss rewrite each sentence in three different ways, using the words given. Check the answers with the whole class.

> **OPTIONAL VARIATION**
>
> With stronger classes, if Ss have clearly understood the use of the phrases, you may prefer to do this as a whole class oral activity.

> Answers
> 1 a <u>When</u> they offer me the job, I will take it. (They are definitely going to offer me the job.)
>   b If they offer me the job, I <u>might</u> take it. (I'm not sure that they will offer me the job, or that I will take it.)
>   c <u>As soon as</u> they offer me the job, I will take it. (I won't hesitate to take the job.)
> 2 a <u>As soon as</u> I see Tom, I'll tell him. (I'll tell him immediately.)
>   b <u>If</u> I see Tom, I'll tell him. (I'm not sure if I will see him.)
>   c When I see Tom, I <u>can</u> tell him (I'll be able to tell him. (an offer))

b ▶ As this is a more difficult structure, you may want to do the first question as an example. Write sentence 1 on the board. Make sure Ss understand that they have to rewrite it using *unless*. Then Ask Ss: *Where does 'unless' go in the sentence?* (at the beginning). *Which part of the sentence follows it?* (the first part: you don't pay the bill) *Do you have to make any changes to it?* (Yes, you have to change it from a negative to a positive.) Then elicit the full answer. Ss rewrite the remaining sentences individually before checking in pairs. Get feedback from the whole class.

> Answers
> 1 Unless you pay the bill on time, you'll get a fine.
> 2 Unless there is something urgent to discuss, he won't phone us.
> 3 I won't help you unless you help me.
> 4 Unless Sandro finds an apartment soon, he'll have to stay at home.
> 5 Unless you work hard, you won't do well in your exams.
> 6 It will be a great day out unless it rains.

Speaking

9a ▶ Focus Ss on sentence prompts 1–5. Give them time to write complete sentences which are true for them. Go round and check Ss' sentences for correct use of the First and Zero Conditional structures.

b ▶ Put Ss in pairs to discuss their sentences. Encourage them to ask follow-up questions. Change the pairs and repeat the activity. Get feedback from the whole class.

Listening and speaking

10 ▶ Ss look at the advertisements and discuss the questions in pairs. Get feedback from the whole class.

11a ▶ ◉ 1.36 Elicit ideas for what behavioural advertising might be. Write Ss' ideas on the board but don't confirm the answer at this point. Play the recording. Make sure that Ss have understood the meaning before moving onto the next exercise.

> Answers
> Behavioural advertising sends adverts to specific people based on their interests and Internet browsing habits.

b ▶ Ss read through the statements and try to remember if they are true or false. Play the recording for Ss to check and complete their answers. Get feedback from the whole class.

> Answers
> 1 T
> 2 T
> 3 F
> 4 F
> 5 T

c ▶ Ss discuss the questions in pairs. Get feedback from the whole class..

12a ▶ ◉ 1.36 Read the title of the How to... box. Elicit possible situations when you might ask for clarification. Give Ss time to read the phrases and then play the recording. Ss tick the phrases that are used. Drill the phrases as a whole class and individually and then elicit any other phrases that Ss might use to ask for clarification.

> Answers
> Sorry, I'm not with you.
> Are you saying that ... ?

b ▶ Ss choose a topic from the list and prepare what they are going to say.

c ▶ Put Ss in pairs and tell them that they now have three minutes to give a talk to their partner. Tell partners they should use at least three phrases to ask for clarification during the talk. Monitor and note down any errors for the class feedback session.

4 Vocabulary | confusing words

In this lesson Ss practise using words which are easily confused such as *rob* and *steal*. The exercises will help Ss analyse the differences between these words.

1 ▶ Go through the first set of words as an example with the Ss. Write the two words on the board. Focus on *credit card* and elicit the meaning. Then elicit the meaning of *debit card*. Check that Ss understand the different meanings by eliciting examples. Ss then discuss the remaining items in pairs. Get feedback from the whole class.

> **OPTIONAL VARIATION**
>
> With weaker classes you could do this as a dictionary activity, where Ss check the dictionary in pairs for the meanings and the differences.

Answers
1   If you pay by *debit card*, the money comes straight out of your account. If you pay by *credit card*, you pay later but have to pay interest on the money borrowed.
2   A *receipt* is a piece of paper that shows you have paid for something. A *bill* is a piece of paper that shows what you have to pay.
3   A *coin* is metal money. A *note* is paper money.
4   A *fare* is the amount you pay to travel by train, plane, bus, taxi, etc. A *fine* is money you pay as a punishment for breaking a law or rule.
5   The *price* is how much it costs to buy something. A *fee* is money you pay for professional services (e.g. lawyer) or to do something (e.g. a course).
6   A *reduction* is a decrease in price. A *refund* is when the money you have spent on something is returned to you.
7   *Change* means coins. *Cash* refers to real money (notes or coins) as opposed to a credit card or debit card.

2 ▶ Ss do the activity in pairs. Allow Ss to compare their answers with another pair. Check the answers with the whole class and then, in small groups, Ss discuss the difference between each pair of words. Get feedback from the whole class.

Answers

1	a	miss		5	a	job
	b	lost			b	work
2	a	trip		6	a	lend
	b	travel			b	borrow
3	a	fun		7	a	remind
	b	funny			b	remember
4	a	told		8	a	robbed
	b	said			b	stolen

3 ▶ Read through the first paragraph of the Lifelong learning box with the Ss and check understanding. Discuss the importance of recording how to use new vocabulary and explain how a good dictionary can be helpful in this respect. Focus Ss on the examples. Give Ss time to read them and then, in pairs, Ss write similar notes for the other words in italics from exercise 2. Check the answers with the whole class.

> **Example notes:**
> *lose/miss:* If you *lose* something, you cannot find it. If you arrive too late for something, e.g. a bus, you *miss* it.
> *work/job:* Work is what you do to earn money. A *job* is the particular type of work that you do.
> *lend/borrow:* If you *lend* something to someone, you give it to them so that they can use it for a short time. If you *borrow* something from someone, you take something that belongs to them, use it, and return it.
> *remember/remind:* If you *remember* something, it comes back into your mind. If you *remind* someone to do something, you let them know they need to do it.

4 ▶ Tell Ss to cover the words from exercises 1 and 2. They then complete the sentences with an appropriate word. Remind Ss to change the form of the word when necessary to fit the context of the sentence. Check the answers with the whole class.

Answers

1	told		8	job
2	lend		9	funny
3	bill		10	missed
4	stolen		11	credit
5	change		12	refund
6	trip		13	fee
7	fine			

5 ▶ Ask Ss to find ten words that they have trouble with from the lists on the page. Ss then write true sentences about themselves and their life to show their understanding. They should write these on a piece of paper without adding their name. Go round the class and check what Ss are writing, giving help where necessary. Collect all the papers and put them in a bag. Each student then pulls out a paper, reads it and tries to guess who wrote it, giving reasons for their answer.

4 Communication

In this lesson, Ss look at some of the most expensive things in the world. Ss then consider whether these things are a waste of money or not.

> **OPTIONAL WARMER**
>
> In pairs, Ss discuss how much they would be willing to pay for a meal in a restaurant. Get feedback and discuss whether Ss think that spending a lot of money in a restaurant is a waste of money or not. Elicit from Ss which things they would be prepared to spend a lot of money on.

1a ▶ Focus Ss on the photos. In pairs, Ss decide what each photo shows and how much money was spent on each item. Ss match the figures to the photos. Get feedback from the whole class but don't confirm any answers at this point.

b ▶ Ss read the text quickly first to check their answers. Tell Ss not to worry about any words they don't understand at this stage. Check the answers with the whole class. Then ask Ss to read the text again more carefully. Ask Ss if there are any words they don't understand. Tell Ss to try to explain words to each other before asking you.

Answers		
1 B	2 C	3 A

2a ▶ 🔘 1.37 Read through the questions and then play the recording. Ss answer the questions. Get feedback from the whole class but don't confirm the answers.

b ▶ Play the recording again. This time Ss look for reasons for the answers from exercise 2a. Check the answers with the whole class.

Answers
1. the Jackson Pollock painting: because he thinks the painting is a 'dribble a child could produce'
2. sending a man to the moon: as it has some meaning for man and the problems we face on this planet
3. the Hadron Collider: because it's too risky, so much could go wrong and it's not important to know how Earth came into being
   the Wagyu sandwich: because it's too expensive, it's full of fat and it's a waste of carbon to bring the beef from Chile every day.

3a ▶ Divide the Ss into two groups (A and B). Group A chooses three facts from the text and decides why they think these are/were a terrible waste of money. Group B chooses three facts from the same text and decides why they are/were a good use of money. Read through the examples with the Ss to check they understand the task.

b ▶ Put Ss into A/B pairs . Ss discuss their facts and why they think they were a waste of money or worth spending money on. Monitor the conversations and take note of errors. Write the errors on the board and encourage Ss to work together to correct them.

> **OPTIONAL VARIATION**
>
> After Ss have finished exercise 3a, divide Groups A and B into two separate groups and then match one Group A with one Group B. Tell the Ss that they will now have a mini-debate. Whatever one group presents, the other group must disagree with and try to convince the whole group why they disagree. Allow two minutes for discussing each point. When the time is up, the groups should vote individually on whether they agree with the original statement or not. Go round the class monitoring while this activity takes place, taking note of any problems or errors for the feedback session.

4a ▶ Ss work in pairs and choose one topic. They should then find three reasons for either agreeing or disagreeing with the statement.

b ▶ Put Ss in different pairs to discuss the topics they chose in exercise 4a. Tell Ss that they should disagree with their partner's point of view and give reasons for their opinions. Monitor this activity and take notes of errors or important points. Get feedback from various Ss then write errors on the board and encourage the Ss to self-correct.

Review and practice

1 ▶

Answers					
1	can I	4	didn't she	8	have they
2	don't I	5	isn't it	9	should I
3	won't they	6	aren't I	10	didn't you
		7	aren't we		

2 ▶

Answers									
1	c	3	i	5	e	7	b	9	d
2	g	4	j	6	f	8	a	10	h

3 ▶

Answers	
At the meeting we agreed on some rules.	✓
All staff should look smart to	to
at all times but workers don't never have	never
to wear a suit unless requested. Staff	✓
must to go outside to smoke and should	to
try not to blow smoke in through the	✓
windows. Workers mustn't not leave dirty	not
cups in the workspaces and food must not	✓
to be consumed in the office. Staff do	to
not have to be eat in the canteen, but	be
lunch breaks must not have exceed one hour.	have

4 ▶

Answers			
1	mustn't	4	doesn't have to
2	don't have to	5	mustn't
3	mustn't	6	doesn't have to

5 ▶

Answers					
1	If	3	Unless	5	if
2	unless	4	when	6	If

6 ▶

Answers
1 If I ~~will~~ see you tomorrow, I will give you the book.
2 She won't act in the film unless ~~that~~ she receives her normal salary.
3 We'll go as soon <u>as</u> the taxi arrives.
4 If I drink another cup of coffee, I will <u>not be</u> able to sleep tonight.
5 I can't hear you unless you ~~don't~~ shout.
6 When I next go shopping, I'll ~~to~~ buy some milk.
7 Unless you drive carefully, you ~~won't~~ <u>will</u> crash.
8 As soon as you ~~will~~ see him, call me.

7 ▶

Answers					
1	run	4	picked	8	trip
2	value	5	figures	9	refund
3	up	6	around	10	lend
		7	advert		

Writing bank

See page 156 in the Students' Book

1a ▶ Ss discuss the question in pairs. Get feedback from the whole class.

b ▶ Ss read the report and compare the findings with their ideas. Get feedback from various Ss.

2a ▶ Ss complete the How to... box with the underlined linkers from the report.

Answers	
1	In addition
2	However
	In fact
	On the other hand
3	In conclusion

b ▶ Ss choose the correct words in *italics*.

Answers	
1	Nevertheless
2	Moreover
3	Furthermore
4	However
5	Overall

3 ▶ Ss read the report again and underline the answers to points 1–3. Check the answers with the whole class.

Answers	
1	The purpose of this report is to present the findings of …
2	Most of the class said that … , fewer people said that … , just one person … , Nearly everyone we spoke to … , several people said that … , some people would … , Relatively few people decided that … , a few people claimed … , most people would …
3	In conclusion, it appears that … , our survey also showed that …

4a ▶ Ss refer back to the results of their survey from exercise 12 on page 55. Ss prepare to write a report on this survey by deciding on the key points they want to present. Monitor and help where necessary.

b ▶ Ss write a report about the findings of their survey, using linkers from the How to... box and phrases from exercise 3.

5 Free time

Overview

CEFR Can do objectives
5.1 Describe your response to a picture
5.2 Describe a pastime
5.3 Describe a restaurant
Communication Make a short presentation
Writing bank Write a detailed description of an object

CEFR Portfolio ideas
a) Choose a photo or painting you really like. Write an online article under the title 'Great Pictures'. Describe the picture and explain how it affects you and why you like it so much. Don't forget to add the picture to your description.
b) Find out about an unusual pastime that your friends won't know much about, e.g. T'ai Ch'i. Prepare a presentation video about what it is and why it is so much fun or so useful.
c) Write a short description of a great technological invention. Describe the product and explain why it is so important.

Lead-in

OPTIONAL WARMER
Make sure Ss understand the meaning of *free time*. Then each student mimes a free-time activity and the other Ss have to guess what it is. Put the activities on the board and then rank them in order of class popularity.

1 ▶ Focus Ss' attention on the photos. Put Ss in pairs to discuss the questions. Get feedback from the whole class and write useful adjectives on the board.

2a ▶ In small groups, Ss decide which column each word should go in. Draw the table on the board. Check the answers with the whole class and write the words in the table on the board.

b ▶ 🔵 1.38 Check that Ss remember what stress is. In pairs, Ss mark the stress on the words. Then play the recording, pausing after each word for Ss to check their answers. Check the answers and pronunciation with the whole class.

Answers			
Play	**Go**	**Do**	**No verb**
cards computer games football a musical instrument squash volleyball	climbing cycling dancing horse riding jogging sailing skiing snowboarding surfing swimming	aerobics athletics exercise karate photography	cooking drawing painting reading socialising

3 ▶ Ss work in pairs to think of three activities they enjoy and discuss what equipment is necessary for each one. Get feedback from the whole class. Practise any words which cause pronunciation problems.

Answers
belt – karate board – surfing, snowboarding boots – climbing, football, horse riding, skiing, snowboarding brush – painting canvas – painting costume – swimming goggles – swimming helmet – climbing, cycling, horse riding, snowboarding net – football, volleyball poles – skiing racquet – squash rope – climbing, sailing saddle – cycling, horse riding trainers – aerobics, athletics, cycling, jogging, squash, volleyball

4 ▶ In pairs, Ss discuss the three questions. Get feedback from various Ss by asking them to report something they found out about their partners.

5.1 Are you creative?

In this lesson, Ss look at the topic of creativity. Ss listen to people's feelings about some paintings. This introduces the language of how to respond to a picture and suitable adjectives. The listening also provides the context for studying the Present Perfect Continuous and Present Perfect Simple. Ss also learn about becoming more creative.

Giuseppe Arcimboldo (1527–1593) was an Italian painter, best known for creating imaginative portrait heads made out of objects, vegetables or animals. His portrait, made from fish, called *Water* is shown here. This painting has been used as an album cover.

Sir Hubert von Herkomer (1849–1914) was a British painter, film director and composer. His painting, *Hard Times*, depicting the hard life of peasants in Britain in 1885, is shown here.

Paul Gauguin (1848–1903) was a leading post-Impressionist French artist, sculptor and writer. His experiments with colour had a profound effect on modernist art. He lived much of his later life in Tahiti and the islands of the Pacific, where his painting *The Siesta*, shown here, was created.

George Frederic Watts (1817–1904) was a popular Victorian artist, often associated with the symbolist movement. He was as famous for his sculptures as he was for his paintings. *The Rain it raineth every day*, shown here, is one of his less well-known paintings, showing a weary girl waiting for the rain to stop.

Speaking and listening

OPTIONAL LEAD-IN

Write the lesson title on the board. Check Ss understand the meaning of *creative*. Ask Ss to answer the questions and give their reasons. Get feedback from the whole class and elicit jobs that involve creativity.

1 ▶ Ss work in pairs and discuss the paintings and their feelings towards them. Get feedback from the whole class and write any adjectives they use on the board.

2a ▶ 🔊 1.39 Play the recording. Ss number the pictures in the correct order. Check the answers with the whole class and elicit reasons for their choices.

Answers
1 Top right painting of family by the road (Hubert von Herkomer)
2 Middle right painting of women sitting down (Paul Gauguin)
3 Top left portrait made from fish (Giuseppe Arcimboldo)
4 Bottom right painting of woman sitting in a chair (George Frederic Watts)

b ▶ Focus Ss' attention on the box and practise saying the phrases. Play the recording for Ss to tick the phrases they hear. Play the recoding again. Ss listen and repeat the phrases.

Answers
It makes me feel …　　I like the way …
It reminds me of …　　It looks (as if) …

c ▶ Read through the adjectives with the Ss. Elicit which adjectives Ss can remember hearing and for which paintings. Then play the recording for Ss to match the adjectives with the paintings. Check the answers with the whole class. Let Ss listen again to check the meaning of the adjectives. To demonstrate understanding, encourage Ss to provide examples of things the adjectives could describe (e.g. sitting in the rain is depressing).

Answers
1 depressing, sad　　3 disturbing, unusual
2 striking, vivid　　　4 intriguing

OPTIONAL EXTENSION

Brainstorm other adjectives that could be used to describe the paintings and check understanding in the same way as in exercise 2c.

3 ▶ Refer Ss back to the paintings. In pairs, Ss choose a painting and describe it using the phrases from the How to… box and the adjectives from exercise 2c. Tell Ss they can use more adjectives if they wish. Then ask different pairs to read out their descriptions. If all the pairs have chosen a painting on the page, ask the rest of the class to guess which painting they are referring to.

4a ▶ Put Ss into different pairs. Tell Ss to look at the list of activities and decide which activities are creative, giving reasons for their answers. Change the pairs and repeat the activity. Then get feedback from the whole class.

OPTIONAL VARIATION

In pairs, Ss rank the activities according to their level of creativity, with 1 being the most creative and 7 the least creative. They should also be prepared to explain their rankings. Then put pairs into groups of four and ask Ss to compare their rankings and agree on a final list. Get feedback from the whole class and try to agree on a class ranking.

b ▶ Ss read through the definitions and decide which ones they agree with and why. Do this activity with the whole class. Ask Ss: *Based on this definition, do you think you are creative? Why/Why not?*

OPTIONAL EXTENSION

Ss come up with their own definition of *creativity* that the whole class agrees on.

5a ▶ 🔊 1.40 Read through the instructions and questions with the Ss. Then play the recording. Ss answer the questions and then check in pairs. Get feedback from the whole class.

Answers
1 Mike agrees with the first definition. Tom agrees with the third definition. Ruth agrees with the second definition.
2 Mike makes origami. Tom makes up his own recipes. Ruth looks after her children and encourages their creativity.

b ▶ Ss read the questions and try to answer them before listening. Play the recording for Ss to check their answers. Check the answers with the whole class.

Answers	2	Mike	4	Tom
1 Tom	3	Ruth	5	Mike

c ▶ Put Ss in pairs to talk about any creative activities they do. Partners should comment on whether they agree that the activity is creative or not and why. Ss then report their discussion to the whole class.

Grammar | Present Perfect Continuous and Present Perfect Simple

OPTIONAL GRAMMAR LEAD-IN

Write the following gapped sentence on the board. *I've been studying English for _____ years*. Tell Ss to complete the sentence so that it is true for them. Elicit Ss' answers and ask how long they have been studying English. Then elicit the name of structure in this sentence (Present Perfect Continuous).

6a ▶ Focus Ss' attention on the sentences from exercise 5b. In pairs, Ss write *S* next to sentences which use the Present Perfect Simple and *C* next to sentences which use the Present Perfect Continuous. Check the answers with the whole class.

Answers	2	S	4	S
1 C	3	C	5	C

b ▶ Ss read the Active grammar box and match the example sentences with the grammar rules. Let Ss compare their answers in pairs before checking the answers with the whole class. Ask Ss to turn to Reference page 75 and give them time to read through the notes. Point out that the Present Perfect Continuous emphasises the continuation of an activity (recently finished or unfinished) rather than the result.

Active grammar

A 2   B 3   C 1

7 ▶ Focus Ss' attention on sentences 1–5. Ss work in pairs to explain why the tenses are incorrect. Get feedback from the whole class. Ss can also supply the correct tenses.

Answers
1 The question is about how long something has taken, so the Present Perfect Continuous is better.
2 The Present Perfect Simple indicates that the cleaning has recently been finished. Use the Present Perfect Continuous to show that it is incomplete.
3 The Present Perfect Continuous indicates that the attempt to give up is incomplete. Use the Present Perfect Simple to show that it is now complete.
4 The continuous form can't be used with state verbs.
5 The Present Perfect Continuous is better to emphasise the repetition of the activity.

Pronunciation | weak forms

8a ▶ 🔊 1.41 Read through the instructions and elicit ideas. Then play the recording and get feedback from the whole class. Refer Ss to the Pronunciation bank on page 164 to read more about the use of weak forms.

Answers
The weak forms of *have* and *been* are used: *have* is shortened or 'contracted' to /əv/ and the weak form of *been* is used: /bɪn/.

b ▶ Play the recording again. Pause after each sentence to let Ss repeat the sentences, as a whole class and individually.

9a ▶ Ss read the blog and complete the sentences. Point out that sometimes both forms could be possible. Let Ss compare their answers in pairs before getting feedback from the whole class.

Answers
1 have been
2 have been working
3 have never exhibited
4 has started
5 has made
6 have been looking/have looked
7 have been staying
8 have seen

b ▶ Give Ss about ten minutes to write a blog entry similar to the one in exercise 9a. Remind Ss to use Present Perfect Simple and Present Perfect Continuous where possible. Monitor and help where necessary.

c ▶ In pairs, Ss read each other's blogs and ask questions. Ask Ss to report their findings to the whole class.

OPTIONAL VARIATION

Give Ss a few minutes to make a list of things they have done in the last few weeks. Then in pairs, Ss ask and answer questions about each other's activities and take notes. Then Ss use their notes to write a blog for their partner. They then show their partner the blog, who checks it and makes corrections.

Reading

10 ▶ Focus Ss on questions 1–4. Ask Ss if there are any words they don't understand and encourage them to explain difficult words to each other before doing it yourself. Ss then discuss the questions in pairs or small groups. Get feedback from the whole class.

11a ▶ Ss read the first paragraph of the article and answer the question. Tell Ss not to worry about any vocabulary they don't understand at this stage. Check the answers with the whole class. Put Ss in pairs and ask them to discuss ways in which they use imagination and creativity in their daily lives.

Answers
The first paragraph discusses question 1 and mentions questions 3 and 4.

b ▶ Ss read the rest of the article quickly and match the headings with the paragraphs. Let Ss compare their answers in pairs before checking with the whole class.

Answers
1 c   2 a   3 b

12 ▶ Ss read the article more carefully and answer the questions. Check the answers with the whole class. Ask Ss if there are any words or phrases in the text that they don't understand. Write the words and phrases on the board and encourage Ss to explain them to each other. If there are still words or phrases that Ss don't understand, explain them to the class yourself.

Answers
1 c   4 b
2 a   5 c
3 b

Speaking

13a ▶ Refer Ss to page 147 and give them time to read through the problems. Then put Ss in small groups to discuss how to solve the problems. Encourage Ss to use the creativity techniques they read about in exercises 11 and 12.

b ▶ Put Ss in pairs so that they are working with a student from a different group. Ask Ss to summarise what their group discussed, the creativity techniques they used and what solutions they found. Monitor the conversations, taking note of errors and examples of correct language. Get feedback from the whole class and ask the class to decide which group found the best solutions. Write the errors on the board and encourage Ss to self-correct. Write up examples of correct language Ss used and praise them for using it correctly.

c ▶ Refer Ss to page 148 so they can check the solutions to the problems and compare them with their own ideas. Get feedback from the whole class.

5.2 Time well spent?

In this lesson, Ss find out about what people do in their free time. They listen to a film-maker planning a film about free-time activities. This provides the context for the grammar focus on -ing and infinitives. This is followed by a reading activity on reviews. The reading provides the vocabulary focus for describing pastimes.

Listening

1a ▶ Ss look at the words in the box and do the activity individually.

b ▶ Put Ss in pairs to discuss their answers. Get feedback from the whole class.

2 ▶ ⏺ 1.42 Ss read about Hannah Cheung and look at the diagram. Check that Ss understand the amount of time she dedicates to each activity by asking Ss what percentage of time she spends doing each one. To help students understand the meanings of these percentages, ask how many days twenty percent of one month would be. (Based on a month of thirty days twenty percent is six days.) Play the recording. Ss complete the information in the diagram. Check the answers with the whole class.

Answers			
1	Shopping	3	10 percent
2	15 percent	4	Cooking and eating

3a ▶ Play the recording again. Ss complete the notes about what Hannah says. Let Ss compare their answers in pairs, but don't confirm any answers at this point.

b ▶ Refer Ss to the audioscript on page 170 to check their answers. Elicit the correct answers.

Answers			
1	shopping	5	to cook
2	doing	6	friends
3	to do	7	to do
4	starting	8	to change

Grammar | -ing and infinitive

OPTIONAL GRAMMAR LEAD-IN

Write the following sentence prompts on the board.
I can't stand …
I enjoy …
When I was younger I decided …

Ss copy the prompts into their notebooks and complete the sentences so they are true for them. Go round and check the sentences Ss have written, correcting the verb forms if necessary. Ss tell a partner what they have written about. Get feedback from the whole class and focus Ss on the form of the verb which follows *can't stand*, *enjoy* and *decided*. Tell Ss that there are some verbs which are followed by the -ing form and some which are followed by an infinitive (*to* + verb).

4a ▶ Give Ss time to read through the Active grammar box. Then ask Ss to look back at exercise 3a and match the words in bold with the headings A–D. Let Ss compare their answers in pairs. Copy the headings onto the board. Then check the answers with the whole class and write the verbs under the correct headings on the board.

Active grammar

A   enjoy, look forward to, love
B   manage, seem, 'd like
C   invite
D   try

b ▶ Ss add the verbs from the box under the correct headings in the Active grammar box. Check the answers with the whole class and write the verbs under the headings on the board. Focus Ss' attention on Reference page 75. Give Ss time to read through the notes. Check that Ss realise that there is no rule for verb patterns and that they must try to remember the patterns. Ask Ss: *If I 'stop eating', do I eat first, then stop?* (Yes) *If I 'stop to eat', do I stop what I am doing to eat?* (Yes)

Active grammar

A   hate, adore
B   agree, refuse, decide
C   remind, allow, advise
D   remember, stop

5 ▶ In pairs, Ss choose the correct verb form in sentences 1–6. Check answers with the whole class.

Answers			
1	doing	4	doing
2	to do	5	to do
3	doing	6	to go

Speaking

6 ▶ Put Ss in small groups to ask and answer the questions from exercise 5. Elicit any interesting information that Ss found out during the discussion.

Reading

OPTIONAL LEAD-IN

Before the lesson, make a list of books, films and plays on a slide or on the board. Divide Ss into groups and tell them they have to identify which titles are books, which are films and which are plays. Some titles may fall into more than one category. Ss have to give reasons for their answers, e.g. the film starred Jared Leto.

7a ▶ Ss discuss the questions in pairs. Get feedback from the whole class.

b ▶ Discuss the first question with the whole class. Give Ss a minute to read the opinions and then check understanding. Put Ss in pairs to discuss the remaining questions, giving reasons for their answers. Get feedback from the whole class to find out what the majority view is.

OPTIONAL LEAD-IN

Ss cover the texts so that they can only see the pictures. Ask Ss: *Which title is a film? How do you know? What do you think it is about?* Then ask the same questions for the book and the play.

8a ▶ For this activity, you just want Ss to get a general idea of the film/book/play, so tell Ss to read the titles only. In pairs, Ss close their books and tell each other which review appeals to them the most and why. Get feedback from the whole class with Ss reporting what their partners said.

b ▶ Ss read the full reviews and answer the questions. Let Ss compare their answers in pairs before getting feedback from the whole class. Make sure Ss give reasons for their 'false' answers. Ask Ss if there are any words or phrases that they didn't understand. Encourage Ss to answer each others' questions before asking you. You could also find out if Ss have changed their minds about question 8a after reading the reviews in detail.

Answers
1 T
2 F (the reviewer hasn't seen the film yet)
3 T
4 T
5 T
6 F (it's a real page-turner)
7 T
8 F (the ending is rather sudden)
9 T
10 F (the performances are rather dull)
11 F (the reviewer likes the soundtrack)
12 T

Vocabulary | describing pastimes

9 ▶ Read through the Lifelong learning box with the Ss. Check that Ss understand the meaning of *phrase* and the differences between the types of phrase. Get Ss to find the example information for books in the book review. Then ask them to add the other book review words in bold to the correct column of the table. Check the answers with the whole class. Ss then do the same thing for the play and film reviews. Check the answers with the whole class.

Answers

	Noun or noun phrase	Verb or verb phrase	Adjective or adjectival phrase
Books	a modern classic the main character descriptions dialogue the plot a real page-turner first chapter	took my breath away couldn't put it down	out of print full of atmosphere beautifully written
Theatre/Musicals	on stage puppets sound effects dramatic lighting musical score melodies lyrics amazing spectacle applause audience	adapted from tells the story of steal the show	well-rounded
Film	sequel heart throb fans performances leading characters plot soundtrack album	plays the role of stars as	

Pronunciation | sounds and spelling: 'a'

10a ▶ 🌐 1.43 Play the recording. Ss decide whether the underlined letter in each word is pronounced /æ/ or /eɪ/ and add the words to the table. Let Ss compare answers in pairs before getting feedback from the whole class.

Answers	
/æ/	/eɪ/
abandoned	based
album	danger
chapter	page
character	
classic	
soundtrack	
vampire	

b ▶ Read through the rubric with the Ss and brainstorm ideas with the whole class. Then refer Ss to the Pronunciation bank on page 163 to check their ideas.

Answers
'ai' (pain, strain)
'ay' (play, stay)

Speaking

11a ▶ Read through the instructions with the Ss. Remind Ss to use their notes from the Lifelong learning box. Ss make notes and prepare their description.

b ▶ Put Ss in pairs to discuss their books/films/plays. Tell Ss to ask questions to find out more information and take notes on what their partner says. Monitor the conversations and make notes of any errors for the feedback session. Then ask Ss to tell the rest of the class about the book/film/play their partner described.

OPTIONAL EXTENSION

Ss write a review of a book or film to put up in the class for the next lesson. Ss can use pictures, photos or realia to make the review more interesting. Then, in the next lesson do a class survey of the best book or best film from the reviews.

5.3 Memorable meals

Iran is a country with a rich cuisine. Iranian cuisine is famous for soups made from rice, herbs and meat. Main courses include rice and meat or chicken dishes. 'Chelo kebabs' are rice served with roasted meat. Its desserts include many delicious dishes often made from yoghurt and almonds.

Argentinian food is quite similar to European food. They predominantly use red meat in their dishes and eat a lot of bread. Most common dishes are barbecued meat, dulce de leche (a milk caramel dessert) and empanadas (stuffed bread or pastries).

Belgian food is considered as good as French cuisine but is usually served in large quantities. Well-known dishes include mussels and chips, Flemish beef stew, patés, (e.g. boar paté) and waffles.

The lesson begins with Ss listening to someone talking about Argentinian food and through this context Ss study food vocabulary. They then read a story about a restaurant in Iran. The text provides the context for the grammar focus on countable and uncountable nouns. Ss listen to a woman talking about a restaurant and study and practise language for describing a restaurant.

Vocabulary | food

1a ▶ Ss discuss the questions in pairs. Get feedback from the whole class.

b ▶ 🌐 1.44 Focus Ss' attention on the notes and check understanding. Then play the recording. Ss listen and complete the text. Let Ss check their answers in pairs and then play the recording again. Check the answers with the whole class.

Answers			
1	meat	5	hot or cold
2	garlic, oil and herbs	6	dessert/sweet
3	'Empanadas'	7	boiling milk and sugar
4	different fillings	8	cake or biscuits

c ▶ Ask Ss to find all the words in italics and check understanding. Then tell Ss to prepare a description of a local dish that includes at least two of the phrases in italics. Put Ss in pairs. Each student describes their dish for their partner to guess. Monitor and make a note of interesting language and errors to check in the feedback session. Then get feedback from various Ss in the class.

Reading

2a ▶ Focus Ss' attention on the photos. In pairs, Ss decide what country this might be and what type of food they might eat. Get feedback from the whole class. Tell Ss to cover the right-hand column of words in exercise 2a. Ask Ss to make expressions by adding words to the words in the left-hand column. Check the expressions with the class and write correct expressions on the board. Ss uncover the right-hand column and match the two sets of words. Check the answers with the whole class.

Answers

1	c	3	d	5	b
2	a	4	f	6	e

b ▶ Ss work in pairs and use the photos and the expressions from exercise 2a to predict what happens in the story. Put Ss in different pairs to explain the predictions they have made. Get feedback from the whole class and write their predictions on the board.

3 ▶ Ss read the story quickly to check their ideas. Tell Ss not to worry about any words they don't understand at this point. Check whether any Ss made correct predictions. In pairs, Ss then discuss why they think the man never found the café again. Get feedback from the whole class.

4 ▶ Ss read the story more carefully. Ask Ss if there are any words or phrases in the text that they don't understand. Encourage Ss to answer each others' questions. Ss read the summary and find eight mistakes. Ss compare their lists in pairs and correct their mistakes. Check the answers with the whole class.

Answers

1 They were not driving through *a busy area*, they were driving through an isolated place.
2 They didn't stop in a *small city*, they stopped in a village.
3 The owner didn't speak *a little* English, he spoke perfect English.
4 The meal was *not expensive*, it was astonishingly cheap.
5 His friends didn't think it was possible to find a *good* restaurant in such a remote area.
6 The engineer didn't return with his *wife*, he returned with his colleague.
7 They couldn't find the café, not the *train station*.
8 The local man had been there for forty years, not *thirty* years.

Grammar | countable and uncountable nouns

OPTIONAL GRAMMAR LEAD-IN

Write the following sentences on the board.
1 *There are much restaurants in the centre of London.*
2 *Have you got many furniture in your house?*
In pairs, Ss correct the sentences. Check the answers, then swap *much* and *many* in the sentences on the board. Ss write six more sentences and questions; three with *much* and three with *many*.

5a ▶ Give Ss a few minutes to read part A of the Active grammar box. In pairs, Ss complete the gaps in part A. Get Ss to compare their answers with another pair before getting feedback from the whole class.

Active grammar

1	countable	4	rice
2	uncountable	5	and
3	restaurant	6	counted

b ▶ Ss read through the table in part B of the Active grammar box and complete it by referring to the underlined examples in the text on page 70. Let Ss check their answers in pairs before getting feedback from the whole class.

Answers

	None	A small amount	A large amount
Countable		A <u>few</u> months later … A <u>couple</u> of bowls of soup …	Outside one of the <u>many</u> huts …
Uncountable		We didn't have <u>much</u> hope … A <u>little</u> sugar …	
Countable and uncountable	We do not get … <u>any</u> foreigners here.	<u>some</u> weak tea …	I told <u>a lot of</u> friends about the meal …

6 ▶ Refer Ss to Reference page 75. Give Ss time to read through the notes and answer any questions before doing this exercise. Ss do the activity individually and then check their answers in pairs. Check the answers with the whole class, making sure the corrections have been done properly.

Answers

1 How <u>much</u> ~~many~~ money do you have?
2 We need to buy ~~a~~ (some) new furniture.
3 Sam ate almost all the chocolates in the box. (correct)
4 She has ~~a~~ beautiful long blonde hair.
5 I don't have ~~some~~ <u>any</u> luggage.
6 Would you like some rice with that? (correct)

OPTIONAL EXTENSION

Divide the class into teams of three or four Ss. Label these teams A and B. Each team A member will compete against one B team member. Ss prepare six sentences, which can be correct or incorrect. However, at least two sentences must be incorrect. Ss then play a quiz with one team reading out a sentence and the other team deciding if it is correct or correcting any incorrect sentences. For this task to work, books must be closed.

7 ▶ Ss work in pairs and complete the sentences with quantifiers. Check answers with the whole class.

Answers

1	couple	3	any/much	5	many
2	many	4	a little	6	a few

Speaking

8 ▶ In pairs, Ss ask and answer the questions from exercise 7 and write down their partner's answers, checking for correct use of quantifiers. If some Ss finish early, they can change pairs and report their previous partner's answers. Monitor the activity and note down any errors to review in the class check.

Listening

> **OPTIONAL LEAD-IN**
>
> Ask Ss to describe the photo and elicit which country they think it is. Then elicit possible foods from this country or the ingredients that might be used.

9 ▶ 🔊 1.45 Read through the instructions with the Ss and give them time to read the four summaries. Play the recording and ask Ss to tick the correct summary. Check the answers with the whole class.

Answers	summary 2

10 ▶ Remind Ss to use a maximum of three words in each sentence. Ss read through the sentences and try to remember or predict the missing words. Let Ss check their ideas in pairs. Then play the recording and get feedback from the whole class.

Answers		
1	her boyfriend's birthday	3 sit outside
2	a cathedral	4 steak
		5 fish and meat

11 ▶ 🔊 1.45 Give Ss time to read through the How to... box. Check that Ss understand the vocabulary and expressions. If they don't understand any vocabulary, encourage them to answer each other's questions before providing the explanations yourself. Play the recording again. Ss tick the expressions they hear and compare their answers in pairs. Check the answers with the whole class.

Answers	Menu: It's famous for …
Location: in the centre of	Service: The service is
Atmosphere: peaceful,	quite slow.
relaxing	Prices: quite expensive

Speaking

12a ▶ Tell Ss to think about a restaurant they like. Focus Ss on the How to... box and tell them to use these expressions to describe their restaurant. Give Ss a few minutes to prepare what they are going to say. Monitor and help with vocabulary if necessary.

b ▶ Put Ss in groups of four to tell each other about their restaurants. Encourage Ss to ask follow-up questions after listening to each description. Monitor the conversations and note down any errors. Write the errors on the board. Discuss them with the class and write up the correct form. Get feedback by asking each group to decide which of the restaurants they heard about was the best and why.

5 Vocabulary | explaining what you mean

In this lesson, Ss look at common expressions for clarifying what you are talking or writing about and for giving further explanation. These expressions have similar meanings but collocate with either countable or uncountable nouns. Ss also review the use and correct order of adjectives to describe shape, weight, size and texture.

> **OPTIONAL WARMER**
>
> In pairs, Ss look back through their books and write a list of ten new words they have seen. Now put Ss in different pairs. Ss take turns to explain a word and their partner tries to guess what the word is.

1a ▶ Ss think of different situations in which they need to explain something, using all of the prompts.

b ▶ Put Ss in pairs to compare their situations. Make sure they use full sentences, as in the example. Get feedback from the whole class.

2a ▶ 🔊 1.46 Play the recording. Ss try to decide what is being described. Let Ss compare their answers in pairs before getting feedback from the whole class. Refer Ss to page 148 to check the answers.

Answers			
1	surfing	4	vacuum cleaner/
2	curry		Hoover
3	mud/earth	5	bookshelves

b ▶ Read through the Lifelong learning box with Ss. Ss then practise saying the phrases. Ss can also suggest endings for the phrases. Play the recording again. Ss listen and complete the sentences. Check the answers with the whole class. Then focus Ss' attention on *thing* and *stuff*. Elicit which is used for countable nouns (thing) and which is used for uncountable nouns (stuff). Tell Ss that *type*, *kind* and *sort* can be used for countable and uncountable nouns and have the same meaning in these situations. *What type of car do you have? What kind of music do you like? What sort of food do you want to eat tonight?* If you are saying that something is partly true or are not being exact, use *sort of* or *kind of* rather than *type of*. E.g. *It was a sort of square shape.*

> **Answers**
> 1 It's a type of sport which you do in the sea.
> 2 It's a kind of meal you get in Indian restaurants.
> 3 It's the stuff you find under the grass.
> 4 It's something you use for cleaning the house.
> 5 They are usually made of wood. They're a useful thing to have in the house.

c ▶ Elicit the answer from the whole class.

> **Answers**
> thing – countable
> stuff – uncountable

3 ▶ Ss work in pairs to put the words in the correct order. Let them compare their answers with another pair before checking the answers with the whole class. Ss then match the sentences with the pictures.

> **Answers**
> 1 It's something you find in front of windows. F
> 2 It's a type of cheese which you put on pasta. A
> 3 It's something you use for opening wine bottles. B
> 4 It's a kind of rice dish from Spain. E
> 5 It's the stuff you use for washing your hair. D
> 6 It's a large figure made of stone. C

4a ▶ Ss complete the notes in groups of four. Tell Ss to use a dictionary if there are any words they don't understand or to ask you. Get feedback from the whole class.

b ▶ 🔘 1.47 Play the recording. Ss check if their ideas from exercise 4a are mentioned in the recording.

c ▶ 🔘 1.48 Play the recording, pausing after each word for Ss to repeat the words individually and then as a whole class.

5 ▶ Write *crossword* on the board and ask Ss to explain to you what a crossword is. Help Ss if necessary and say that horizontal words in a crossword are known as the 'across' words and that vertical words are known as the 'down' words. Read through the instructions with the Ss and put them in two groups (A and B). Group A Ss turn to page 149 and group B Ss to page 152. Each group prepares definitions for the words in their crossword. Now put Ss in A/B pairs. Ss take turns to explain and guess words. Check the answers with the whole class.

5 Communication

In this lesson, Ss listen to someone talking about Capoeira, a martial art which originated in Brazil. Ss then prepare a talk about a skill they enjoy or are good at and tell the class.

1a ▶ Focus Ss on the photo. In pairs, Ss quickly discuss what they think the people in the photo are doing. Get feedback from the whole class.

b ▶ 🔘 1.49 Tell Ss that the people in the photo are doing Capoeira. Give Ss a few minutes to read through the gapped notes at the bottom of the page. If there are any words or expressions that Ss don't know, encourage them to answer each others' questions or to ask you. Play the recording. Ss listen and number the sections in the order they hear them. Check the answers with the whole class.

> **Answers**
> 2 Personal qualities necessary
> 3 Main actions/Activity
> 4 Afterwards
> 5 Other information/Future plans

2 ▶ Encourage Ss to read through the gapped notes and try to remember or predict the missing words. Let Ss compare their ideas in pairs and then play the recording again. Check the answers with the whole class.

> **Answers**
> 1 martial art
> African slaves in Brazil
> the songs tell the story of capoeira and the slaves struggle
>
> 2 very fit and strong
> use your hands to balance
> have good control of your body
>
> 3 sits around in a circle
> you see the other person's hand or foot coming towards you
> doesn't kick you
> you lose
> how skilful you are
>
> 4 talk about the fight
> the evening together
>
> 5 three years
> I first started
> a trainer/Master

3 ▶ Tell Ss to think of a skill which they are good at or enjoy doing. Give Ss a few minutes to prepare what they can say about this skill. Encourage Ss to use the expressions in bold from the notes about Capoeira. Monitor and help where necessary.

4 ▶ Do this activity in groups or with the whole class. Ss tell the rest of the group/class about their skills. Tell Ss that while they listen they should write down a few questions to ask at the end of the talk. Take note of errors while the Ss are talking. At the end of each talk, other Ss can ask their questions. When all the Ss have finished talking, write the errors on the board and discuss them with the whole class.

Review and practice

1 ▶

Answers

1	been working	5	finished
2	known	6	been learning
3	been dancing	7	played
4	we've met	8	been watching

2 ▶

Answers

1. A: You look exhausted. What <u>have</u> you been <u>doing</u> (do)?
   B: <u>I've been playing</u> (play) squash.
2. A: You're late! <u>I've been waiting</u> (wait) for nearly an hour.
   B: I'm sorry. <u>I've been working</u> (work) late in the office.
3. A: I'm really hungry. I <u>haven't eaten</u> (not/eat) all day.
   B: Sit down. <u>I've</u> just <u>finished</u> (finish) making dinner.
4. A: I haven't seen you for hours. What <u>have you been doing</u> (do)?
   B: <u>I've been playing</u> (play) with the dog.
5. A: <u>Have</u> you <u>left</u> (leave) any messages for him?
   B: Yes, <u>I've left</u> (leave) four messages.
6. A: There's paint on your clothes! <u>Have</u> you <u>been decorating</u> (decorate)?
   B: Yes, <u>I've been painting</u> (paint) the living room. It's nearly finished.

3 ▶

Answers

1	check	5	listening	9	to bring
2	seeing	6	to go	10	to ask
3	to give	7	to entertain	11	to leave
4	to stay	8	going out	12	to bring

4 ▶

Answers

1	Coffee; a coffee	4	rooms; room
2	a hair; hair	5	chickens; chicken
3	a noise/noises; noise		

5 ▶

Answers

1. In the evening I love listening to music.
2. We went out to <u>a</u> lovely restaurant.
3. Hurry up! We don't have <u>much</u> time.
4. I don't think I can come to the theatre, because I <u>don't have much/only have a little</u> money.
5. Would you like (<u>some</u>) milk in your coffee?
6. I've got bad news – the show has been cancelled.
7. I'm going to the market to buy some bread.

6 ▶

Answers

1	sequel	3	set	6	dialogue
2	a net	4	climbing	7	stuff
		5	lyrics	8	made with

Writing bank

See page 157 of the Students' Book

1 ▶ Check Ss understand *family heirloom*. Ss read the extract quickly and identify the object being described.

Answers
B

2 ▶ Ss read the How to... box and tick the words and phrases used in the extract.

Answers
Explaining:
It's a kind of ...
It's made of ...
It's used for ...

Talking about how it looks:
oval
narrow, long
decorated

Giving background information:
It used to belong to ...
She kept it on ...
I love it because ...

3a ▶ Ss choose their own family heirloom or one of the objects on the page. Ss make notes using the prompts.

b ▶ Ss write about their object for the magazine, using their notes and language from the How to... box.

6 Holidays

Overview

Lead-in	Vocabulary: Holidays, Describing landscape
6.1	Can do: Describe a memorable photo Grammar: Past Perfect Simple Vocabulary: Descriptive language Speaking and Pronunciation: How to... describe a memorable photo Reading: Extracts from *Travels Across Africa* Listening: Travel photos
6.2	Can do: Get around a new place Grammar: Uses of *like* Vocabulary: Places in a city Speaking and Pronunciation: How to... get around a new place Intonation in questions Reading: Danii Minogue in Melbourne Listening: Travelling around Australia
6.3	Can do: Talk about unexpected events Grammar: Articles Vocabulary: Travelling Speaking and Pronunciation: Sentence stress Reading: Strange things happen when you travel ... Listening: Lady Mary Wortley Montagu
Vocabulary	Expressions with *get*
Communication	Suggest and respond to ideas
Writing bank	Write a detailed description of a place How to... write a description of a place
Extra resources	ActiveTeach and ActiveBook

CEFR Can do objectives
6.1 Describe a memorable photo
6.2 Get around a new place
6.3 Talk about unexpected events
Communication Suggest and respond to ideas
Writing bank Write a detailed description of a place

CEFR Portfolio ideas
a) Imagine you work in a tourist information centre. With some friends, record a typical day in the life of a tourist information centre. Respond to different people's queries and requests about the town you live in.
b) Look at a news website and find a story that interests you. Write an email to a friend in another country, retelling the story in your own words.
c) What is the holiday location of your dreams? Write a description or prepare a short promotional video, describing the place and explaining why it is so special.

Lead-in

OPTIONAL WARMER
Brainstorm different types of holidays with the Ss. They may not need to use the right names as long as they can describe them. Write the Ss' suggestions on the board. In pairs, Ss then choose the holiday they would most like to go on and tell their partner why they would like to go on that holiday. Get feedback from the class and rank the holidays in order of preference with 1 being the best and 4 being the worst.

1a ▶ Focus Ss' attention on the types of holidays in the box. Put Ss in pairs to match the holidays with the photos. If Ss don't understand the vocabulary, tell them to use their dictionaries or to ask you. Check the answers with the whole class.

> **Suggested Answers**
> Main photo: safari
> Top photo: package holiday
> Middle photo: sailing holiday
> Bottom photo: camping holiday

OPTIONAL EXTENSION
In pairs, Ss mark the syllable stress on the words from the box. Check the answers with the whole class and write the words on the board with the stress marked. Practise saying any words Ss have difficulties with.

b ▶ Ss decide which category they would put the types of holiday in and why. Ss compare their answers in pairs. Then get feedback from the whole class.

2 ▶ Write *holiday* and then *camping* on the board. Elicit how the two words can go together (*camping holiday*). Remind Ss that this is a collocation. Elicit other words that collocate with *holiday* (adventure, beach, package, sailing). Write *tour* on the board. Ask Ss whether this collocates with holiday (no). Now focus Ss on the words in exercise 2 and check that Ss understand all the vocabulary. Ss do the activity individually and then check their answers in pairs. Get feedback from the whole class with Ss providing reasons for their answers.

> **Answers**
> 1 pebbly   3 snow-capped   6 snow-capped
> 2 sandy   4 pebbly   7 sandy
>   5 lush

OPTIONAL EXTENSION
In pairs, Ss prepare a question similar to the ones in exercise 2. It doesn't have to be about holidays. Then put two pairs together to answer each other's question. Ss can then nominate the best question to ask the whole class.

3 ▶ Put Ss in pairs to discuss the questions. Get feedback from the whole class.

6.1 Across Africa

Travelling in Africa has become much easier and organised safari tours are now very common. However, there are still many people who prefer to travel in Africa on their own.

The Victoria Falls is a waterfall on the Zambezi river, between Zambia and Zimbabwe. It has some of the largest falls in the world and is considered to be one of the Seven Wonders of the World.

The Okavango Delta is the largest delta (an area of land formed at the mouth of a river when it enters the sea) in the world. It is part of the Moremi National Park in Botswana and is famous for its wide variety of wildlife.

In this lesson, Ss read about a holiday in South Africa, which provides the context for vocabulary practice and the grammar focus on the Past Perfect Simple. Ss then listen to people talking about photos. This provides the opportunity for Ss to practise the language of describing a photo.

Reading

1a ▶ Ask Ss to close their books. Write *keep a _____ , take _____ , buy _____ , send postcards/letters/_____* on the board. In pairs, Ss think of ways of completing these phrases. Get feedback from the whole class. Ss then open their books and complete the task. Check the answers with the whole class.

Answers		2	photos	4	emails
1	diary	3	souvenirs		

b ▶ Ss discuss the question in pairs. Then get feedback from various pairs.

2 ▶ Focus Ss on the photo before Ss discuss the questions in pairs. Get feedback from the whole class and elicit more information from anyone who has been to Africa.

3 ▶ Ss read the text and answer the questions. Tell Ss not to worry about any words they don't understand at this stage. Let Ss compare their answers in pairs before getting feedback from the whole class.

Answers
1 They are in the Karoo desert in South Africa.
2 Ss' own answers
3 Daniel likes to use a camera; Sophie (the narrator) likes to write down her experiences in notebooks.

4 ▶ Ss read the extract again and do the activity individually. Tell Ss to underline any words or expressions they don't understand. Give Ss no more than five minutes for this. Ss then compare their answers in pairs. Get feedback from the whole class and ask Ss to correct the false statements. Review the words and phrases that Ss don't understand. Ss can use their dictionaries, help each other or ask you.

Answers
1 F (They 'shot through' the desert means they moved very quickly and the road was empty not busy.)
2 T
3 NG
4 T
5 F (He was asleep.)
6 NG
7 F (The horses were 'almost close enough to touch'.)
8 F (She tried but he only woke up an hour later.)

Vocabulary | descriptive language

5 ▶ Write *shoot/shot/shot* on the board and ask Ss what this verb usually means. Elicit/explain that it is normally used for the action of firing a gun. Focus Ss on line 1 of the text and ask them what they think *shot* means in this context. Elicit that it means *moved very fast*. Ss then look at the descriptive language from the text and do the activity individually before comparing their ideas in pairs. Check the answers with the whole class.

Answers
1 incredible (Drinking alcohol normally makes people drunk.)
2 makes a loud noise (Lions normally roar.)
3 it became silent (Rain falls from the sky. People slip on icy ground and fall over. The temperature falls at night.)
4 noticed something and looked at it (You can catch a ball or catch a bus/train.)
5 very well

OPTIONAL EXTENSION

In pairs, Ss make two sentences using the phrases from exercise 5. One sentence is correct and one is incorrect. The pairs swap sentences with another pair and identify the correct sentences.

Grammar | Past Perfect Simple

OPTIONAL GRAMMAR LEAD-IN

Write the following sentences on the board.
1. I ate breakfast.
2. I left the house.
Ask Ss: *Which action was first? Which was second?*
Underneath the two sentences write:
After _____ the house.

In pairs, Ss complete the sentence so that it has the same meaning as the first two sentences. Check the sentences Ss have written. Write the answer on the board and underline the verb forms: *After I had eaten breakfast, I left the house.* In pairs, Ss discuss what the underlined tenses are and why they are used. Elicit that the first underlined structure is the Past Perfect Simple and the second is the Past Simple.

6a ▶ In pairs, Ss read the Active grammar box and answer the questions. Check the answers with the whole class and then ask Ss to choose the correct alternatives. Get feedback from the whole class. If Ss are having problems, draw a timeline on the board and ask Ss to label the two points in the example from the grammar box.

Active grammar

1   *We saw things* happened first.
    We use the Past Perfect to make it clear that one event happened before another one in the past.
    We make the Past Perfect simple with *had/hadn' t* + past participle.

---

b ▶ Ss find other examples of the Past Perfect Simple in the text on page 78. Let Ss check their answers in pairs before getting feedback from the whole class. Give Ss time to read the notes on Reference page 89 and then check understanding.

Answers
I <u>had</u> already <u>finished</u> three notebooks and was into the fourth, a beautiful leather notebook I'<u>d bought</u> in a market.
The road was empty – we <u>hadn't</u> <u>seen</u> another car for hours.
I didn't know how long they <u>had been</u> there next to us.
When Daniel woke up an hour later I told him what <u>had happened</u>.

---

7 ▶ Ss do the activity in pairs. Make sure Ss are prepared to explain why they chose a particular tense. Check the answers with the whole class.

Answers
1	had told	4	smelt
2	were	5	was/had been
3	had decided	6	had been abandoned
		7	arrived

8a ▶ Ss do the activity individually. Encourage Ss to write true sentences if possible. Monitor and check Ss sentences, but don't get feedback at this stage.

b ▶ Put Ss in pairs. Ss take turns to read out their sentences and ask follow-up questions. e.g. *Which city were you in? How did you find your way again?* Ss can invent information if necessary. Monitor and note down any errors. When Ss have finished, put some of the important errors on the board and ask various Ss to come up to the board and correct the errors. Praise Ss for correct use of target language.

OPTIONAL EXTENSION

Play the following chain game. Say: *By the time I got home last night ... .* The first student has to complete the sentence, e.g. *my favourite TV programme had finished*. This student then uses the same ending to form the beginning of the next sentence, e.g. *By the time my favourite TV programme had finished...* and the next student has to complete the ending.

Listening and speaking

9 ▶ Focus Ss on the photos. Put Ss in pairs to describe the photos and answer the questions. Monitor and help Ss with vocabulary where necessary. Get feedback from the whole class and ask Ss if they have been on holidays similar to the ones shown in the photos.

OPTIONAL VARIATION

Put Ss into pairs (A and B). Student A looks at the photos on page 80 and describes them to Student B. Student B draws the pictures into his/her notebook. When Student A has finished describing all the photos, Student B opens the book and compares the drawings with the photos. Ss then discuss questions 1–4. You can bring other photos into class to continue this activity with A and B changing roles.

10a ▶ ● 2.1 Read through the instructions with the Ss. In pairs, Ss brainstorm words they think the people might use to describe each photo. Get feedback from the whole class and write the words on the board. Play the recording and then check the answers with the whole class. Elicit the words that helped Ss decide.

Answers
Helen B	Matthew C	Tracy A

---

b ▶ Read through the instructions with the Ss and play the recording again. Let Ss compare their notes in pairs before getting feedback from the whole class.

Answers
where they took the photo:
    H – the island of Koh Samui in Thailand
    M – Scotney Castle, Kent (UK)
    T – from a tram in the centre of Hong Kong
what the weather was like:
    H – very hot and it was monsoon season so sometimes it would suddenly rain
    M – it started raining after he took the photo
    T – really nice: not too hot or cold
what else they had done that day:
    H – had breakfast on the beach; sat on the beach reading
    M – walking in the countryside; found the castle by accident
    T – walking around, taking trams and finding places to visit

c ▶ Give Ss time to read through the How to... box. If they have any problems with the vocabulary, encourage them to help each other or to ask you. Play the recording again for Ss to tick the phrases they hear. Check the answers with the whole class.

Answers
This is a photo I took in ...
In the foreground you can see ...
On the left-hand side you can see ...
We suddenly stumbled on ...
We had a really amazing day.

11 ▶ Give Ss a few minutes to choose a photo and decide which expressions from the How to... box they can use while describing the photo. Remind Ss that they can use a photo from page 148. In pairs, Ss take turns to describe their photos and ask follow-up questions. Monitor and note down any errors. At the end, write any major errors on the board and ask Ss to correct the errors in pairs. Elicit the corrections and write them on the board.

OPTIONAL EXTENSION

In small groups, Ss look at the photos on pages 80 and 148 and rank the types of holidays in order of relaxation with 1 being the most relaxing and 3 the least relaxing. Now put Ss in pairs to work with a student from a different group and compare their rankings. Get feedback from the whole class and discuss whether Ss prefer the idea of a relaxing holiday or doing dangerous/adventurous things on holiday.

6.2 Down under

Down under is an informal way of referring to Australia.

Aussie is an informal way of referring to Australians.

St Kilda is an inner city suburb in Melbourne, Australia. It is the Bohemian sector of Melbourne, similar to Greenwich village in New York.

The Great Barrier Reef, situated off the coast of Queensland, Australia, is the largest reef system in the world. CNN labelled it as one of the Seven Wonders of the World and it can be seen from space.

Twelve Apostles Rock is a collection of eight limestone rock stacks off the coast of Victoria, Australia. It is a major tourist attraction and attracts approximately two million visitors a year.

Danni Minogue is the younger sister of Kylie Minogue and is a world-famous singer, actress and TV presenter in her own right.

The topic of this lesson is Australia. Ss begin by looking at vocabulary to describe places and then talk about places in a city. They then listen to two people talking about their trip to Australia. This introduces the language of getting around a new place. They then read a text which provides the context for Ss to learn about the uses of *like*.

Vocabulary | places in a city

OPTIONAL LEAD-IN

Ask Ss to close their eyes. Tell them you are going to say a word and then they will have thirty seconds to think about it with their eyes closed. Next, they open their eyes and have another thirty seconds to write down all their thoughts. Say the word *Australia* and do the task. After one minute, Ss compare their notes in pairs. Elicit the most interesting ideas and write the most useful language on the board.

1a ▶ Put Ss in pairs to discuss the differences in meaning between each pair of words. Read through the example sentence and make sure Ss take note of the format used. Ss then write a sentence for each pair of words to explain the difference between them. Get feedback from the whole class.

Suggested Answers

2 A museum is a place where people can see important objects related to art, science or history for example, but an art gallery only has art on display.

3 A pub specialises in selling wine and beer although it may also sell food, but a café specialises in selling simple food and drink and the drinks are usually non-alcoholic.

4 A park is a public space, but a garden is a private space attached to a house which may sometimes be open to the public.

5 A lake is a large area of water surrounded by land, but a fountain is a structure, often in the middle of a lake, that sends water up into the air.

6 You can buy books from a bookshop, but you can only borrow them from a library.

7 A shop is a building where you can buy things, but a market is a large building or outside area where different people sell things from tables or stalls.

8 A square is an open area with buildings around it, but a roundabout is a circular area where roads meet and which cars must drive around.

9 A hostel and a hotel are both places to stay when you are travelling or away from home, but a hostel is cheaper; often for students and may have shared dormitories.

10 A canal is a long, man-made area of water, created for boats to travel along, but a river is a long, natural area of water which flows across land to the sea.

b ▶ Read through the instructions with the Ss and model the example. Give Ss a few minutes to prepare what they are going to say. Encourage them to use the vocabulary from exercise 1a where possible. Put Ss in pairs to talk about their choices and give reasons. Get feedback from the whole class. Ask Ss: *Are there are any places in exercise 1a that you would not be interested in visiting? Why?*

OPTIONAL VARIATION

Ss work in pairs (A and B). Ss A tells B their top three things to visit when travelling to a new city. Ss B must disagree with Ss A and try to convince them that their three places to visit are more interesting.

Listening

2 ▶ 🔊 2.2 Read through the instructions with the Ss and then play the recording. Let Ss check their answers in pairs before getting feedback from the whole class. Encourage Ss to explain their answers.

Answers
1 in a train station
2 on a street
3 on a street
4 on a bus/in a bus station
5 in a train station

3 ▶ Play the recording again and ask Ss to answer the two questions for each dialogue. Let Ss check their answers in pairs before getting feedback from the whole class.

Answers
Dialogue 1
1 two standard-class tickets from Melbourne to Adelaide
2 Train delays are expected.
Dialogue 2
1 directions to the National Railway Museum
2 The museum is closed.
Dialogue 3
1 directions to a post office
2 It closed at five o'clock.
Dialogue 4
1 the bus to Werribee Park
2 It's the wrong bus and you need to buy a ticket in advance.
Dialogue 5
1 two student tickets
2 She's forgotten her student card and has to pay the full price.

OPTIONAL EXTENSION

Put Ss in groups of three or four to discuss problems they have had while travelling and how these problems were solved. Get feedback from the whole class.

4 ▶ 🔊 2.3 Give Ss time to read through the How to... box. Then put Ss in pairs to predict how the sentences in the box could be completed. Elicit ideas from the whole class. Play the recording and then check the answers with the whole class.

Answers
What time does the museum <u>open</u>?
Is there a <u>bank</u> near here?
How much is a <u>return</u> to the city centre?
<u>Does</u> this bus go to the airport?
Excuse me. Could you tell me what time the train <u>leaves</u>?
Excuse me. Do you know where <u>platform 1</u> is?
Can you tell me the way to the <u>station</u>?
Just go straight on. It's on your <u>left</u>.

Pronunciation | intonation in questions

5a ▶ 🔊 2.4 Read the example questions with the Ss. Ss try to match the questions with the intonation patterns. Then play the recording for Ss to check their predictions. Get feedback from the whole class.

Answers
1 b   2 c   3 a

b ▶ Elicit the types of questions in the How to... box. Then drill at least one example of each question type, individually and as a whole class. Refer Ss to the Pronunciation bank on page 164.

Answers
What time does the museum open? – *wh-*
Is there a bank near here? – *yes/no*
Can you recommend a good restaurant? – *yes/no*
How much is a return to the city centre? – *wh-*
Does this bus go to the airport? – *yes/no*
Excuse me. Could you tell me what time the train leaves?
  – indirect
Excuse me. Do you know where platform 1 is? – indirect
Can you tell me the way to the station? – *yes/no*

OPTIONAL EXTENSION

In pairs, Ss write a question for each intonation pattern on a piece of paper (but not necessarily in the same order). Ss then give their piece of paper to another pair, who try to read out the questions with correct intonation.

Speaking

6 ▶ Ss work in pairs (A and B). Student A reads at the information on page 148. Student B reads the information on page 152. Make sure Ss understand the situations and give them time to prepare their questions using structures from the How to… box. Student B asks Student A questions to get the information they need about trains. Then Student A asks Student B questions to find out about the art gallery. Monitor carefully, checking for correct intonation in questions.

OPTIONAL EXTENSION

Ss think of five questions to ask about the city or town where they are studying at the moment. Ss write the questions using expressions from the How to… box. Ss stand up and mingle to ask other Ss their questions. The winner is the student who is able to get answers to his/ her questions first.

Reading and speaking

7a ▶ Elicit descriptions of the two photos. Encourage Ss to use language from the How to… box on page 80. Then elicit the country.

b ▶ Ss discuss the things to do in pairs. Get feedback from the whole class. Make sure Ss give reasons for their answers.

c ▶ Read through the introduction with the Ss. Ask Ss if they know who Danni Minogue is. Ss read the article to look for the activities from exercise 7b. Check the answers with the whole class.

Answers
1, 2, 3 and 6

8 ▶ Ss read the article more carefully and answer the questions. Ss then compare their answers in pairs and check the reasons for their answers. Get feedback from the whole class and then go through any vocabulary that the Ss do not know.

Answers
1   because people from there have travelled a lot
2   to eat food from seventy-five different countries
3   beachside cafés
4   fruit and vegetables
5   rock formations, rainforest, beaches and resort towns
6   Queensland and the Barrier Reef
7   because you need a private boat or helicopter
8   change into pyjamas

OPTIONAL EXTENSION

Elicit from Ss what they liked/didn't like about Danni's article. Ask Ss: *Would you like to visit Melbourne? Why/ Why not? What particular places seemed interesting to you?*

Grammar | uses of *like*

OPTIONAL GRAMMAR LEAD-IN

Write *like* on the board. In pairs, Ss think of as many different ways of using this word as they can. Elicit and write all their ideas on the board.

9a ▶ Read through the instructions and example sentences with the Ss and make sure they understand the two different ways that *like* can be used. Ss then decide if *like* is used as a verb or a preposition in the sentences from the text. Let Ss compare their answers in pairs before getting feedback from the whole class.

Answers
1	preposition	4	verb
2	preposition	5	preposition
3	verb	6	preposition

b ▶ Ss read through the Active grammar box and match the sentences from exercise 9a with the different uses of *like* in the box. Check the answers with the whole class. Refer Ss to Reference page 89 and give Ss time to read through the notes.

Active grammar

B   4
D   1, 2
      6
E   5

10 ▶ Ss do the activity in pairs. Let Ss compare their answers in pairs before getting feedback from the whole class.

> **Answers**
> 1   's it like
> 2   would you like to
> 3   like
> 4   do you like
> 5   does (he) look like
> 6   tasted like
> 7   don't (really) like, look like
> 8   if you like

Speaking and writing

11a ▶ Ss read the questions about the town or city they were born in or a place they know well. Give Ss time to make notes and tell them they don't have to write full sentences. In pairs, Ss take turns to talk about their towns and ask follow-up questions. Monitor and take note of any important errors. Get feedback from the whole class and go over any errors with Ss coming to the board to correct them.

b ▶ Individually, Ss write a short article (probably no more than 75 words) about a city or area they know well. To make this as interesting as possible, try to avoid too many people writing about the same place. Before they start, refer them to the expressions used in the article on page 82 and check they understand how to use them. The writing can be done for homework. Encourage Ss to use dictionaries or ask each other when they need help with vocabulary.

c ▶ Do this activity at the end of the lesson, or at the start of the next lesson. Ss swap articles or you could put them on the wall. Encourage Ss to ask each other follow-up questions as they read. Ss decide which of the cities they would like to visit and why. Get feedback from the whole class.

> **OPTIONAL VARIATION**
>
> Put Ss in groups of three or four. Ask Ss to present their articles to the rest of the group and encourage the listeners to ask follow-up questions. At the end of the presentations ask Ss to choose their favourite place.

6.3 Travellers' tales

In this lesson, Ss learn vocabulary connected with travelling. They then listen to a radio programme about Lady Mary Wortley Montagu and study more vocabulary for describing people's characters. The listening provides the context for Ss to practise sentence stress. Ss then read an article about strange experiences that happen when people travel. The text provides examples of how articles are used.

> St Mark's Square is the central square in Venice, Italy. It is the social, political and religious centre of Venice and is one of the few places in Europe where you cannot hear any motorised traffic.
>
> The Rocky Mountains are a major mountain range in western North America. It is a popular tourist destination for hiking, camping, mountaineering, fishing, hunting, skiing and snowboarding.
>
> Hawaii only became a US state in 1959 and it is the only state made up entirely of islands. Because it is in the central Pacific, it has a lot of North American and Asian influences. It also has its own distinct, native culture.

> **OPTIONAL WARMER**
>
> Write the words *tourist* and *traveller* on the board. Elicit the difference between the two words. Elicit some example sentences using each word and write them on the board. Ask Ss if they know the names of any travellers. You could also discuss whether an explorer is also a traveller, e.g. Columbus, Vasco da Gama, Henry the Navigator, Captain Cook.

Vocabulary | travelling

1a ▶ Ss may need dictionaries for this task. Ss read the texts and complete them using the words from the box. Tell Ss not to worry about words they don't know at this stage. Ss compare their answers in pairs. If Ss have dictionaries, they can use them now. Then get feedback from the whole class and check the meaning of the words in the box.

> **Answers**
>
> A 1 new   B 1 cultural
>   2 famous   2 tropical
>   3 sandy   3 barren
>   4 package   4 local
>   5 independent
>   6 unforgettable

> **OPTIONAL EXTENSION**
>
> Encourage Ss to make new sentences with the following words to check that they have understood the meaning: *barren, cultural, independent, package, sandy, unforgettable, tropical.*

b ▶ Elicit the topic of each text from the Ss (definitions of *tourist* and *traveller)*. Ss then discuss the questions in pairs. Get feedback from the whole class.

2 ▶ Before doing the activity, elicit collocations from the texts in exercise 1a that use the vocabulary from the box, e.g. *new experiences*, *famous landmarks*. Elicit any other collocations Ss can think of using the words from the box. Then put Ss in pairs to discuss the questions. Encourage them to use the vocabulary from exercise 1a. Monitor and take note of how Ss use the vocabulary. Get feedback from the whole class and go over any errors you heard.

Listening and vocabulary

3a ▶ Ss may need dictionaries for this exercise. Discuss the first two questions with the whole class. Then elicit the meanings of the words in the box and let Ss use dictionaries if necessary. Put Ss in pairs to discuss question 3 before getting feedback from the whole class.

b ▶ 2.5 Play the recording and ask Ss to check their predictions from exercise 3a. Tell Ss that there is no definitive answer to this task and that they should decide which adjectives could describe Lady Mary based on what they hear. Get feedback from the whole class.

Suggested Answers
1   She lived in the eighteenth century.
2   She lived in England and Turkey.
3   She was not beautiful as smallpox had scarred her face. She was open-minded about new cultures and was probably confident and adventurous. She also seems to be clever and intelligent.

4a ▶ Ask Ss to read the text and try to remember or guess which words complete the gaps. Remind them to use a maximum of three words in each gap. Elicit ideas but don't confirm any answers at this point. Play the recording and then check the answers with the whole class.

Answers
1	women travellers	5	after her death
2	her husband	6	culture
3	1716	7	polite
4	letters	8	son

b ▶ Again ask Ss to remember or guess the answers before they listen. Play the recording again and then check the answers with the whole class.

Answers
1   Most women travellers went abroad to accompany their <u>husbands</u>.
2   Lady Mary <u>enjoyed</u> living in Turkey.
3   She wore <u>Turkish</u> clothes.
4   She had caught smallpox as <u>an adult</u>.
5   She had her son inoculated against smallpox in <u>Turkey</u>.
6   She helped to introduce inoculation to <u>England</u>.

OPTIONAL EXTENSION

Ss close their books. Go round the class or choose Ss randomly. Each student should say one thing they remember about Lady Mary Wortley Montagu.

Pronunciation | sentence stress

5a ▶ 2.6 Check that Ss remember what stress is. Play the first sentence of the recording only and elicit which word is stressed. Check by reading the example in the book. Play the first sentence again, to confirm that Ss have heard the stress. Ss then listen and write the stressed word in the remaining sentences. Play the whole recording for Ss to check and then get feedback from the whole class.

Answers
2   Lady Mary <u>enjoyed</u> living in Turkey.
3   She wore <u>Turkish</u> clothes.
4   She had caught smallpox as an <u>adult</u>.
5   She had her son inoculated against smallpox in <u>Turkey</u>.
6   She helped to introduce inoculation to <u>England</u>.

b ▶ Elicit the answer to the question and refer Ss to the Pronunciation bank on page 164 to check. Drill the sentences as a whole class and individually.

Answers
These words wouldn't usually be stressed, but are in this case to show contrast and emphasise which information has been corrected. For example, in sentence 2, *enjoyed* is stressed to contrast it with the incorrect *didn't enjoy* in the original sentence.

6a ▶ Read through the instructions with the Ss and make sure they understand the task. Give Ss time to read the text and write their sentences. Go round and check Ss' sentences for language errors.

b ▶ Ss work in pairs and swap sentences. Ss identify their partner's incorrect facts and respond with a correct sentence, emphasising the corrected information. Get feedback by asking various pairs to read out the incorrect and corrected versions of a sentence. Pay attention to the intonation.

Reading and speaking

7a ▶ Focus Ss' attention on the three pictures. Put Ss in pairs and give them a couple of minutes to discuss what they can see in each picture. Get feedback from the whole class.

b ▶ Ss read the article to check their predictions. Tell Ss not to worry if there are any words they don't understand. Get feedback from the whole class.

Answers
A   A lost dog made a difficult 3,000-mile journey to get home.
B   A woman found a ring on a beach where she had lost it ten years earlier.
C   A whale jumped out of the ocean into a family's boat.

8 ▶ Ss read the article again and answer the questions. Let Ss discuss their answers in pairs before getting feedback from the whole class. Ask Ss if there are any words or phrases in the text that they don't understand. Encourage Ss to answer each other's questions before explaining them yourself.

> **Answers**
> 1 The article isn't very serious. The stories don't have serious consequences and the writer doesn't draw any conclusions from the stories. The aim of the writer is to surprise/entertain the reader.

9 ▶ Focus Ss on the words in the box and the key words in 1–4. In pairs, Ss take turns to retell the stories from the article. Monitor and note down any important errors. Then, ask various Ss to repeat the stories for the rest of the class. Finally, write the errors on the board and encourage Ss to self-correct.

> **OPTIONAL EXTENSION**
> In pairs, Ss use words from the box in exercise 9 to tell strange travel stories that have happened to them or that they have heard.

Grammar | articles

> **OPTIONAL GRAMMAR LEAD-IN**
> Write the first lines of this children's song on the board with the articles underlined: *I knew an old woman who swallowed a fly, I don't know why she swallowed the fly, perhaps she'll die.* In pairs, Ss discuss the use of articles in the song.

10 ▶ Give Ss time to read the Active grammar box. Then put Ss in pairs to match the example sentences with the grammar rules. Check the answers with the whole class. Refer Ss to Reference page 89. Give Ss time to read through the notes then ask the following questions. *What do we use when we mention a subject for the first time?* (a/an) *What do we use with jobs?* (a/an) *Do we use a when we are talking about something we have mentioned previously?* (No) *What do we use if the subject is unique?* (the) *What do we use with superlatives?* (the) *When do we not need to use an article?* (when we make generalisations with plurals and uncountable nouns) Check Ss understand the use of articles in place names. Ask them to write two more places for each place name category on the reference page. Check the Ss' answers and write them on the board.

> **Active grammar**
>
> | | | | |
> |---|---|---|---|
> | A | 8 | E | 7 |
> | B | 5 | F | 3 |
> | C | 1 | G | 4 |
> | D | 6 | H | 2 |

11 ▶ Ss do the activity individually. Tell Ss that there may be more than one mistake in each sentence. Let Ss compare their answers in pairs before getting feedback from the whole class.

> **Answers**
> 1 ~~The~~ Travellers should always respect other people's culture.
> 2 ~~The~~ Europe is not <u>the</u> most beautiful continent.
> 3 ~~The~~ <u>A</u> good way to see a country is to go by train.
> 4 It'd be really relaxing to go on <u>a</u> trip along a river, like <u>the</u> River Nile, for example.
> 5 ~~The~~ Delayed flights are one of <u>the</u> greatest problems travellers face these days.
> 6 Before going abroad, you should learn a few words of <u>a</u> <u>the</u> local language.
> 7 ~~The~~ Travel is a bit boring for me.
> 8 I hate travelling in ~~the~~ aeroplanes.

12 ▶ Ss read the stories and then do the activity in pairs. Let Ss compare their answers with another pair before getting feedback from the whole class.

> **Answers**
>
> | | | | | | |
> |---|---|---|---|---|---|
> | 1 | a | 4 | a | 8 | the |
> | 2 | The | 5 | – | 9 | – |
> | 3 | the | 6 | a | 10 | the |
> | | | 7 | the | 11 | the |

> **OPTIONAL EXTENSION 1**
> When you have checked the answers to exercise 12, ask Ss to close their books. Write the words which follow the articles in each story on the board in two columns. At the top of the column with the words from the story about the guitar, write *guitar*. At the top of the column with the words from the story about the hotel in Warsaw, write *Warsaw*. Ss retell the stories in pairs, using the words on the board as prompts. Monitor for correct use of articles and take note of any errors. When Ss have finished telling the stories, write the errors on the board and discuss them with the class.

> **OPTIONAL EXTENSION 2**
> In groups of three or four, Ss plan a trip round the world. Tell Ss they can visit any places they like: countries, rivers, deserts, oceans, cities. They must also make a list of things they would like to take with them, and who will be responsible for buying these items. Before starting to make plans, refer Ss back to the Active grammar box and the rules about using articles. While Ss are discussing their trip monitor closely for correct use of articles. Get feedback by asking different groups to present their plans for the trip to the rest of the class.

Speaking

13 ▶ Read through the instructions with the Ss. Ss read the sentences from exercise 11 again and decide if they agree with each sentence, disagree or don't know. Put Ss in groups of three or four to discuss their answers. Tell Ss that they should come to an agreement about each statement. Put Ss in pairs to work with a student from a different group. Ss take turns to explain what their group decided and why. Get feedback from the whole class.

6 Vocabulary | expressions with get

In this lesson, Ss use a mind map to look at different expressions formed with *get*. Ss then go on to write a story using these phrases.

OPTIONAL WARMER

In pairs, Ss make a list of all the expressions they know with *get*. Elicit feedback and write correct expressions on the board. Make sure Ss know the meaning of all the expressions on the board.

---

1 ▶ Focus Ss on the mind map. In pairs, Ss read through the map and tick any expressions they know. Ss compare their lists with another pair and explain expressions to each other where possible. Finally, get feedback from the whole class and ask various Ss to explain the expressions. If there are any expressions Ss have not seen before, explain them to the class.

2 ▶ Ask Ss if they have ever used maps like the *get* map before. If the answer is yes, ask them to describe their maps, telling the class what kind of language it recorded and how useful it was. Discuss how this can be an effective way of recording and remembering vocabulary and encourage Ss to use maps to record vocabulary in the future. Ss do the activity in pairs. Then check the answers with the whole class.

Answers									
a 3		b 6		c 1		d 3		e 2	

3 ▶ Ss do the activity individually. Remind Ss that they need to use the correct tense, as well as identifying the expression. Let Ss compare their answers in pairs before getting feedback from the whole class.

Answers		
1	getting on	5 get off
2	get on	6 got
3	get it into	7 get away with
4	got out of	

OPTIONAL VARIATION

Before the lesson, copy the text (including the gaps) and cut it up into the seven parts. Mix up the pieces and give one to each student. Note that you may need to cut up more than one text and Ss may have more than one part, depending on how many Ss you have in your class. Each student has to complete his/her section and then find the rest of the story and check their answers. Do a class check but don't confirm the answers. Collect in all the papers. Then give Ss two minutes to complete the text in their books before checking the answers with the whole class.

4a ▶ Put Ss in groups of three or four. Focus Ss on the expressions in the box. Ss check that they know the meaning of all the expressions. If there are any expressions Ss don't know, encourage them to answer each others' questions before asking you. Ss then prepare a story in their groups. Remind them that they can use any expressions with *get* not just the phrases from the box. If Ss need help with vocabulary, encourage them to use their dictionaries or to ask you.

b ▶ In their groups, Ss write up their stories, leaving spaces where there is an expression with *get*. Check the stories for correct use of language. Ss swap stories with another group. Each group reads a story and tries to complete the gaps. Ss then check their answers with the group who wrote the story.

6 Communication

Buckingham Palace is the official London home of the royal family in England. It is the place where all official gatherings take place and has been a meeting place for the British people at times of great joy or crisis. Originally, it was the home of a duke and was not given to the Royal family to use until 1761.

Les Mis or *Les Miserables* is an award-winning musical adaptation of the famous Victor Hugo novel. It is the third-longest running show on Broadway in history and the only musical to have three productions taking place at the same time in one city.

The British Museum is the museum of history and culture in London and is most notable for its archaeological artefacts. It has more than seven million objects and has the second largest numbers of visitors in the world annually, after *The Louvre* in Paris.

In this lesson, Ss read information about events and activities in London. Ss then plan a day trip to London and tell the rest of the class about their plans.

1 ▶ Put Ss in groups of three or four to discuss the question. Get feedback from the whole class.

OPTIONAL WARMER

Write *London* on the board. In groups of three or four, Ss brainstorm everything they know about London. Get feedback and write Ss ideas on the board. Ask Ss if anyone in the class has been to London. If someone has visited London, ask them to tell the rest of the class about the city. Finally, with the whole class, elicit which places Ss would like to visit in London.

---

2 ▶ Ss read the leaflet about London and find the items (1–6). Tell Ss not to worry about words they don't understand at this stage. Check the answers with the whole class. Ss read through the information again and underline any words or expressions they don't know. Encourage Ss to explain vocabulary to each other or to ask you.

Answers
1   a Big Red Bus tour
2   30 minutes
3   *Les Misérables*
4   The Royal Festival Hall
5   Madame Tussaud's and The British Museum
6   Harrods

3a ▶ ⊙ 2.7 Read through the instructions and elicit the three things Ss will be listening for. Then play the recording. Let Ss check their answers in pairs before getting feedback from the whole class.

Answers
1   a London walk and Camden Market
2   *Les Miserables*
3   The British Museum

---

b ▶ Refer Ss to the audioscript on page 171. Ask Ss to underline all the phrases that speakers use to give suggestions and respond to ideas. Let Ss check their answers in pairs before getting feedback from the whole class.

Answers
Make suggestions:
It would be good to ...
I like the idea of ...
Are you guys OK with ... ?
I quite like the sound of ...
(Are) you guys OK with that, too?
Can we go to ... , too? I('ve) heard it's really good.
How about ... ?

Respond to ideas:
I'm happy with that.
Yeah, I think so.
OK, let's do that then.
Yeah, I think we should.
I('ve) heard that, too.
I like the sound of that.

4a ▶ Read through the instructions with the Ss. Then put Ss in groups of four to plan their day using the information in the leaflet. Encourage Ss to use the phrases for making and responding to suggestions from exercise 3b. Monitor and help where necessary.

b ▶ Get feedback by asking each group to tell the rest of the class about their plans for the day out. Ss can vote on which group came up with the best plan.

OPTIONAL EXTENSION

Ss plan a day out in their own city. In a monolingual class, Ss work in pairs to plan the day out and tell the rest of the class what they have planned to do. In a multilingual class, Ss plan a day out in a city they know well in their own country and tell their partner about the day out.

Review and practice

1 ▶

Answers
1	had left	6	had all gone
2	had lived	7	kissed
3	got, had cooked	8	had grown, had
4	went	9	hadn't seen
5	had never seen		

2 ▶

Answers
1 I don't feel like to go going tonight.
2 He's like really nice.
3 It tastes like coffee. (correct)
4 Would you like having to have a drink?
5 What was/is Madrid like?
6 We could eat out tonight, if you like. (correct)
7 I like going to restaurants. (correct)
8 Can you hear that noise? It sounds like Joe's car.
9 I'll come round tomorrow and help clear up, if you're liking you like.
10 I'd like two tickets please.

3 ▶

Answers
1	the	4	the	7	the	10	–
2	–	5	the	8	–	11	the
3	the	6	–	9	the	12	the

4 ▶

Answers
1	the hotel	3	aeroplanes	6	A
2	The food	4	the	7	the most
		5	Cats	8	a

5 ▶

Answers
1	go	6	unforgettable
2	travel	7	get
3	getting	8	getting
4	sandy	9	get
5	tropical	10	Get

6 ▶

Answers
1	garden	4	Hostels
2	lake	5	square
3	bookshop		

Writing bank

See page 158 of the Students' Book

1 ▶ Ss read the competition entry and decide which view is being described.

Answers
C

2 ▶ Check Ss' understanding of the adjectives in the box. Ss read the competition entry again and complete it with adjectives from the box.

Answers
1 traditional
2 lush
3 snow-capped

3 ▶ Ss complete the How to... box with words and phrases from the competition entry in exercise 1.

Answers
The view from my window is so green and peaceful.
It's a beautiful sunny day.
On the left, there is a traditional Swiss church.
Nearby, there are a few houses.
In the distance I can see the snow-capped mountains.
A little nearer (there is) a mountain covered with trees.
A little way off on the right there's a small road.
The whole scene is so perfect.
It makes me feel glad to be alive.

4a ▶ Ss choose a view they want to write about and make notes.

b ▶ Ss write their own entry for the competition, using their notes and language from the How to... box.

Overview

Lead-in	**Vocabulary:** Learning and education
7.1	**Can do:** Describe a learning experience **Grammar:** Subject and object questions **Vocabulary:** Learning **Speaking and Pronunciation:** **How to...** describe a learning experience **Reading:** Mistakes that work ... **Listening:** Learning experiences
7.2	**Can do:** Describe a teacher from your past **Grammar:** *Used to* and *would* **Vocabulary:** Personal qualities (2), Word building **Speaking and Pronunciation:** Word stress in word building **Reading:** Extract from *Matilda* **Listening:** Memorable teachers
7.3	**Can do:** Carry out an interview **Grammar:** Modals of ability, past and present **Vocabulary:** Education **Speaking and Pronunciation:** Connected speech **How to...** carry out an interview **Reading:** It's never too late **Listening:** U3A, Old age
Vocabulary	Learning: idioms and phrasal verbs
Communication	Discuss options and make a decision
Writing bank	Summarise a short article **How to...** write a summary
Extra resources	ActiveTeach and ActiveBook

CEFR Can do objectives
7.1 Describe a learning experience
7.2 Describe a teacher from your past
7.3 Carry out an interview
Communication Discuss options and make a decision
Writing bank Summarise a short article

CEFR Portfolio ideas
a) With a friend, imagine you are interviewing applicants for a teacher's job in your school. Take turns to be the interviewer and interviewee. Video the interviews and the discussion that you have afterwards, discussing what you learned from the experience about teaching and about interviews.
b) You have received an email from a friend. Tomorrow morning, he has to travel from his house on one side of town to attend an interview on the other side of town at 10:00 a.m. Reply to the email, suggesting all the possible travel options and then recommend the best option. Your friend doesn't have a car. Remember to mention all possible forms of transport.
c) Choose an article that interests you from the Internet or from a magazine or newspaper and write a summary of it. Use the How to... box on page 159 to help you.

Lead-in

OPTIONAL WARMER

Write *education* on the board. Ss write down five words connected with education. Put Ss in pairs (A and B). Student A describes his/her words to student B without saying the word. Student B guesses the words. Ss swap roles and Student B describes their words for Student A to guess.

---

1 ▶ Focus Ss on the photos of different learning situations. Put Ss in pairs to discuss the first question. Get feedback from various pairs. Then discuss the second question with the whole class.

2 ▶ Focus Ss on the box and the table. Ss think of as many verb/noun collocations as they can and add the nouns to the correct column of the table. Monitor and help Ss with the meanings of any words they don't know. Copy the table onto the board. Ask various Ss to write nouns in the table on the board to create correct collocations. In pairs, Ss add more nouns to each verb in the table. Check the words Ss have added and write them in the correct column of the table on the board.

Answers
get: a degree, good marks
take: an exam, notes, a subject
do: a degree, an exam, a course, some research, a subject, your best, well at something
pass: an exam, a subject
fail: an exam, a subject
revise: notes, a subject
go: to a lecture, to class
make: a decision, a mistake, notes, progress, a suggestion
graduate: from university

3a ▶ Ss do the activity individually. Remind Ss that they may have to change the form of the verbs. Let Ss compare their answers in pairs before checking the answers with the whole class.

Answers
1	revise	3	taken	5	get
2	make	4	go	6	do, do

---

b ▶ Ss discuss the questions in pairs. Monitor and note down any errors. When Ss have finished, tell them you are going to read out some errors. Read out the errors and elicit the correct form from Ss.

OPTIONAL EXTENSION

If you feel Ss need extra practice, tell them to write five questions of their own using some of the collocations from the table. Then put Ss in pairs and tell them to take turns to ask each other their questions. Encourage Ss to self-correct. Go round the class and correct errors if necessary.

7.1 Learning from experience

Thomas Edison (1847–1931) was an American inventor, scientist and businessman. He is credited with inventing the phonograph (the first record player), the motion picture camera and the light bulb. He was also one of the first people to use mass production.

Benjamin Franklin (1706–1790) was one of the founding fathers of the US. However, he was also a politician, a scientist, an inventor, a statesman and a diplomat. He was a major figure of the American enlightenment. He invented lightning rods and bifocals (glasses for people with more than one eye problem). He also founded the first public library and the first fire department in the US.

In this lesson, Ss listen to people talking about how they learned to do something. They then look at vocabulary connected with learning and through the listening they learn how to describe a learning experience. Ss then read about mistakes that work. This context provides practise in subject and object questions. There is also advice on how to use a correction code.

Listening

OPTIONAL LEAD-IN

Put Ss in pairs (A and B). Ss A look at the pictures in exercise 1. Ss B have the book closed. Student A describes the pictures to Student B. Student B listens and decides what the pictures have in common. Get feedback from the whole class and check what Ss B think the pictures have in common. Ss B open the book and check their ideas.

1 ▶ 🌐 2.8–2.12 In pairs, Ss discuss what they think the people are doing in each picture. Get feedback from the whole class. Then play the recordings (five tracks) for Ss to match the speakers with the pictures. Let Ss compare their answers in pairs before checking the answers with the whole class. Discuss whether the Ss predictions about what the people are doing were correct.

Answers
A 1   B 5   C 4   D 2   E 3

2a ▶ Ss read through the sentences from the listening and try to remember or predict the answers. Remind Ss to use a maximum of three words in each gap. Then play the recordings again and let Ss compare their ideas in pairs before getting feedback from the whole class.

Answers
1   five, seven
2   a year, German
3   time to
4   eighteenth, seven or eight
5   six, four teachers

b ▶ Put Ss in pairs to discuss the five learning experiences they heard about. Elicit feedback from each pair to find out which experience most Ss thought was the most interesting/difficult/exciting.

Vocabulary | learning

3a ▶ Focus Ss on the five sentences and check Ss' understanding of the words in the box. Ss do the activity in pairs. Then get feedback from the whole class.

Answers
1   heart   4   thrown
2   picking   5   crash
3   steep

b ▶ Ss do the activity individually. Then check the answers with the whole class.

Answers
a   crash course
b   learn by heart
c   was just thrown into, thrown
d   had a really steep learning curve
e   picking it up

OPTIONAL EXTENSION

Divide Ss into five groups and assign one phrase from exercise 3a to each group. Each member of the group has to make up a sentence, true or false, about themselves, using the phrase. Then create different groups so that everyone in each group has a different phrase. Ss then tell each other their sentences and the rest of the group has to guess whether it is true or false.

4 ▶ 🌐 2.8–2.12 Give Ss' time to read through the How to… box. Play the recordings from exercise 1 again for Ss to tick the expressions they hear. Check the answers with the whole class.

Answers
About a year ago I took an interest in …
I took a one-day crash course in …
I used to practise … over and over …

I was amazed how quickly I started picking it up.
I'm not sure I'd want to do it again.
It was a great experience, even though it was hard work.
I really didn't know what to expect …

5a ▶ Ask Ss to think about a good or bad learning experience they have had. Then put Ss in pairs to make questions from the prompts. Check the answers with the whole class and write the questions on the board. Drill the questions with the whole class if you think it's necessary.

Answers

1 What were you learning? Why?
2 Why was the experience good or bad?
3 How did you learn?
4 Did you learn in a group or on your own?
5 Was it easy or difficult to learn?
6 How did you make progress?
7 Did you learn (any) useful techniques?

b ▶ Ss answer the questions individually and make notes about their learning experience. Go round and help Ss with vocabulary where necessary.

c ▶ Tell Ss they are going to describe their learning experience. Encourage Ss to think about how they can use the vocabulary from exercise 3 and the language from the How to... box in their descriptions. Ss then work in pairs, taking turns to describe their learning experiences and ask follow-up questions. Monitor the conversations and note down errors. Get feedback by asking Ss to tell you about their partner's experience and why it was good or bad. When Ss have finished, put some of the important errors on the board and ask various Ss to come up to the board and correct the errors. Praise Ss for correct use of target language.

OPTIONAL VARIATION

When you have got feedback about all of the learning experiences, ask Ss to choose the top five most difficult learning experiences the Ss have mentioned. In groups, Ss discuss which Ss had the most difficult learning experiences and why. Get feedback from the whole class.

Reading

6 ▶ Write the following words on the board: *light bulbs, crisps, bread, post-it notes*. Give Ss thirty seconds to work in pairs and discuss what the connection between the items might be. If Ss find this difficult, you could let them look at the title of the article as well. Get feedback from the whole class. Ss then read the text quickly to find the connection. Tell Ss not to worry about words they don't understand at this stage. Check the answer with the whole class.

Answers
The items were all invented after failures or mistakes.

7 ▶ Ss close their books. Write the numbers on the board and elicit how to say them. In pairs, Ss try to remember what the numbers refer to in the text. Ss then read the text again and write questions for the answers. Get feedback from the whole class. Elicit words or expressions in the text which Ss don't understand. Encourage Ss to answer each others' questions or to use a dictionary, before giving the explanations yourself.

Suggested Answers

1 How many ideas did Benjamin Franklin have that didn't work?/How many of Benjamin Franklin's ideas didn't work?
2 When was bread invented?/In which year BC was bread invented?
3 When did Spencer Silver invent a weak glue?/When was a weak glue invented?
4 When did Art Fry invent the post-it note?/When was the post-it note invented?
5 How much did an employee's mistake cost IBM (in dollars)?

8 ▶ Put Ss in groups of three or four to discuss the questions. Get feedback from the whole class.

9 ▶ Focus Ss' attention on the text at the bottom of the Lifelong learning box. Ask Ss: *Is there anything wrong in this text?* (Yes, there are mistakes). Explain that when we make mistakes, we need to understand what type of mistakes they are before we can correct them. Read through the Lifelong learning box with the whole class. Look at the example given in the text and then put Ss in pairs to check the text for mistakes and identify them using the correction code. Get feedback from the whole class and elicit corrections for each mistake. Ask Ss: *Do you use a code like this? Would it be helpful? Why/Why not?*

Answers
I started learning ~~to~~ drive (WF) when I ~~am~~ was (WT) seventeen. I was (M) very nervous. My father ~~tort~~ taught (sp) me ~~in his car to drive~~ to drive in his car (WO) and ~~everyctime~~ every time (Sp) I ~~did~~ made (WW) a mistake he shouted ~~to~~ at (WW) me. ~~it~~ It (P) took me a (M) long time to learn.

Grammar | subject/object questions

OPTIONAL GRAMMAR LEAD-IN

Write the following questions on the board.
1 What time did the class start?
2 Who arrived last in the class today?
In pairs, Ss answer the questions. Elicit full-sentence answers and write them on the board below the questions. Ask Ss if they can see a difference between the two questions. Elicit that the first question contains an auxiliary verb and the second question doesn't. In pairs, Ss discuss why there is an auxiliary in the first question but not in the second. Get feedback from various pairs and elicit/explain that the first question is an object question, the second a subject question. Go on to look at the Active grammar box.

10 ▶ Put Ss in pairs to discuss the questions. Then get feedback from the whole class.

11 ▶ Read through the instructions with the Ss. Ss read through the Active grammar box and complete the rules. Let Ss compare their answers in pairs before checking the answers with the whole class. Then Refer Ss to Reference page 103 and give them time to read the notes.

Ask *Ss: When a Wh- question word is the object of the question, what word order do we use?* (normal question word order: question word + auxiliary + subject + verb) *When a Wh- question word is the subject of the question, what word order do we use?* (order of an affirmative sentence: question word + verb + object) *Do we need an auxiliary verb in a subject question?* (No). *Which is the most common type of question: subject or object questions?* (object questions)

Active grammar

Object questions: object
Subject questions: subject

12a ▶ Put Ss in pairs (A and A or B and B). Individually, Ss look at their own quiz statements and write a question for each statement. Remind Ss to decide whether an object or subject question is required. Ss compare their questions in pairs. Monitor and help where necessary.

Answers
Quiz A
1 Who painted *Guernica* in 1937?
2 When did Mozart start composing music?
3 Who discovered penicillin in 1928?
4 Which of the world's greatest scientists lived from 1879–1955?
5 Which famous city is nicknamed *The Big Apple*?
6 What invention is Guglielmo Marconi responsible for?
7 Which is the largest desert in the world?
8 Who wrote the best-sellers *The Da Vinci Code* and *The Lost Symbol*?
9 Which country is the oldest surviving republic in the world?
10 When did Tom Daley become the youngest ever male Olympics competitor?

Quiz B
1 Which islands did Christopher Columbus discover in 1492, before he discovered America?
2 Who painted the Sistine Chapel?
3 What song about London was a huge hit for Lily Allen in 2006?
4 Which European country has the smallest area?
5 Which team bought Cristiano Ronaldo for $163 million?
6 Who wrote the song *Imagine* in 1971?
7 What did Laszlo Biro invent?
8 Which is the world's longest river?
9 Which of the world's most famous writers lived from 1564–1616?
10 When did Hong Kong become part of China again?

b ▶ Now put Ss in different pairs so each Student A is working with a Student B. Ss ask each other their quiz questions. Ss give their partners a point for each question answered correctly. When they have finished, Ss count the points and check who won the quiz. Get feedback from the whole class and discuss which questions Ss found most difficult.

13 ▶ In pairs, Ss write their own quiz questions and answers. Encourage Ss to include both subject and object questions in their quiz. Go round and check the questions Ss are writing. Ss read out the questions for other pairs and see if they can answer them.

OPTIONAL EXTENSION

Put Ss into pairs. Ss think of five facts they think they know about their partners. Ss write down the five things. Ss then think of questions for these five facts. The questions must include subject and object questions. If the original five questions don't include both subject and object questions, tell Ss to change some of them to include both types of questions. Ss now ask their partner the questions and compare their partners' answers with the answers they predicted.

7.2 Great teachers

Roald Dahl wrote many very successful books for children such as *James and the Giant Peach* which was turned into an animated film and *Charlie and the Chocolate Factory*, which was also made into a film, starring Gene Wilder. A new version of the film was released in 2005, starring Johnny Depp. *Matilda* was also turned into a film, starring Danny De Vito. Roald Dahl also wrote for adults. His short stories are famous for having an unexpected twist at the end of them. Some of his stories were televised in Britain as *Tales of the Unexpected*.

In this lesson, Ss read about a young girl's experience of her very first teacher and learn more vocabulary connected with personal qualities. They then listen to two people talking about their teachers. Through this context they learn about word building and how to stress different forms of the same word. This is also the context for the grammar focus on the uses of *used to* and *would*. Finally, Ss talk about a good or bad teacher from their past and write an entry about them for a website.

Reading and speaking

OPTIONAL LEAD-IN

Dictate the following words taken from the *Matilda* extract: *exercise book*, *pencils*, *headmistress*, *strict discipline*, *argue*, *liquidise*, *laugh*, *eager*. Check that Ss understand these words and phrases. In pairs, Ss discuss how these words and phrases could be related to a first day at school. Get feedback from the whole class.

1 ▶ Put Ss in pairs to discuss the questions. Then get feedback from the whole class.

2a ▶ Ss look at the picture and discuss the question. Let Ss compare their ideas with another pair before getting feedback from the whole class. Write the Ss ideas on the board.

b ▶ Tell Ss that the teacher in the picture is Miss Trunchbull from *Matilda* by Roald Dahl. Ss read the extract quickly to check their predictions from exercise 2a. Tell Ss not to worry about any words or expressions they don't understand at this stage. Get feedback from the whole class.

Suggested Answers
Miss Trunchbull sounds very strict and quite frightening. She 'insists upon strict discipline', 'can liquidise you like a carrot' and 'deals very severely with anyone who gets out of line'.

3 ▶ Ss read the text again more carefully and do the task individually. Ask Ss to underline the parts of the text which give them the answers and to correct the false sentences. Let Ss compare their answers in pairs before checking the answers with the whole class.

Answers
1 T
2 F ('You have all brought your own pencils, I hope.')
3 T
4 F (eleven years of schooling, six of which are spent at Crunchem Hall)
5 F (Miss Trunchbull is the headmistress.)
6 T
7 F (She advises them not to argue with Miss Trunchbull.)
8 T (eager)

4 ▶ Ss do the activity individually and then compare their answers in pairs. Check the answers with the whole class. Check if there are any other words or expressions in the text that Ss don't understand.

Answers
1 making people obey rules
2 do what I suggest
3 act like a good child
4 disagree with someone by talking or shouting
5 reply rudely
6 punishes

5a ▶ Ss do the activity individually and then compare their answers in pairs. Check the answers with the whole class.

Answers
1 behave
2 (strict) discipline
3 take, advice
4 argue
5 deals severely

b ▶ Ss change three of the sentences so that they are true for them and then compare their sentences in pairs. Elicit new sentences from various Ss.

Vocabulary | personal qualities

6a ▶ Ss may need dictionaries for this exercise. Ss check the meaning of the words in the box in pairs, using dictionaries if necessary and decide which words are the qualities of a good or a bad teacher. Let Ss compare their answers with another pair. Then get feedback from the whole class and check understanding.

Answers
Good: calm, clear, encouraging, enthusiastic, imaginative, inspiring, interesting, knowledgeable, patient, tolerant, understanding
Bad: boring, frightening, strict
Note: *strict* can also be a positive quality if it is fair and not too severe.

b ▶ Ss do the activity individually and then check their answers in pairs. Check the answers with the whole class.

Answers

1 boring	4 knowledgeable
2 patient	5 strict
3 understanding	6 encouraging

OPTIONAL EXTENSION

Each student chooses one word from exercise 6. Ss shouldn't tell anyone their word. They then have thirty seconds to behave in a way that illustrates that personal quality. The rest of the class guess which quality is being shown.

Listening

Rastafarianism or the Rastafari movement is an African-centred religious movement which developed in Jamaica in the 1930s. Its followers worship Haile Selassie, the former Emperor of Ethiopia. It is not a highly organised religion, more a way of life. Many male believers style their hair in dreadlocks.

OPTIONAL LEAD-IN

Write the word *mathematics* on the board. Elicit from Ss that this is a school subject. Also elicit what Ss expect to learn about in a mathematics lesson. Give Ss thirty seconds to brainstorm more school subjects and then put them all on the board. Make sure all Ss understand what is taught in each lesson.

7a ▶ 2.13 Read through the instructions with the Ss and then play the recording. Check the answers with the whole class.

Answers

Mr Halsworth – History	Mrs Sharp – Physics
Miss Matthews – Music	Mr Ford – Religious Studies

b ▶ Tell Ss that the words from exercise 6a will help with this activity. Make sure Ss understand that they should note down all the important points they hear about the teachers, not just their good and bad points. Then play the recording and let Ss compare their answers in pairs before checking the answers with the whole class. Get feedback on the other points Ss noted down.

Answers

Mr Halsworth – boring, shouted a lot
Miss Matthews – inspiring, patient
Mrs Sharp – frightening, strict (she would punish you)
Mr Ford – knowledgeable, patient (never lost his temper)

Vocabulary | word building

8a ▶ Write *interest, to interest, interesting* on the board and elicit the names of the different forms (noun, verb, adjective). Tell Ss that we can make different word forms by changing them slightly. This is called word building. Explain or elicit how you can change words (use a prefix or suffix). Ss then complete the table individually. Tell Ss they may find some of the answers on page 96. Ss then check their answers in pairs before getting feedback from the whole class. Don't confirm any answers at this point.

Answers

1 imagine, imaginative
2 knowledge, knowledgeable
3 frighten, frightening
4 encouragement, encouraging
5 inspire, inspiration
6 tolerate, tolerant
7 boredom
8 clarification

OPTIONAL VARIATION

This activity could be done as a dictionary task to give Ss confidence in finding different word forms in a monolingual dictionary.

---

b ▶ Focus Ss on the suffixes 1–7. Make sure Ss remember what a suffix is and refer them back to page 45 if necessary. Ss do the activity in pairs. Ask them to think of an example for each suffix. Then get feedback from the whole class. Finally, see if Ss can come up with any other suffixes that could be used e.g. *-ist, -ism, -al*.

Answers

2 N		5 N	
3 A		6 A	
4 N		7 A	

Pronunciation | word stress in word building

9a ▶ 2.14 Read through the words with the Ss and check the differences in meaning/form. Elicit the meaning of stress and how to mark stress. Put Ss in pairs to practise saying the words and mark the stress. Then play the recording for Ss to check their ideas. Check the answers with the whole class.

Answers

1 bored – boring
2 inspire – inspiration
3 encourage – encouragement
4 enthusiasm – enthusiastic
5 fright – frightening
6 imagine – imagination
7 knowledge – knowledgeable

b ▶ Ss do the task quickly individually. Then check the answers with the whole class. Finally, play the recording again and drill the words chorally and individually.

> **Answers**
> *-tic* and *-tion* change the stress

c ▶ Put Ss in pairs to practise saying the words. Then play the recording and drill chorally and individually.

Grammar | *used to* and *would*

> **OPTIONAL GRAMMAR LEAD-IN**
> Write the following sentence prompts on the board.
> 1 *When I was five I* <u>used to</u> *like ___ at school.*
> 2 *When I was five I* <u>would</u> *often ___ at school.*
> Ss complete the sentences so they are true for them and then compare their answers in pairs. Elicit sentences from various Ss. Ask Ss why we use the underlined words.

10a ▶ Refer Ss to the audioscript on page 172 and ask them to complete sentences 1–5 first. Ss then read the rules A–D and choose the correct options. Check the answers with the whole class. Refer Ss to Reference page 103. Give Ss time to read through the notes and ask any questions.

> **Active grammar**
>
> A repeated actions
> 1 'd/would
> 2 used to
>
> B *used to* + verb
> 3 used to
> 4 didn't use to
>
> C *Would*
> 5 'd
>
> D *use to*

b ▶ Ss do the activity individually. Let Ss compare their answers in pairs before checking the answers with the whole class.

> **Answers**
> He <u>used to shout</u> so much he <u>'d go</u> red …
> She <u>used to make</u> me sit at the front …
> … she <u>would punish</u> you.
> He <u>used to teach</u> us …
> … not even when we <u>used to</u> …

11 ▶ Ss do the activity individually. Let Ss compare their answers in pairs before checking the answers with the whole class.

> **Answers**
> 1 use to   4 used to be
> 2 both   5 both
> 3 both   6 used to be

12 ▶ Ss do the activity in pairs and then compare their answers with another pair. Get feedback from the whole class.

> **Answers**
> 1 use to be
> 2 used to like
> 3 didn't use to watch
> 4 used to live
> 5 didn't use to go
> 6 use to eat
> 7 used to do
> 8 didn't use to behave

13a ▶ Ss do the activity individually. Make sure Ss notice that numbers 1 and 6 are questions which they should answer.

b ▶ Put Ss in pairs to compare their sentences. Encourage Ss to ask follow-up questions. Monitor and note down any errors. Get feedback from various pairs. Then write any important errors on the board and encourage Ss to self-correct.

Speaking

14a ▶ Ss think about a good or bad teacher from their past that they do not have now and write notes using the questions 1–6. Tell Ss that it isn't necessary to write full sentences. Monitor and help Ss as necessary.

b ▶ Put Ss in groups of three or four. Ss take turns to talk about their teachers and ask follow-up questions. Encourage Ss to use *used to*/*would* as appropriate. Monitor the conversations and note down any errors. When Ss have finished, write the errors on the board and encourage Ss to correct them. Finally, praise Ss on the correct use of *used to* and *would*.

Writing

15 ▶ Ss write a website entry about a favourite teacher from their past, using their notes from exercise 14. Monitor and help Ss where necessary. When Ss have finished writing, ask various Ss to read out their entries for the class.

7.3 It's never too late

In this lesson, Ss listen to a radio programme about a university for older people and read texts about people starting a new career late in life. Through this context, Ss learn more vocabulary connected with education and the modals of ability, past and present. They also study the pronunciation of connected speech and, at the end of the lesson learn and practise the language of conducting an interview.

Vocabulary | education

OPTIONAL LEAD-IN

Write *university* on the board. Give Ss one minute to brainstorm words they can think of related to universities. Then get feedback from the whole class. Ask Ss: *What subjects can you learn at university? What other activities can you do at university? At what age do you go to university?*

---

1 ▶ Read through the instructions and questions with the whole class. Check understanding of the words in bold. Put Ss in pairs to discuss the questions and then get feedback from the whole class, discussing the reasons for their answers.

OPTIONAL EXTENSION

In pairs, Ss construct sentences with the words they studied in exercise 1 to show that they have understood the meaning.

Listening

2a ▶ 🔘 2.16 Read through the instructions and tell Ss to take notes on what makes this university different from the universities they described in exercise 1. Play the recording. Let Ss check their answers in pairs before getting feedback from the whole class.

Answers
You can't take a degree or any kind of formal assessment.
The students are all over fifty-five.
There are branches all over the world.

---

b ▶ Put the Ss into pairs (A and B). Play the recording again. Ss A answer the first set of questions and Ss B answer the second set. Don't ask for feedback at this point.

c ▶ Ss A and B now share the answers to their questions. Check the answers with the whole class.

Answers
Student A
1   3,000
2   They find out what people want to learn and bring them together.
3   It keeps their brain active./It's their first chance to do something which interests them./It's a social activity.
4   They made a return visit to South Africa.
5   They go to lectures with the regular university students.

Student B
1   200,000
2   Philosophy/Mandarin Chinese/Latin
3   It keeps their brain active./It's their first chance to do something which interests them./It's a social activity.
4   They went on a twenty-one day study tour of Central Europe.
5   They do community work, such as teaching English.

---

d ▶ Play the recording again. Ss underline the words in bold in exercise 1 that are used during the listening. They should also listen to what is said about them. Get feedback from the whole class.

Answers
1   courses, academic, subjects
2   formal assessment, exam
3   lecture, seminar
4   distance learning
5   degree, subject

Reading

3a ▶ Put Ss in pairs (A and B). Ss A read the three texts on pages 98–99. Ss B read the three texts on page 149. While reading, Ss make notes on each of the four topics. Tell Ss not to copy directly from the text, but to write the information in their own words. If there are any words or phrases that Ss don't understand, encourage them to answer each other's questions or to use a dictionary before asking you.

b ▶ In their pairs, Ss take turns to describe the three people they have read about. Ss then decide which of the old people is the most remarkable and why. Let Ss compare their answers with another pair before getting feedback from the whole class.

Speaking and listening

4 ▶ Put Ss in different pairs to discuss the questions. Get feedback from the whole class.

5 ▶ 🔘 2.17 Read through the instructions and the questions with the Ss. Play the recording and then check the answers with the whole class.

Answers
1   N   2   P   3   E   4   P   5   N

Play the recording again. This time, Ss take notes on how Eben and Polly answer the questions from exercise 4. In pairs, Ss then compare their notes with their own answers to exercise 4. Get feedback from the whole class.

Grammar | modals of ability, past and present

OPTIONAL GRAMMAR LEAD-IN

Write five sentences on the board about yourself and your present and past abilities. Use the following modals of ability in your sentences: *can*, *could*, *was able to* and *managed to*. Ss can ask you follow-up questions to find out more about your abilities. Discuss the use of the modal verbs of ability in the sentences with the class.

6a ▶ Use this task as a revision activity. Make sure Ss have covered the texts on pages 98–99. Ss then do the task individually. Get feedback from the whole class but don't confirm any answers.

b ▶ Put Ss in pairs to compare their answers and then check the texts for the correct answers. Finally, check the answers with the whole class.

Answers
1 managed to
2 can
3 can't
4 can
5 couldn't
6 managed to
7 was able to
8 couldn't

7 ▶ Ss work though the Active grammar box in pairs. Then get feedback from the whole class. Go back to exercise 6a and elicit reasons for each answer, using the information in the Active grammar box. Then refer Ss to Reference page 103. Give Ss time to read through the notes and ask any questions they might have.

Active grammar

	General ability	Succeed in actually doing something
can/can't	✓	
could/couldn't	✓	
be able to/not be able to	✓	✓
manage to/not manage to		✓

OPTIONAL VARIATION

When Ss have finished reading the Reference, ask Ss: *Which modal verb do we use when we are talking about general ability in the present?* (can) *Which modal verb do we use when we are talking about general ability in the past?* (could) *When do we use* was able to? (when we talk about general ability in the past or a particular situation in the past) *Which modal verb do we use if we want to emphasise that the action is difficult?* (manage to) *Which modal verbs can we use in the negative when we are talking about one particular moment?* (couldn't, wasn't able to, didn't manage to)

8 ▶ Make sure Ss understand that there could be more than one answer. Ss do the activity individually and then compare their answers in pairs. Make sure Ss give reasons for their answers. Finally, check the answers and reasons with the whole class.

Answers
1 been able to, managed to
2 can't
3 be able to
4 wasn't able to, couldn't
5 was able to, managed to

9 ▶ Ss complete the task individually. Let Ss check their answers in pairs before checking the answers with the whole class. Make sure Ss can give reasons for their answers.

Answers		
1 managed to	4 managed to
2 managed to	5 could
3 managed to	6 managed to
	7 could

Pronunciation | connected speech

10a ▶ 2.18 Focus Ss' attention on the pairs of sentences. Play the recording for Ss to tick the sentence they hear. Let Ss compare their answers in pairs before getting feedback from the whole class.

Answers		
1 I could do it.	3 They were able to play.
2 He wasn't able to stop.	4 I managed to do it.

b ▶ 2.19 Read through the instructions and the three examples of connected speech. Make sure Ss understand them. Play the recording and ask Ss to listen for examples. Get feedback from the whole class.

Answers
1 wa<u>s a</u>ble, wasn'<u>t a</u>ble, weren'<u>t a</u>ble
2 couldn'<u>t d</u>o, manage<u>d to</u>
3 we<u>re a</u>ble

c ▶ Play the recording again and drill the sentences chorally and individually, correcting any problems.

> **OPTIONAL EXTENSION**
>
> Put Ss in pairs and give them some time to prepare example sentences with other words (not *could, were able to, managed to*) to show the three examples of connected speech. Pairs then say their sentences for the rest of the class. The class has to identify which example of connected speech is being exemplified.

Speaking

11a ▶ Read through the instructions with the Ss. Then give Ss time to think and make notes.

b ▶ 🔵 2.20 Play the recording. Ss take notes on what Jake says in response to the prompts from exercise 11a. Get feedback from the whole class.

> **Answers**
> 1 He can knit.
> 2 He can drive and cook.
> 3 He could sing.
> 4 He managed to climb three peaks (mountains).

c ▶ Remind Ss that Jake was taking part in an interview. Elicit the questions that the interviewer asked. Ss then turn to the audioscript on page 172 to check. Give Ss time to read through the How to... box. Elicit the difference between initial questions and follow-up questions. Elicit/ explain that initial questions are indirect questions. Ss then prepare their own questions to ask their partners.

> **OPTIONAL EXTENSION**
>
> As part of exercise 11c, you can play the recording again, stopping after each question and drilling the questions with the Ss to get the pronunciation right. Ss can also mark the stress.

d ▶ Put Ss in pairs to interview each other. Ss use their prepared indirect initial questions and follow-up questions and the notes they prepared in exercise 11a. Monitor and make a note of any problems. Then ask some of the Ss to report their discussions to the rest of the class. Go over any problems you heard whilst monitoring.

7 Vocabulary | learning: idioms and phrasal verbs

In this lesson, Ss find out about idioms and phrasal verbs and practise them. They are also encouraged to find out about the origins of idioms.

> **OPTIONAL WARMER**
>
> Write the following on the board.
> *hit the roof*
> *get cold feet*
> *over the hill*
> Elicit from Ss what the words mean. Tell Ss that these are examples of *idioms*. In these phrases, the words don't mean what they seem to mean. Encourage Ss to think, in their own language, about what the phrases might mean. If Ss still cannot guess, then provide example sentences to help them work out the meaning. Put Ss in pairs and encourage them to translate idioms from their own language into English. Get feedback from the whole class.

1a ▶ Read through the instructions and the example with the Ss. Make sure Ss understand that they are identifying the school subject. Ss do the activity individually and then check their ideas in pairs. Finally, check the answers with the whole class.

> **Answers**
> 2 Mathematics
> 3 Biology
> 4 Music
> 5 Art
> 6 Geography
> 7 Foreign languages
> 8 Chemistry/Physics/Science

b ▶ Elicit from Ss what the words in bold are (*idioms*). Ss then do the activity individually before checking answers with their partner. Get feedback from the whole class.

> **Answers**
> a 6   c 2   f 1
> b 8   d 5   g 3
>   e 4   h 7

2 ▶ Do this activity with the whole class. Elicit why Ss think the pictures match the idioms. Encourage Ss to think of pictures for the remaining idioms.

> **Answers**
> A bookworm
> B give someone a hand
> C teacher's pet
> D pass with flying colours

3 ▶ Focus Ss on the Lifelong Learning box and read the first sentence. Put Ss in pairs (A and B). Refer Ss A to page 149 and Ss B to page 150 and give them time to read. While Ss are reading, write the following idioms on the board: *haven't got a clue, bookworm, learn by heart, teacher's* *pet, pass with flying colours, a piece of cake*. Write more idioms on the board as distractors if you wish. Ss tell their partner about the idioms without mentioning the idiom directly. Partners should guess which idiom from the board is being described. Finally, get feedback from the whole class, making sure Ss have identified the correct idioms. Ask Ss if they know the origin of any idioms in their own language.

OPTIONAL LEAD-IN

Write the following phrasal verbs on the board: *pick up, pass out, put off*. Ask Ss what types of verbs these are (phrasal verbs). Ask Ss what makes up a phrasal verb (a verb and a particle or particles). Make sure Ss understand that the preposition changes the meaning of the verb. Encourage Ss to guess what the phrasal verbs mean. If Ss cannot guess, then provide example sentences to help them work out the meaning. Once Ss understand, brainstorm any other phrasal verbs that Ss know and put them on the board. Encourage Ss to make sentences to show what they mean.

4a ▶ Ss do the activity individually. Let Ss check their answers in pairs before getting feedback from the whole class.

Answers			
1	b	4	c
2	e	5	a
3	d		

b ▶ Ss do the activity individually. Then check the answers with the whole class.

Answers			
1	down to	4	up
2	about	5	through
3	up		

5a ▶ Make sure Ss understand that they only need to complete five of the sentences. Ss do the activity individually.

b ▶ Put Ss in pairs to compare their sentences. Ss must ask at least one follow-up question for each of their partner's sentences. Monitor and take note of important errors. Write the errors on the board and encourage Ss to self-correct. Praise Ss for correct use of the idioms about learning.

7 Communication

In this lesson, Ss practise memorisation and learn how to memorise things. Through this context, they learn language for discussing opinions and making decisions.

OPTIONAL WARMER

Ask Ss to think about the earliest memory they have. Ss share their earliest memories with a partner. Then get feedback from various Ss. Elicit why they think they remember this memory. Explain that there is usually a reason why we remember something.

1a ▶ Make sure Ss have their books closed before you begin this activity. Tell Ss that they are going to look at a picture and will have one minute to remember everything. Tell Ss to open their books and time one minute before getting them to close their books again.

b ▶ With their books closed, Ss quickly write down as many objects as they can remember.

c ▶ With the whole class, check what Ss remembered and find out who remembered the most and the fewest objects. Then elicit which method Ss used for remembering the objects.

2 ▶ Give Ss a few minutes to read the article or read it as a whole class. Check for understanding and any new vocabulary. Then put Ss in small groups to discuss the questions. Get feedback from the whole class.

3 ▶ Keep Ss in the same groups. Give the groups a minute to decide which memorisation technique they are going to use.

4a ▶ Tell Ss that will have three minutes to look at another page and memorise all the phrases. Tell them to turn to page 149 and start the clock.

b ▶ At the end of the three minutes, Ss close their books. Give Ss time to write down as many words and phrases as they can, using their chosen memorisation technique. Ss then check their answers in their groups.

c ▶ Get feedback from the whole class. Elicit which group did best/worst and which technique they used. Elicit from Ss which technique they think is the most effective.

Review and practice

1 ▶

Answers
1 Who phoned me last night?
2 When does he get the train?
3 Who taught her to play the piano?/Who did Maria teach to play the piano?
4 Why did he fail the exam?
5 What fell on the floor?
6 Who lives in that house?
7 Which office did she run into?
8 How did they meet?

2 ▶

Answers
1 would get   7 used to live
2 would stay   8 would spend
3 use to have   9 use to go out
4 used to love   10 would stay
5 use to study   11 would read
6 used to think   12 would dream

3 ▶

Answers
1 Sam used to smoke but now he has given up.
2 (correct)
3 Tomas would ~~to~~ go to the market every day with his father.
4 Emil used to love riding horses on the beach.
5 (correct)
6 Tom didn't use to have a girlfriend, but now he has lots!
7 Myra used to ~~being~~ be a dancer when she was younger.
8 She ~~would dance~~ danced for me one time when I came to visit.

4 ▶

Answers
1 be able to
2 are you able to
3 could, was able to
4 managed to, was able to
5 can't
6 couldn't, wasn't able to

5 ▶

Answers				
1 d	2 c	4 d	6 d	
	3 a	5 c	7 a	

Writing bank

See page 159 of the Students' Book

1 ▶ Ss read the article and answer the questions.

Answers
1 because she has always considered Asia her home
2 for low income people to access basic English lessons using a voice call or text
3 Yes, because all the mobile phone operators are offering the service at discount rates and in less than two weeks they've had half a million calls.

2a ▶ Ss read the article again and match the summaries with the paragraphs.

Answers
1 D   5 C
2 G   6 F
3 E   7 A
4 B

2b ▶ Ss decide which three paragraph summaries from exercise 2a are not main points of the article.

Answers
1, 4 and 7

3 ▶ In pairs, Ss read the two summaries and choose the best one. Get feedback from the whole class, with Ss giving justifications for their answers.

Answers
A is the best summary because it includes all the main ideas.

4 ▶ Ss complete the How to... box by choosing the correct words in italics.

Answers
1 the main idea
2 Cut out
3 shorter text

5 ▶ Ss read the article on page 93 and then use the How to... box to help them write a summary. Ss then share their summaries with a partner who suggests corrections. Finally, build a model summary on the board.

Overview

CEFR Portfolio ideas
a) Choose a website that you use a lot. Write a review of the website, describing what you like and what you don't like and suggest changes that would improve the site.
b) Write an article or a record a video piece on the topic 'How people's decisions changed the world'. Think about three to five different moments in history when a person's decision changed the world, e.g. Christopher Columbus' decision to look for an easier route to India, and imagine what would have happened if they had done something else.
c) You have just been promoted to a new job in the US. Write a personal email to a friend, telling him or her how you feel about the move and all the changes you expect to happen in your life.

Lead-in

OPTIONAL WARMER

Ask Ss to think about their life ten years ago. Ask Ss to write down all the changes that have happened to them personally and in the world in the last ten years. Get Ss to mingle and tell each other about one change in the last decade. When they have finished discussing all their changes, they should sit down. The last person standing is the winner with the most changes. Finally, get feedback from the whole class.

1a ▶ Put Ss in pairs to look at the photos and discuss the question. Get feedback from the whole class.

b ▶ Ss discuss the questions in pairs. Get feedback from the whole class.

2 ▶ Elicit what *collocation* means. Write *climate change* on the board. Elicit/explain that *climate* and *change* come together to make a collocation. Then focus Ss on the words and phrases in the box. Ss do the activity individually and then check their ideas in pairs. Check the answers with the whole class. Identify which answer is an idiom (change your tune) and its meaning (to start to express a different attitude). Then elicit any other words or phrases Ss think might collocate with *change*.

Answers	the subject	your mind
an arrangement	your address	your name
direction	your clothes	your password
places	your hairstyle	your tune

3a ▶ ⏺ 2.21 Read through the instructions with the Ss and then play the recording. Get feedback from the whole class.

Answers
Carol changed her mind (and may change her name in the future).
Stig changed his address and his job.

b ▶ Play the recording again. Ss answer the questions and then check with a partner. Finally, get feedback from the whole class.

Answers
1 because it was much easier to pronounce and to spell than her maiden name
2 because they were living in China and it was complicated to change her passport and other details
3 It was dark, cold and near a main road (noisy).
4 a year

4 ▶ Ss do the activity in pairs. Get feedback from the whole class by asking Ss to report their partner's answers.

8.1 Changing the rules

New York, nicknamed *the Big Apple*, has always had a reputation for being a bustling, noisy, dangerous city where anything goes. Recently, however, that reputation has changed, largely because of a city-wide ban on smoking in public places. The smoking ban and other new laws have infuriated some citizens and been applauded by others.

Central Park is a public park in the centre of Manhattan, New York. It is the most visited urban park in the US, with around twenty-five million visitors annually. It used to have a reputation as a dangerous area for crime, especially at night as it was difficult to police, but in recent years crime levels have fallen dramatically.

Vanity Fair is a magazine of popular culture, fashion and politics. Published since 1983, it has four different European editions, as well as the US edition. It is famous for its controversial photography and has been behind some of the breaking stories of the last two decades, for example, revealing the identity of 'deep throat', the man behind the Watergate scandal.

In this lesson, Ss read about New York and how changes in the laws have made it a safer place. Through the text, Ss learn about the Second Conditional and use it to talk about new laws in the town they are studying in. Finally, Ss study vocabulary related to cities, discuss problems in their own city and suggest changes.

Reading

OPTIONAL LEAD-IN

Ask Ss to draw two columns in their notebooks. Ss write *New York* at the top of the first column and the name of their town or city at the top of the second column. Ss write words in each column to compare the two places, e.g. *subway* in the first column and *bus* in the second column. Get feedback from the whole class and discuss how Ss think New York is different from their own towns or cities.

1a ▶ Ss do the activity in pairs without looking at the text. Get feedback from various Ss but don't confirm any answers at this point.

b ▶ Ss read the first paragraph of the text to check their answers. Check the answers with the whole class and correct the false information. Ask Ss: *Are you surprised by this information? Why do you think this is the case?*

Answers
1 T
2 F (36 percent)
3 F (the Big Apple)
4 F (Washington DC)
5 F (it has fewer crimes per head than 193 other US cities)

2a ▶ Ss discuss the issues in pairs and discuss why some issues are illegal. Get feedback from the whole class.

b ▶ Ss do the activity individually and then check their answers in pairs. Check the answers with the whole class.

Answers
They all are illegal except keeping a gun at work.

Vocabulary and speaking

3a ▶ Discuss the first question with whole class. Then put Ss in pairs to discuss questions 2 and 3. Get feedback from the whole class. Ask Ss: *Are there any laws in your country that are unusual?*

b ▶ Ss read the article and underline the words in the box. Tell Ss that they should now try and work out meaning from the context, by looking at the words before and after the underlined words. Get feedback from the whole class.

OPTIONAL VARIATION

Once Ss have tried to work out the meaning from the context, get feedback from the whole class but do not confirm any answers. Then make sure each pair has a dictionary and ask Ss to compare their own ideas with the definitions in the dictionary. Get feedback from the whole class.

c ▶ Put Ss in pairs to discuss the questions. Encourage Ss to use words and phrases from exercise 3b when possible. Monitor and ask some pairs to report their discussions to the rest of the class. Get feedback from the whole class, discussing reasons for their answers.

Grammar | Second Conditional

OPTIONAL GRAMMAR LEAD-IN

Write the following sentence prompt on the board. *If I spoke English perfectly ... .* Ss complete the sentence and compare in pairs. Get feedback from various Ss and write correct sentences on the board. Ask Ss what type of sentence this is. Elicit that it is a Second Conditional sentence. In pairs, Ss discuss why this type of conditional is used in English (to talk about unreal/imaginary/ hypothetical situations and their consequences).

4 ▶ Give Ss time to read through the Active grammar box. Ss then choose the correct options in pairs. Check the answers with the whole class. Refer Ss to Reference page 117. Ss read through the notes. Ask Ss: *Which conditional structure do we use with an unreal, imaginary or hypothetical situation?* (Second Conditional) *What is the form of the Second Conditional?* (if + Past Simple + would ('d)/wouldn't t) *Does the 'if clause' always have to come first?* (No, it can come first or second) *If the 'if clause' is the second phrase, do we need a comma?* (No) *Is it possible to say 'If I were'?* (Yes) *Which conditional structure do we use to talk about possible or real situations?* (First Conditional)

Active grammar

an imaginary situation
the Past Simple.
imaginary (hypothetical)
not sure

First and Second Conditional:
In a real situation we use the First Conditional.
In an imaginary situation we use the Second Conditional.
The First Conditional uses the Present Simple + *will*.
The Second Conditional uses the Past Simple + *would*.

5 ▶ Ss do the activity in pairs. Check the answers with the whole class.

Answers
1 were, would you arrest
2 wouldn't like, lived
3 would/could you go, wanted
4 wouldn't be, had to pay
5 didn't have, would find
6 existed, would they be
7 would be, had

6 ▶ Read through the instructions and situations with the Ss and check understanding of vocabulary. Ask Ss to write *R/P* next to situations that are real or possible in their lives. In pairs, Ss then discuss what they *will/would* do in each situation. Get feedback from the whole class.

OPTIONAL VARIATION

Put Ss in pairs (A and B). First, Ss think about what they *will/would* do themselves in each of the situations. Then Ss think about what their partner *will/would* do in each of the situations. Ss A tell Ss B what they think B *will/would* do in each situation. Ss B tell Ss A if their guesses are correct. Ss B then tell Ss A what they think Ss A *will/would* do in each situation and Ss A confirm if they are correct.

Speaking and listening

7a ▶ Tell Ss to imagine they are representing the mayor of their town or city. Give Ss a few minutes to think of five new laws that they would introduce individually. Then put Ss in groups of three or four to discuss their ideas. Encourage Ss to use the Second Conditional and ask them to make a note of the laws they agree on.

b ▶ Ask each group to tell the rest of the class about their laws/proposals. Encourage the Ss listening to ask follow-up questions. At the end, Ss vote for the five best laws/proposals.

Vocabulary | cities

8 ▶ Ss will need dictionaries for this activity. Read through the words and phrases in the box with the Ss. Check Ss understand the headings in the table and tell them that some words can go under more than one heading. Ss then do the activity individually before comparing their answers in pairs. Get feedback from the whole class but don't confirm any answers. Then let Ss check their answers with a dictionary before confirming that Ss have understood the meaning of each word or phrase.

Answers
Noise: building work, construction, drilling, horns honking
Congestion: building work, construction, roads being blocked, rush hour, traffic jams
Pollution: exhaust fumes
Weather: heatwave, terribly cold

OPTIONAL EXTENSION

Do a chain activity. Start a story using one word from the box. Each student then continues the story until they have used another one of the words or phrases and then another student continues. This can be done as a group activity.

9a ▶ ● 2.22 Read through the instructions with the Ss and then play the recording. Let Ss compare their answers in pairs before checking the answers with the whole class.

b ▶ Play the recording again for Ss to make notes. Get feedback from the whole class.

Answers
Madrid:
noisy (traffic, horns honking)
construction (building work)
congestion (due to building work, construction and roads being blocked)
pollution (in summer)
Edinburgh:
congestion (traffic jams while a tram system is being built)
weather (terribly cold)
architecture: (beautiful buildings in city centre but ugly tower blocks on the outskirts)

c ▶ Elicit the answers to this question. Then play the recording again for Ss to check their ideas.

Answers
Madrid: vibrant, lots of things going on, famous nightlife
Edinburgh: beautiful buildings, historical, interesting, pleasant place to live

10a ▶ Read through the instructions with the Ss and check understanding. Ask Ss to make notes on their home town or city. Then tell Ss that they are going to share their information in pairs. Give Ss time to read through the How to... box and think about how they can use the phrases in their own descriptions.

b ▶ In pairs, Ss take turns to present their information, using language from the How to... box. Monitor and note down any errors. Now put Ss in different pairs to repeat the activity. Get feedback by asking Ss to report what their second partner told them. Spend time correcting the errors you noted.

OPTIONAL VARIATION

If Ss all come from the same city or there are groups of people from the same city, this task can be done as a group activity.

OPTIONAL EXTENSION

In groups, Ss prepare a presentation on how they would deal with the problems in their city or town if they were the mayor. Ss could collect photos and realia and give the presentation in the next lesson.

8.2 Change the world

In this lesson, Ss read about an actor's experience of earning money for charity by running consecutive marathons. This introduces vocabulary related to global issues which they practise. They also practise pronouncing the different sounds of the letter 'o'. They then listen to two people discussing how the world has changed since they were children. Through this context, they learn about adverbs, which they practise and use to talk about conditions around the world.

Eddie Izzard (1962–) is a British comedian and actor. Regarded as one of the best stand-up comedians (on stage) in Britain, he is also a successful actor, having starred in *Ocean's Twelve* and *Thirteen* and *Valkyrie*. He is a pro-European campaigner and does a lot of work for charity.

Reading

OPTIONAL LEAD-IN

Write the word *charity* on the board. Ss write down all the things that they associate with this word. Get feedback from the whole class. Ask Ss: *What charities do you know about? Who do they support? What do you think is a worthy cause for a charity? What are the best ideas for raising money?*

1a ▶ Tell Ss to cover the article on page 109. Put Ss in pairs to do the activity and write three questions. Get feedback from the whole class, writing the best questions on the board.

b ▶ Ss read the article and answer their questions. Tell Ss not to worry about any words they don't understand at this stage. Elicit the answers to the questions you have on the board and get feedback from various Ss on other questions they answered.

2 ▶ Ask Ss to cover the article again. In pairs, they try to answer the questions from memory. Get feedback from the whole class but don't confirm any answers. Ss then uncover the text and check their answers. Check the answers with the whole class and elicit any words or expressions that Ss don't understand.

Answers
1 He's a forty-seven-year-old comedian.
2 *Sports Relief*, an international charity
3 six weeks
4 Blisters caused some toenails to fall off and other toes to swell up. He had sleepless nights. He looked lean and muscular and his legs looked good.
5 He learned to associate himself with sport again.

---

3 ▶ Put Ss in pairs to discuss the questions. Get feedback from the whole class and make sure Ss give reasons for their answers.

Vocabulary | global issues

OPTIONAL LEAD-IN

In pairs, Ss make a list of the five most important problems facing the world today. Monitor and help with vocabulary if necessary. Ss compare their lists with another pair. Get feedback from the whole class and try to agree on the five most important global problems.

4 ▶ Put Ss in pairs. Ask Ss to discuss the questions and make a list of other ways to initiate change. Get feedback from the whole class.

5 ▶ Ss do the activity individually and then compare their answers in pairs. Remind Ss that some words and phrases can go under more than one heading. Get feedback from the whole class. Accept different answers if Ss can provide reasons. Make sure Ss understand the meaning of all the words and phrases.

Suggested Answers
Environment: climate change, global warming, intensive farming, organic farming, pollution, recycling, solar power
Global economic issues: debt(s), fair trade, poverty, standard of living, wealth
Global political issues: conflict, peace, war
Health: cure, disease, mortality rate

6a ▶ Tell Ss that they may need to change the form of some words or phrases. Ss do the activity individually. Let Ss compare their answers in pairs before checking the answers with the whole class.

Answers
1 pollution, climate change/global warming
2 organic farming, intensive farming
3 fair trade
4 cure, diseases
5 debts

b ▶ Put Ss in pairs to discuss the questions from exercise 6a. Let Ss compare their ideas with another pair before getting feedback from the whole class.

OPTIONAL EXTENSION

In pairs, Ss use the remaining words and phrases from exercise 5 to make their own gapped sentences. Ss swap sentences with another pair and try to complete the gaps.

Pronunciation | sounds and spelling: 'o'

7a ▶ 🔊 2.23 Play the recording. Ss decide whether the letter 'o' in each word is pronounced /ɒ/, /ɔː/ or /əʊ/ and add the words to the table. Let Ss compare answers in pairs before getting feedback from the whole class. Confirm that Ss have matched the correct phonetic symbol with the correct sound.

b ▶ 🔊 2.24 Ss add the words in the box to their table from exercise 7a, according to the pronunciation of 'o'. Play the recording for Ss to check their answers and then check the answers with the whole class. Play the recording again and drill the words chorally and individually.

Answers

/ɒ/	/ɔː/	/əʊ/
conflict	mortality	global
poverty	organic	solar
hot	floor	coast
pocket	short	cold
	your	open
		own
		phone
		road
		throw

OPTIONAL EXTENSION

Encourage Ss to add more words to the table.

c ▶ Read through the instructions with the Ss. Now put Ss in pairs to write at least one word in each column. Elicit ideas from the whole class, making sure Ss pronounce the words correctly. Refer Ss to the Sound-spelling correspondences table in the Pronunciation bank on page 163.

Possible Answers
ou: your
au: taught
al: small
aw: awful
ar: warm
oo: door

Listening and speaking

8 ▶ 🔊 2.25 Read through the instructions with the Ss. Give Ss a minute to look back at the issues from exercise 5 and then play the recording. Let Ss compare their answers in pairs before getting feedback from the whole class.

Answers
Health (cures for diseases)
Environment (pollution and climate change)

9 ▶ Give Ss time to read through the How to... box. Then play the recording again for Ss to tick the phrases they hear. Check the answers with the whole class.

Answers
Express your attitude:
Luckily, ...
Unfortunately, ...
(Not) surprisingly, ...

Respond to an opinion:
You have a point there.
Well, that's your opinion.
I don't know about that.
Oh, come on!

OPTIONAL EXTENSION

Focus Ss on the 'Express your attitude' section of the How to... box. Elicit which word class these words belong to (adverbs). Elicit other adverbs that could be used to express attitude, e.g. *happily, sadly*. Briefly describe a situation and ask Ss to respond using one of the adverbs from the How to... box, e.g. *There's been an accident outside. Luckily, nobody has been hurt.*

Speaking

10a ▶ Divide the class into two groups or an even number of groups with a maximum of five Ss per group. Number the groups 1 and 2. Read through the instructions with the Ss and check they understand *optimist* and *pessimist*. Give Ss time to discuss their ideas and think of ways to justify their opinions.

b ▶ Each Group 1 now works with a Group 2. In the new groups, pair each Group 1 student with a Group 2 student. Ss take turns to read one sentence each. Their partner in the other group should respond in a positive, neutral or negative way, using the phrases from the How to... box. Monitor and note down errors. At the end, write the important errors on the board and encourage Ss to self-correct.

Grammar | adverbs

OPTIONAL GRAMMAR LEAD-IN

Write the following sentence on the board. *The situation is quickly getting worse and worse* Ask Ss what type of word *quickly* is. Elicit that it is an adverb. Focus Ss' attention on the *-ly* ending and explain that this is a typical ending for adverbs. Ask Ss if there are any typical endings for adverbs in their own languages. Tell Ss to look at audioscript 2.25 on page 173 and underline all the adverbs. Get feedback from the class and write the adverbs on the board. (really, probably, luckily, unfortunately, quickly, surprisingly)

11a ▶ Give Ss time to read through the Active grammar box and match the example sentences with the uses A–D. Let Ss compare their answers in pairs before checking the answers with the whole class.

Active grammar

A	4	B	3	C	1	D	2

b ▶ In pairs, Ss choose the correct options to complete the rules in the Active grammar box. Elicit the answers from various Ss. Then refer Ss to Reference page 117. Give Ss time to read through the notes and ask any questions.

Active grammar

A after
B before
D beginning

12 ▶ Focus on the adverbs in the box and check that Ss understand them all. Put Ss in pairs and ask them to mark the syllable stress on each adverb. Check the stress with the class and write the adverbs (with stress) on the board. Ss practise saying the adverbs in pairs. In pairs, Ss then match the adverbs with their uses 1–6. Check the answers with the whole class.

Answers
1 fortunately
2 surprisingly
3 hopefully
4 personally
5 basically
6 obviously

Speaking

13a ▶ Put Ss in groups of three or four to discuss the questions. Get feedback from the whole class and write the different groups' predictions on the board.

b ▶ Refer Ss to the answers on page 150. Ss check their answers and then complete the sentences with their own opinions. Go round and check the sentences Ss write.

c ▶ In their groups, Ss discuss whether they found any of the facts surprising, interesting or shocking. Encourage Ss to use adverbs while doing so. Monitor and check for correct use of adverbs and then get feedback from the whole class.

OPTIONAL EXTENSION

In groups or pairs, Ss look at one of the issues from exercise 13a and decide what changes they could introduce to make things better, e.g. *How can we help the continent that has the most people?* Ss prepare mini-presentations. Tell Ss that they should use the grammar (Second Conditional and adverbs) and language from lessons 8.1 and 8.2.

8.3 Making the right decisions

In this lesson, Ss read a problem page and the advice given by readers. They also listen to people talking about important decisions they have made in their lives. Through these contexts, Ss learn and practise the Third Conditional and sentence stress. Ss discuss their own ability to make decisions, the decisions they have taken and their effect. To finish the lesson, they write about an important turning point in their lives.

Reading and vocabulary

> **OPTIONAL LEAD-IN**
>
> Tell Ss about a moment in your life when you had to make a decision about something important. In pairs, Ss guess what the decision was and what happened to you as a result. Get feedback from the class and check if any Ss correctly guessed your decision and its consequences. Ask Ss if they think it was the right decision to make.

1 ▶ Ss read the two problems but not the advice. In pairs, Ss discuss what they think Linda, Jack and Suzie should do. Ss then read the advice and see if they agree with any of the suggestions. Get feedback from various pairs.

2 ▶ Ss do the activity individually and then check their answers in pairs. Get feedback from the whole class.

> **OPTIONAL VARIATION**
>
> Put Ss in pairs (A and B). Ss A match the words and definitions from Problem 1 while Ss B match the words and definitions from Problem 2. Ss A then compare their answers with Ss B. Finally, check the answers with the whole class.

> **Answers**
> Problem 1
> 1   take the plunge
> 2   unpaid leave
> 3   volunteer
> 4   promoted
> 5   no real alternative
> 6   regret
>
> Problem 2
> 1   a long distance relationship
> 2   go for it
> 3   a once-in-a-lifetime opportunity
> 4   start a family
> 5   for the best
> 6   landed her dream job

> **OPTIONAL EXTENSION**
>
> Ss work in pairs and make sentences to show that they have understood the meaning of the words and phrases in the texts.

Speaking

3a ▶ Put Ss in pairs to discuss the questions. Then get feedback from the whole class.

b ▶ Focus Ss on the decisions in the list and check that Ss understand the vocabulary. Encourage Ss to answer each other's questions if there are words they don't understand, or to look them up in their dictionaries. Ss then do the activity individually. Monitor and help Ss where necessary.

c ▶ Put Ss in pairs (A and B). Ss take turns to talk about their decisions and ask follow-up questions. Get feedback from various pairs.

> **OPTIONAL EXTENSION**
>
> Put Ss in different pairs. Ss tell each other about their previous partner's decisions and whether it was an easy or difficult decision. Get feedback by asking various Ss to report what they learned about the previous partner's decisions. With the whole class, decide which of the Ss had to make the most difficult decision.

Listening

4a ▶ ● 2.26 Read through the instructions with the Ss and then play the recording. Check the answers with the whole class.

> **Answers**
> Roger: to give up work, to change career, to start your own business
> Tunde: to go to university, to get married
> Sarah: to sell a house, to leave a job, to start your own business

b ▶ Give Ss time to read through the questions and encourage Ss to try and remember the answers. Get feedback from the whole class but don't confirm any answers. Play the recording again for Ss check their predictions.

c ▶ Refer Ss to audioscript 2.26 on page 173 to check their answers.

> **Answers**
> 1   Tunde   5   Sarah
> 2   Tunde and Sarah 6   Roger and Sarah
> 3   Sarah   7   Sarah
> 4   Tunde

d ▶ Put Ss in pairs to discuss the question. Then get feedback from the whole class.

Grammar | Third Conditional

> **OPTIONAL GRAMMAR LEAD-IN**
>
> Refer Ss back to the text on page 104. Ask Ss: *Why was the old lady given a $50 fine?* (because she rested her foot on the subway chair) On the board, write the following jumbled sentence prompt: *hadn't/If/rested/she/chair/on/subway/foot/her/,/she/the*
> In pairs, Ss unjumble and complete the sentence. Get feedback and complete the sentence in the following way: *If she hadn't rested her foot on the subway chair, she wouldn't have been fined/had to pay a fine.* Ask Ss what type of conditional sentence this is. Elicit/explain that it is a Third Conditional sentence and focus Ss on the form of the conditional: *If + subject + past perfect + would(n't) have + past participle.* Tell Ss that the order of the sentence can be inverted and write the following sentence on the board: *The old woman wouldn't have had to pay a fine if she hadn't rested her foot on the subway chair.*

5a ▶ Ss do the activity in pairs. Get feedback from the whole class.

> **Answers**
>
> | 1 No | 2 Yes | 3 Yes | 4 Yes |
> |------|-------|-------|-------|

b ▶ Ss read through the Active grammar box and choose the correct option to complete each rule. Check the answers with the whole class. Refer Ss to Reference page 117 and give them time to read through the notes. Focus Ss on the form of the Third Conditional: *if + past perfect + would have +* past participle. Ask Ss: *If we want to indicate possibility rather than certainty what do we use instead of would have?* (might have/could have) *Is it possible for the hypothetical past situation to have a present result?* (Yes) *How does this change the form of the conditional? if +* past perfect *+ would +* verb.

> **Active grammar**
>
> | imaginary | Second Conditional |
> |-----------|--------------------|
> | past | Third Conditional |

6 ▶ Tell Ss to cover the sentence endings a–h. Ss read the sentence beginnings 1–8 and think of a natural way of completing the sentences. Let Ss compare their ideas in pairs before eliciting full sentences from the class. Write correct sentences on the board. Ss uncover the sentence endings and do the activity individually. Ss compare their answers in pairs. Finally, check the answers with the whole class.

> **Answers**
>
> | 1 c | 3 e | 5 a | 7 d |
> |-----|-----|-----|-----|
> | 2 g | 4 b | 6 h | 8 f |

7 ▶ Give Ss time to read the text. Check the meaning of any words that Ss don't know. Ss then do the activity individually. Le Ss compare their answers in pairs before getting feedback from the whole class.

> **Answers**
>
> 1 If her flight hadn't been delayed, <u>she wouldn't have decided to go for a cup of coffee.</u>
> 2 <u>If there hadn't been a bag on the floor,</u> she wouldn't have tripped over.
> 3 <u>If she hadn't</u> tripped over, she wouldn't have spilt her coffee.
> 4 If <u>she hadn't spilt her coffee (on him), she wouldn't have started</u> talking to Paulo.
> 5 <u>If they hadn't started</u> talking, they <u>wouldn't have got married (a year later).</u>

> **OPTIONAL EXTENSION**
>
> Draw a timeline for the following activities on the board. Alarm clock didn't go off → had to rush → forgot my wallet → went back home → missed my bus → got to work late → missed the meeting → lost my job. Ask Ss to prepare in pairs (or elicit from the class) Third Conditional sentences for each step of the process, e.g. *If the alarm clock had gone off, I wouldn't have had to rush.* You can then ask Ss to make a short flow chart themselves for other Ss to complete.

Pronunciation | sentence stress in the Third Conditional

8a ▶ 🔵 2.27 Focus Ss' attention on the sentence and play the recording. Ss listen and mark the words which are contracted. Elicit the answers from the class.

> **Answers**
>
> *Had* and *have* are contracted.

b ▶ Read through the instructions with the Ss and play the recording again.

> **Answers**
>
> Yes, there is a regular beat. There are four beats in the sentence.

9a ▶ Write the sentence from exercise 8 on the board and ask a student to come up and underline the stressed words. *If I'd <u>left</u> home <u>earlier</u>, I <u>wouldn't've missed the train</u>.* Tell Ss that the stress falls with a regular beat. Then practise saying the sentence with individual Ss and then with the whole class. Ss underline the stressed words in sentences 1–3 and then compare their answers in pairs.

b ▶ 🔵 2.28 Play the recording for Ss to check the words they have underlined. Ss practise pronouncing the sentences in pairs. Encourage Ss to say them with the same rhythm as the recording. Ask a number of Ss to read the sentences aloud for the rest of the class. If they feel confident, tell them they can substitute their own phrases, e.g. If I'd known *you needed the book today*, I would've *brought it in.*

Answers
1 If I'd <u>known</u> the test was <u>today</u>, I'd've <u>done</u> some <u>revision</u>.
2 If I'd <u>gone</u> to bed <u>earlier</u>, I <u>wouldn</u>'t've been so <u>tired</u>.
3 If you'd <u>asked</u> me out to <u>dinner</u>, <u>I</u>'d've said '<u>yes</u>'.

Speaking

10a ▶ Read through the instructions with the Ss. Individually, Ss read the questions and write short answers in the *Now* circle.

b ▶ In pairs, Ss change the questions to questions about the past. Check the questions with the whole class. Individually, Ss write short answers in the *Ten years ago* circle.

Answers
1 Where were you living?
2 What did you do?
3 Who was your closest friend?
4 How did you spend your free time?
5 Did you spend much time with your family?
6 Were you studying anything?
7 Did you play any sports?
8 What music did you enjoy?
9 What were your dreams/ambitions?

11 ▶ Put Ss in pairs to show each other their circles to their partners and tell each other how much their lives have changed in the past ten years. Encourage Ss to ask as many follow-up questions as possible.

12 ▶ Ss do the activity in pairs. Encourage Ss to use the Third Conditional where relevant and to ask follow-up questions. Monitor, and write important errors on the board. Get feedback and then go through the errors, asking Ss to self-correct where possible. Praise Ss for correct use of the Third Conditional.

Writing

13 ▶ Read through the instructions with the Ss. Give them time to think of an important turning point in their lives and then write a paragraph to describe this event. Encourage Ss to include the Third Conditional where possible. Monitor and help Ss with vocabulary where necessary. Put Ss in groups of three or four. Ss read out their paragraphs to the group. Encourage the Ss listening to ask follow-up questions. Get feedback from the whole class and discuss the turning points that Ss have had in their lives.

8 Vocabulary | word building

In this lesson, Ss look at ways of building their vocabulary by using prefixes and suffixes. Ss then speak for a minute on a topic.

OPTIONAL WARMER
Write the following adjectives on the board: *honest, faithful, legal, important*. Tell Ss to write the opposites of these words by adding a prefix. If necessary, refer Ss back to page 45 to remind them of what a prefix is. Get feedback and write the opposites on the board (dishonest, unfaithful, illegal, unimportant). Discuss the use of prefixes and how we use these particular prefixes to make words negative.

1 ▶ Ss read through the examples in pairs and add their own examples to the table. Ss compare their answers with another pair. Write the table on the board while Ss are working. Get feedback from the whole class and add Ss' words to the table on the board.

2 ▶ Ss do the activity individually and then compare their answers in pairs. Check the answers with the class and add them to the table on the board.

Answers
1	over	4	dis	7	dis
2	under	5	in	8	im
3	under	6	in	9	in

3 ▶ Ss read through the information in the table about suffixes. In pairs, Ss add their own examples to the table and then compare their answers with another pair. Write the table on the board while Ss are working. Get feedback from the whole class and add Ss' words to the table on the board.

4 ▶ Ss do the activity individually and then compare their answers in pairs. Check the answers with the class and add them to the table on the board.

Answers
1	education	6	importance
2	employment	7	independence
3	accommodation	8	government
4	treatment	9	direction
5	punishment	10	difference

5a ▶ Ss choose a topic that they feel they can talk about and make notes. Go round and help Ss as necessary. Ss should use words they have previously formed with prefixes and suffixes where possible.

b ▶ Put Ss in groups of three or four. Each student speaks for about one minute on their topic, referring to their notes as necessary. Encourage the Ss listening to ask follow-up questions.

c ▶ Reorganise Ss into new groups of three or four. Ss shouldn't be working with any Ss from their original group. Ss either talk about their original topic again or choose a new topic to talk about. Get feedback by asking Ss what they have learned about their classmates. Praise Ss for correct use of prefixes and suffixes.

8 Communication

In this lesson, Ss find out how they deal with change. Ss then listen to five speakers talking about change, before discussing the same issues themselves.

1 ▶ Ss do the activity in pairs. Encourage Ss to ask follow-up questions. Then put Ss in different pairs to discuss what they learned about their previous partners. Get feedback from the whole class.

2 ▶ Give Ss time to read through the questions and note down their answers. Don't get feedback at this stage, but tell Ss they will use their notes at the end of the lesson.

3a ▶ ⬤ 2.29 Tell Ss they are going to hear five people talking about change. Play the recording and ask Ss to write the question numbers (1–5) next to the photos A–E. Let Ss check their answers in pairs before checking the answers with the whole class.

Answers
A 1
B 3
C 2
D 5
E 4 (She's too young so can't match answer 5.)

b ▶ Ss listen again and take more detailed notes. Put Ss in pairs to discuss what they think the speakers said about change. Let Ss compare their answers with another pair before getting feedback from the whole class. Write the key points that each speaker said in one half of the board.

c ▶ Focus Ss' attention on the example comments and check understanding. Elicit more ideas for how to respond to what the speakers said and write correct phrases on the other half of the board. In pairs, one student reads out an answer from exercise 3b that you have written on the board. Their partner responds with one of the four comments, or a comment from the board. Ss then swap roles and repeat the activity. Get feedback from the whole class.

4a ▶ Ss read and complete the questionnaire individually. If there are words they do not understand, they can look in a dictionary or ask another student.

b ▶ Refer Ss to the feedback on page 150. Give Ss a few minutes to check their answers.

c ▶ Put Ss in pairs to compare and discuss their results. Then get feedback from various Ss.

OPTIONAL EXTENSION

Write *debate* on the board and ask Ss to tell you what a debate is. If they can't tell you, explain quickly how a debate normally works. Divide Ss into two groups (A and B). Group A works together to write down examples of why they think change is good for society. Group B writes down five examples of when society would have been better without change. Refer Ss back to the language in the How to... boxes on pages 108 and 110. Monitor and help Ss where necessary.

Ss hold the debate, taking turns to speak about each point they have written. Encourage Ss to use language from the How to... boxes while doing so. Ss continue speaking until they have discussed all the points. Monitor and take note of errors.

The class now votes either for or against the statement: '*Change is a good thing for society.*' Discuss with the class which group had the best arguments and give feedback, correcting any errors.

Review and practice

1 ▶

Answers
1   If she had Dave's number, she would call him.
2   I'd go out if I didn't have an exam tomorrow.
3   If we had more/enough money, we would/could buy a new car.
4   They'd see the show if there was (more) time.
5   If I had a choice, I'd live in the city.
6   We'd go swimming if the sea wasn't polluted.
7   If it wasn't raining (heavily), we'd go for a walk.

2 ▶

Answers
1   arrives, 'll pick
2   won, 'd buy
3   'd leave, had
4   cook, 'll do
5   studied, 'd pass
6   studies, 'll pass
7   lived, 'd give

3 ▶

Answers
1   I usually go to the supermarket on Saturdays.
2   Susana is so busy that I hardly ever see her anymore.
3   Steve normally drives when we go on long journeys.
4   I exercise regularly in the gym.
5   We certainly don't want to damage the relationship.
6   Personally, I can't see how we can do it any other way.
7   He did a very poor interview. Surprisingly, he got the job.

4 ▶

Answers
1   If I hadn't gone to university, I wouldn't have met Sam.
2   If I had known that England was so cold in the summer, I wouldn't have gone there.
3   If I had decided to study medicine, I wouldn't have worked in an office all my life.
4   If I hadn't listened to the radio this morning, I wouldn't have heard the news.

5 ▶

Answers
1   had asked, would have finished
2   had known, would have cooked
3   had left, wouldn't have missed
4   had told, would have woken
5   had seen, would have been
6   I hadn't drunk, would have fallen asleep
7   hadn't lost, would/could have taken

6 ▶

Answers
1   subject
2   banned
3   pollution
4   environment
5   cure
6   password
7   standard
8   fine

Writing bank

See page 160 in the Students' Book

1 ▶ Ss discuss the questions in pairs. Get feedback from the whole class.

2a ▶ Ss read the emails and answer the questions. Get feedback from the whole class, eliciting the correct answers for any false information.

Answers
1   F (He's planning to move back to Dubai soon.)
2   T
3   T
4   T
5   F (He thinks the metro system will help with the traffic and parking problems.

b ▶ Ss read Bradley's email again and make a list of the changes in Dubai over the past ten years. Get feedback from the whole class and elicit whether Ss think the changes are positive or negative and why.

Answers
There has been a lot of building.
As the city has expanded, the population has grown.
This has created problems with parking and traffic.
The new metro system should help to address these problems.

3 ▶ Ss complete the How to... box with words and phrases used in the emails.

Answers
Thanks for your email.
Hope you and your family are all well.

I have some exciting news.
You asked about what has changed in Dubai.

I suppose it's good that Dubai is expanding.
I personally feel that the population is getting …
On the plus side, we have a new metro system.

Hope to hear from you soon.
Give my regards to your family.
I look forward to meeting up soon/hearing from you.

All the best/Best wishes

4a ▶ Ss make notes about the changes that have taken place where they live in preparation for writing an email to an old friend. Ss should make notes on their opinion of these changes.

b ▶ Ss write an email reply to their friend using their notes and phrases from the How to... box.

9 Jobs

Overview

CEFR Can do objectives
9.1 Ask for clarification
9.2 Take notes while listening
9.3 Describe job skills
Communication Answer interview questions
Writing bank Write a formal email/letter of application

CEFR Portfolio ideas
a) With a friend, prepare and roleplay a difficult conversation between an employee and a manager. The employee wants to complain about a colleague who isn't doing their job properly. The manager has to ask for clarification and deal with the situation diplomatically.
b) A small island in the Pacific has asked for video applications for the post of Island protector. The successful applicant will have to live on Paradise Island, look after the animals and promote the island as a tourist resort. The advert asks for someone who has lots of ideas and loves nature. Prepare your application video, showing why you are the best person for the job.
c) Write an advice booklet for people going to interviews, describing the sorts of questions that they can ask employers and the questions that they shouldn't ask.

Lead-in

OPTIONAL WARMER
Write a list of six jobs that you think Ss will be familiar with on the board. Check that Ss know what all the jobs are by asking various Ss what a person in each job does and what their main responsibilities are. Put Ss in pairs to rank the jobs in order of usefulness to society; with 1 being the most useful and 6 being the least useful. Get feedback from the whole class.

1 ▶ Focus Ss on the jobs in the photos. In pairs, Ss discuss whether they have ever done any of the jobs shown or if they would like to do these jobs. Get feedback from the whole class. Ss discuss the questions in small groups. Get feedback from various groups.

2a ▶ ● 2.30 Give Ss time to read the sentences. Don't help with definitions at this stage. Play the recording and ask Ss to number the sentences in the correct order.

b ▶ In pairs, Ss discuss their answers and help each other to find out the meanings of any unknown words. Get feedback from several Ss but don't confirm any answers.

c ▶ Ss will need dictionaries for this activity. Play the recording again for Ss to check their answers to exercise 2a. Elicit the answers and the meanings of the words and phrases. Do not confirm the meanings, but refer Ss to dictionaries to check.

Answers	4	b	7	g
2 e	5	c	8	i
3 h	6	f	9	d

OPTIONAL EXTENSION
In pairs, Ss construct a job-related story that uses at least five of the words or phrases from exercise 2.

3 ▶ Give Ss a minute to think about their current job or a job they would like to have. In pairs, Ss take turns to ask and answer the questions from exercise 2a. Monitor the conversations and then ask some of the Ss to report their discussions to the rest of the class. Finally, write any important errors on the board and ask Ss to identify and correct the errors.

OPTIONAL EXTENSION
Put Ss in pairs (A and B). Student A chooses a word or expression in bold from exercise 2a and defines it for Student B without mentioning the word or expression. Student B guesses which expression is being defined. Student B then defines a word for Student A to guess. Ss continue taking turns to define the words and expressions until they have all been defined.

9.1 Freedom at work

Semco is a company which sells parts for ships. The company is organised differently from the majority of businesses. Unnecessary jobs were cut by the company boss, Ricardo Semler, with the result that even top managers do the photocopying and dial the phones. Uniforms have been relaxed and employees work flexible hours. This new way of operating has proved successful for Semco.

In this lesson, Ss read a text about the way Semco is run. Through this context Ss look at the grammar of *make*, *let* and *allow*. They also study intonation for pausing and how to ask for clarification and deal with difficult questions. Ss then work in groups to discuss how they would set up a company and report back to the rest of the class about how their company would be run.

OPTIONAL WARMER

Ss think of a job they have done, or a job that someone they know does/has done. Ss think of the types of rules that someone doing that job has to comply with. Write the following prompts on the board to help: *timetable*, *dress code*, *breaks*, *salary*, *bonuses*, *holidays*. Ss tell their partner about their chosen job and the rules associated with it. Encourage Ss to use vocabulary from the Lead-in on page 119. In pairs, Ss decide if these rules are good ones or not, and if not, how they could be changed. Get feedback and discuss how necessary rules are in different jobs.

Speaking and listening

1a ▶ Read through the instructions with the Ss. Ss do the activity individually.

b ▶ Ss compare their ideas in pairs. Get feedback and discuss the quotes with the whole class.

OPTIONAL VARIATION

Put Ss in pairs (A and B). Tell Ss that they must not agree with their partners. Ss A tell Ss B what they think of the first quote. Ss B must disagree and give reasons, trying to convince Ss A of their point of view. Ss then change roles so that Ss B gives their opinion about the second quote and Ss A disagree with this opinion. Ss continue taking turns until they have discussed all the quotes.

c ▶ 🌐 2.31 Read through the instructions with the Ss and give Ss time to read the opinions 1–7. Then play the recording. Check the answers with the whole class. If necessary, play the recording again before confirming the answers.

Answers
1, 3, 5, 6, 7

d ▶ Put Ss in pairs to discuss whether they agree with the opinions from exercise 1c, giving reasons for their answers. Ss can refer to the How to... boxes from lessons 8.1 and 8.2

during this discussion. Monitor and note down any errors. Then ask various Ss to report their discussions to the rest of the class. Finally, go over any errors or problems you heard while monitoring.

Reading

2 ▶ Give Ss time to read through the list of tasks and then check understanding. If there are words or phrases that Ss don't understand, encourage other Ss to explain them before explaining them yourself. Ss then do the activity individually. Let Ss check their ideas in pairs before getting feedback from the whole class. Write Ss' suggestions on the board.

Suggested Answers
decide start/finish times/working hours: managers
do the photocopying: secretaries/PAs
meet guests in reception: receptionists
set salaries: managers
type emails: secretaries, managers, office staff
wear uniforms: factory workers/policemen/hotel staff

3a ▶ Ss read the introduction and answer the questions in pairs. Check the answers with the whole class.

Answers
Ricardo Semler is the boss of his father's business, Semco, which sells parts for ships. He had a medical problem because he was working too hard.

b ▶ Ask Ss to cover the text. In groups, Ss discuss what changes they think Semler made to the way the business was run. Get feedback from the groups and write some of the best ideas on the board. Ss then read the rest of the text to check their ideas. Tell Ss not to worry about any words or expressions they don't understand at this stage. Give Ss time to compare their answers in pairs and then get feedback from the whole class.

4 ▶ Ss read the article and answer questions 1–6. Ask Ss to compare their answers in pairs and then swap partners. Check the answers with the whole class. Ask Ss if there are any words or phrases that they don't understand. Encourage Ss to answer each other's questions or to use a dictionary before explaining them yourself.

Answers
1   Employees set their own salaries, meet guests in reception, do the photocopying, send faxes, type letters, dial the phone and evaluate their bosses.
2   Semco has plants instead of walls and staff can decorate their own workspace; some of the staff wear suits while others wear T-shirts.
3   Rubin Agater is an employee who is important because he knows everything about Semco pumps and how to fix them.
4   Workers can decide their own work hours and use Semco machinery for personal projects.
5   Yes. Profits have increased and the company is growing.
6   'Peer pressure' is the strong feeling that you must do the same things as/be like the people around you. It is important because this is what motivates people to work hard at Semco.

5 ▶ Put Ss in pairs to discuss the questions. Then get feedback from the whole class.

Grammar | *make, let, allow*

OPTIONAL GRAMMAR LEAD-IN

Write three sentences on the board about what you think Ss in a language class should be expected to do. Use *make*, *let* and *allow*, e.g. *The teacher makes us speak in class. The teacher lets us take notes. We are allowed to use a dictionary.* Ss discuss the sentences and decide if they are reasonable things for Ss to do. In pairs, Ss discuss the meanings of *make*, *let* and *allow*.

6 ▶ Ss read the four example sentences and then complete the Active grammar box with *make*, *let* or *allow*. Let Ss compare their answers in pairs before checking the answers with the whole class. Refer Ss to Reference page 131. Give Ss time to read through the notes and ask any questions they may have. Draw Ss' attention to the word order used with these verbs.

Active grammar

A Meaning
  Allow and let mean *give permission to do something*.
  Make means *force to do something*.

B Form
  make someone do something
  Passive: be made to do something

  allow someone to do something
  passive: be allowed to do something

  let someone do something
  Let cannot be used in the passive.

7 ▶ Ss do the activity individually and then compare their answers in pairs. Check the answers with the whole class.

Answers
1 Semler makes the managers do the photocopying.
2 The bosses aren't allowed to shut themselves away.
3 The workers are allowed to decorate the workspace as they want.
4 Semler doesn't make the workers wear suits.
5 Semler lets the workers use the company's machines for their own projects.

8 ▶ Ss do the activity in pairs and then compare their answers with another pair. Get feedback from the whole class.

Possible Answers
1 Our boss is very relaxed. She lets us wear shorts to work.
2 The employees have great holidays. They're allowed to take time off whenever they want.
3 He was wearing dirty clothes in the office. So the boss made him go home and change.
4 It wasn't a very good job. The workers were made to work evenings and weekends.
5 It's my favourite airline. They allow you to bring a lot of luggage free of charge.
6 Don't go near the computer! You're not allowed to use it.

OPTIONAL EXTENSION

In pairs, Ss discuss what they think English teachers are *let*, *made* and *allowed* to do. Ss make a list of the activities in pairs. Ss compare their lists with another pair. Get feedback and tell the class whether their ideas are true (at least for you). Ss decide if these rules are good or bad.

Speaking

9a ▶ Give Ss time to read the statements and decide if they agree with them. Put Ss in small groups to discuss their opinions and give reasons for their answers. Monitor for correct use of *make*, *let* and *allow* and make a note of any errors. Get feedback from the whole class and then go through the errors, encouraging Ss to self-correct.

b ▶ Ask Ss to think about their current job or place of study and write three sentences using the prompts. Put Ss in groups of three or four. Ss read out their sentences and justify their comments. The other Ss then respond by agreeing or disagreeing and saying why. Get feedback from the whole class by eliciting the best ideas from each group.

Listening

10a ▶ 🔘 2.32 Give Ss time to read through questions and then play the recording. Check the answers with the whole class.

Answers
1 a restaurant
2 It will serve food from all over the world (fifty or sixty countries).
3 choose the dishes
4 nine: three chefs and six waiters
5 They will be able to eat in the restaurant for free.
6 World Food

b ▶ Give Ss time to read through the list of functions. Then play the recording again for Ss to take notes. Let Ss compare their notes in pairs before getting feedback from the whole class.

Answers
1 Good afternoon everybody.
2 Today I'd like to tell you about …
3 Our main idea is that … The most important thing for us is …
4 To sum up, …
5 Thank you for listening. Are there any questions?

11 ▶ ● 2.33 Play the recording. Ask Ss to note down questions and answers. Let Ss compare their notes in pairs before getting feedback from the whole class.

Answers
1 Q: Will the food be fresh and if so how can you have such a big menu?
 A: I'm not sure. We'll need to have some pre-prepared food.
2 Q: How will you choose the chefs?
 A: I'm not sure.
3 Q: How did you choose the name of the restaurant?
 A: I'll get back to you on that – it was my wife's idea.

Pronunciation | intonation for pausing

12a ▶ Ss read through the three extracts and mark pauses to divide each extract into three sections. Let Ss compare their answers in pairs.

b ▶ ● 2.34 Play the recording. Ss listen and check their answers. Get feedback from the whole class.

c ▶ Play the recording again. Ss mark where the intonation goes up or down. Ss then discuss the question in pairs. Refer Ss to the Pronunciation bank on page 164. Then check the answers with the whole class.

Answers
1 We'll allow the chefs to choose the dishes (up) // and the menu will be very big, (up) // with something for everybody. (down)
2 We won't make the waiters wear a uniform, (up) // and they will have one special perk: (up) // we'll let them eat free at our restaurant. (down)
3 To sum up, (up) // our restaurant will be small and friendly (up) // but with a great international menu. (down)

13 ▶ ● 2.33 Give Ss time to read through the How to… box and then check understanding. Play the recording from exercise 11 again for Ss to tick the phrases they hear. Get feedback from the whole class.

Answers
What I'd like to know is … ?
Could you tell me a bit more about … ?

That's a very interesting question …
I'm not really sure …
I'll have to get back to you on that.

OPTIONAL EXTENSION
Play the recording again and ask Ss to mark the intonation in the phrases from exercise 13. Then drill the phrases chorally and individually.

Speaking

14a ▶ Read through the instructions with the Ss and put them in groups of three or four. Focus Ss on the company profile. Give Ss time to discuss and complete the profile. Monitor and help where necessary.

b ▶ Ask Ss to decide how the company is going to treat its employees by answering the questions. Ss can add any extra details they want to.

c ▶ Each group presents their ideas to the rest of the class. Tell the Ss listening that they are the future employees of the company. Encourage Ss to make notes about the companies and to ask questions. When all groups have spoken, Ss decide which company would be the best to work for and why. Get feedback from the whole class.

9.2 Skills and experience

In this lesson, Ss listen to descriptions of different management styles. Through this context, Ss look at -ed and -ing adjectives. Ss go on to read a story about a manager and an engineer. Ss use this context to analyse and practise the grammar of reported speech. Ss then listen to people being interviewed for a marketing assistant job. Ss interview their partners to find out if they would make good marketing assistants.

> **OPTIONAL WARMER**
>
> Write the following sentences on the board. *Being a boss is easy. You just tell others what to do.* In pairs, Ss discuss the sentences and decide whether they agree or disagree and why. Get feedback from various pairs.

Listening and speaking

1a ▶ Focus Ss on the picture. Put Ss in pairs to discuss the questions. Get feedback from various pairs.

b ▶ 🌐 2.35 Read through the instructions with the Ss. Elicit typical activities for each of the three management styles and put the most interesting answers on the board. Then play the recording. Check the answers with the whole class and encourage Ss to justify their answers.

> **Suggested Answers**
> autocratic or laissez faire

c ▶ Focus Ss on the notes and then play the recording. Let Ss compare their notes in pairs before checking the answers with the whole class. Finally, compare the answers with the information on the board from exercise 1b.

> **Answers**
> Autocratic
> What it means: The manager makes decisions and tells the staff what to do.
> How the speaker feels about it: finds it a bit annoying.
> When it works well: when it's a question of keeping people safe.
>
> Democratic
> What it means: Everyone can contribute ideas or opinions and then the manager makes the final decision.
> How the speaker feels about it: finds it motivating and likes working this way.
> A disadvantage: It can take a long time for decisions to be made.
>
> Laissez faire
> What it means: The manager leaves the workers to make their own decisions.
> When it works well: when workers have a lot of decisions to make every day.
> A disadvantage: It won't work if workers haven't had enough training.

2 ▶ Ask Ss to think about a boss or teacher they had in the past. Put Ss in pairs to discuss the questions. Get feedback from the whole class.

Vocabulary | -ed and -ing adjectives

3 ▶ Focus Ss' attention on the example sentences. In pairs, Ss read the rules and choose the correct options.

> **Answers**
> 1 feelings
> 2 situations that cause the feelings

4 ▶ Ss do the activity in pairs and then compare their answers with another pair. Check the answers with the whole class.

> **Answers**
> 1 excited   5 tiring
> 2 exhausted   6 depressing
> 3 boring   7 frightened
> 4 frightening   8 relaxing
>   9 confusing

5a ▶ Ss note down answers to the questions individually. Make sure they consider both work/study time and free time. While Ss are completing exercise 5a, write the following question words on the board: *Why? When? How long? Where? What? How often?*.

b ▶ Ss discuss the questions in pairs. Encourage Ss to ask follow-up questions, using the question words on the board as prompts. Monitor and note down any errors. Get feedback from the whole class. Write any important errors on the board and encourage Ss to self-correct.

> **OPTIONAL VARIATION**
>
> Ss write the answers to questions 1–5 in a different order to the questions. In pairs, Ss exchange their answers. Students guess what their partner's answers refer to: *Do you find shopping annoying? No, actually I find it relaxing because … .* Encourage Ss to ask each other follow-up questions.

Reading

6a ▶ In pairs, Ss use the words and phrases from the box to help them predict what the story is about. Let Ss compare their answers with another pair before getting feedback from the whole class. Write the most interesting possibilities on the board.

b ▶ Ss read the story to check their predictions. Get feedback from the whole class, comparing what they read with the predictions on the board.

c ▶ Give Ss time to discuss the question in pairs. Get feedback from various pairs. If there are any words or expressions that Ss don't understand, encourage Ss to help each other to use their dictionaries before explaining the words and phrases yourself.

Grammar | reported speech

7 ▶ Ss do the activity individually. Let Ss compare their answers in pairs before checking the answers with the whole class.

Answers
1   Can you help me?
2   I don't know where I'm going.
3   Everything you've said is technically correct, but I'm still lost.
4   You've made a promise which you can't keep, and you expect me to solve your problem.

8 ▶ Ss read through the Active grammar box and complete it in pairs. Check the answers with the whole class. Refer Ss to Reference page 131. Give Ss a few minutes to read through the notes (tell them not to read the Reported questions section at this point). Ask Ss: *Do time references and pronouns change in reported speech?* (Yes) *If what the person said is still true, do we have to shift the tense back?* (No) Focus Ss on the pronoun changes and on the verb patterns for *say* and *tell*.

Active grammar
1   She told me Carly <u>was in a meeting</u>.
2   He said <u>he was going to meet Marc</u>.
3   He told me <u>Tom had been late every day</u>.
4   She told me he <u>hadn't bought it</u> the day before.
5   He said he <u>would</u> help me.

9 ▶ Ss do the activity in pairs. Check the answers with the whole class.

Answers
1   tell   5   say
2   tell   6   Tell, said
3   said   7   said
4   told   8   told

10 ▶ Ss do the activity in pairs. Remind Ss to start their sentences with the prompts given. Let Ss compare their answers with another pair. Then check the answers with the whole class.

Answers
1   He said (that) he was the new technician.
2   Mum said (that) she would be back the next day/tomorrow.
3   Mara told us (that) she had been stuck in traffic.
4   She said (that) he wouldn't be away for long.
5   He said (that) he would carry our bags for us/my bag for me.
6   He told me (that) they were going on holiday the following week.
7   He told us (that) he had been shopping yesterday/the day before.
8   She told him (that) she was feeling better.

Listening

11a ▶ Ss work in pairs to make a list of questions that might be asked in an interview. Get feedback and elicit corrections for any incorrect questions. Write the best questions on the board.

b ▶ Ss read the job profile. Check understanding of any complex words or phrases, e.g. *negotiate*. Then elicit the difference between *essential* (something you have to have) and *desirable* (something that it would be very nice to have).

c ▶ Ss do the activity individually and then compare their answers with a partner, giving reasons for their answers. Get feedback from the whole class.

Answers
1   Qualifications and training
2   Experience and knowledge
3   Skills
4   Personal qualities

d ▶ 2.36 Read through the instructions with the Ss and then play the recording. Ss make notes. Put Ss in pairs to check their answers and discuss which person they would employ and why. They may use the extra attributes they mentioned in the Optional Extension to help them decide. Check the answers with the whole class. Then ask various Ss to tell the class who they chose and why. Encourage Ss to use the structure from the example.

Answers

Mr Wilkins
Qualifications: degree in Business with Marketing
Experience and knowledge: no experience (but will have an understanding of marketing from degree)
Skills: good communication skills – shown though management of a tennis club
Qualities: probably self-motivated as he ran a tennis club

Miss Southall
Qualifications: degree in English and Art
Knowledge and experience: has worked in marketing for a couple of years
Skills: good organisation skills
Personal qualities: works well alone or with others, creative

OPTIONAL EXTENSION

Refer Ss to the list of questions they wrote on the board in exercise 11a. Elicit which questions were used in the interviews. If Ss can't remember, play the recording again.

12a ▶ Ss do the activity individually. Let Ss compare their answers in pairs or you can play the recording again. Check the answers with the whole class.

Answers
1   Why do you want this job?
2   Do you have any work experience?
3   Are you good at communicating with people?
4   What is your biggest weakness?
5   What skills do you have?
6   Do you work well with others?

b ▶ In pairs, Ss read and complete the Active grammar box. Check the answers with the whole class. Refer Ss to the Reported questions section of Reference page 131. Draw Ss' attention to the pronoun and time/place reference changes as well as the word order for reported questions.

Active grammar

<u>Do</u> you like working in an office?
<u>What</u> is your name?'

c ▶ Ss do the activity individually and then check their answers in pairs. Check the answers with the whole class. Accept answers in the present tense if Ss can argue that what the person said is still true, e.g. *She asked her what skills she has.*

Answers
1   She asked him why he wanted that/this job.
2   She asked him if/whether he had any work experience.
3   She asked him if/whether he was good at communicating with people.
4   She asked him what his biggest weakness was.
5   She asked her what skills she had.
6   She asked her if/whether she worked well with others.

Speaking

13a ▶ Ss write five questions using the prompts.

b ▶ Put Ss in pairs. Ss interview each other using their five questions and take notes. Ss then decide if their partner would be good at the job and why.

c ▶ Ss report their partner's interview answers to the class. Encourage Ss to use reported speech and questions. Take note of any errors which you can correct after Ss have given their feedback.

OPTIONAL EXTENSION

Ss work individually or in pairs to make a short brochure of Dos and Don'ts for interviews. Ss put their brochure on the wall for other Ss to read. Get feedback from the whole class and agree on the five most important Dos and Don'ts for interviews.

9.3 New on the job

TV talent shows like *X Factor* or *Britain's Got Talent* have become extremely popular over the last few years. This type of programme is a competition to find the best talent from a group of people who normally have little or no experience. The winners are often offered contracts and become famous stars. One of these programmes, *Operatunity*, offers amateur opera singers the chance to sing in competition. In 2002, the winners of *Operatunity* ended up singing at the Coliseum in Rome.

The Coliseum is a Roman amphitheatre in the centre of Rome, Italy. Originally used for Roman entertainment, ranging from gladiatorial contests to classical theatre, it is sometimes used today for concerts.

Abbey Road is the location of a famous recording studio in London. It was immortalised by the Beatles who named an album after the studio where they recorded their greatest hits.

Guiseppe Verdi (1813–1901) was a noted Italian composer, mainly of opera. Many of his operas are still very popular today, such as *Rigoletto*, *La Traviata* and *Aida*.

In this lesson, Ss read about the TV talent show *Operatunity*. Through this context, Ss look at the grammar of past obligation and permission. Ss go on to look at vocabulary connected with job requirements and listen to people talking about their jobs. Finally, Ss describe a job they would like to do in the future.

OPTIONAL WARMER

Write *opera* on the board. In pairs, Ss note down anything they know about opera; the names of famous operas, singers, opera houses, musicians, etc. Elicit from Ss their idea of an opera singer, i.e. what they look like, what they do, what skills they need. Get feedback from the whole class and write ideas on the board.

Reading

1 ▶ Put Ss in pairs to discuss the questions. Get feedback from the whole class.

2 ▶ Ss read the article quickly and answer the questions. Tell Ss not to worry about words or expressions they don't understand at this point. Check the answers with the whole class.

Answers
1 opera singer
2 by winning the TV talent show *Operatunity*
3 Denise found waiting for the results difficult. They both found the travelling and childcare arrangements difficult as well as learning to deal with the media.

3a ▶ Ss do the activity individually. Encourage Ss to underline the parts of the text that helped them choose the correct heading. Check the answers with the whole class.

Answers
A 3   B 4   C 2   D 1   E 5

---

b ▶ Ss do the activity in pairs. Let Ss compare their ideas with another pair before getting feedback from the whole class. Write any interesting sentences on the board.

Suggested Answers
A Denise Leigh and Jane Gilchrist won a TV talent show called *Operatunity*, and were changed from working mothers into opera celebrities.
B Before the show, their lives revolved around their families, but winning *Operatunity* has offered them new possibilities.
C They have had a wonderful year, recording and being 'treated like princesses'.
D They had to arrange childcare and found travelling and learning to deal with the media difficult.
E Their advice to people is to try to live your dream.

---

4 ▶ Ss do the activity individually. Let Ss compare their corrections in pairs before checking the answers with the whole class. If there are words or expressions that Ss don't understand, encourage them to answer each other's questions or look in their dictionaries before explaining them yourself.

Answers
Jane and Denise won an <u>opera</u> singing competition on <u>TV</u>, even though Denise is blind. The competition gave them the opportunity to sing <u>Verdi's *Rigoletto*</u> at <u>the Coliseum in Rome</u>, and it changed their lives forever. Although they are both housewives with families – Denise has three children, and Jane has <u>four</u> – they now get the chance to travel and see the world, singing. Their new lives <u>have been</u> very exciting, and they have been treated very well. They found the travelling <u>difficult</u> because <u>they had to arrange childcare</u>. They would recommend the experience to other singers, and say that if your dream is to sing, you should <u>try to do it</u>.

---

5 ▶ Ss discuss the questions in pairs. Get feedback from the whole class.

6 ▶ Focus Ss on the Lifelong learning box. Read through the first sentence with the whole class. Elicit the meaning of *stick together* in this context (stay on topic). Elicit the meanings of *synonym, antonym* and *lexical set*. Don't give the correct answers at this stage. Ss find the related words in the article and check their answers in pairs. Get feedback from the whole class.

Answers
1 transformed
2 full-time mother, cleaner, shop assistant
3 royalty
4 worst, awful, difficult
5 TV, newspapers
6 hobby

Grammar | past obligation/permission

7 ▶ Ss read and complete the Active grammar box in pairs. Check the answers with the whole class. Ss then practise saying the sentences in pairs. Ask various Ss to repeat the sentences for the class. Refer Ss to Reference page 131. Give Ss time to read through the notes and ask any questions they may have.

Active grammar

A   had to
B   didn't have to
C   were allowed to
D   could
E   weren't allowed to
F   couldn't
G   weren't allowed to

8 ▶ Ss do the activity in pairs. Remind Ss that more than one answer may be possible. Check the answers with the whole class.

Answers
1   had to
2   weren't allowed/couldn't
3   were allowed to/could
4   didn't have to
5   weren't allowed to/couldn't, had to
6   had to
7   allowed to/could
8   didn't have to

9a ▶ Ss do the activity individually. Check the answers with the whole class.

Answers
1   I wasn't ~~be~~ allowed to stay out late.
2   We could ~~to~~ eat chocolate all day long.
3   ~~Did you were~~ <u>Were</u> you allowed to buy new clothes?
4   We ~~didn't~~ <u>weren't</u> allowed to watch television.
5   I couldn't ~~to~~ use the telephone because it was too expensive.
6   We didn't ~~had~~ <u>have</u> to help with the housework.
7   We had to ~~studying~~ <u>study</u> very hard.

b ▶ Put Ss in pairs to discuss the question. Get feedback from the whole class.

Speaking

10 ▶ Put Ss in small groups to discuss the questions. Monitor for correct use of language for past obligation and permission. Get feedback from various groups. Write any important errors on one side of the board and write examples of correct or interesting language on the other side of the board. Discuss them with the class.

Vocabulary | job requirements

11 ▶ Ss will need dictionaries for this activity. In pairs, Ss discuss the meanings of the phrases in the box and match them with the definitions. Elicit answers from various Ss but don't confirm any answers. Ask Ss to check their answers using dictionaries.

Answers
1   delegating
2   prioritising
3   persuading people
4   working in a team
5   solving problems
6   making decisions
7   explaining things clearly
8   controlling budgets

12a ▶ Ss will need dictionaries for this activity. Ss do the activities in pairs. Get feedback from the whole class but don't confirm any answers. Let Ss check the answers in their dictionaries. Ensure that Ss know which answers are adjectives and which are nouns.

Answers
1   flexible
2   stamina
3   methodical
4   good communication skills
5   creative
6   fit
7   formal qualifications
8   positive and encouraging

b ▶ Ss do the activity individually and then compare their answers in pairs. Check the answers with the whole class.

Answers		
1	stamina	5 fit
2	flexible	6 Good communication
3	formal qualifications	skills
4	positive and	7 methodical
	encouraging	8 creative

c ▶ Give Ss time to match a student in the class with each quality. Focus Ss on the example dialogue. Ss then walk around the class checking if they matched people correctly. Get feedback by asking questions, e.g. *What quality has Irena got?*

Listening

13a ▶ ⊙ 2.37–2.39 Focus Ss on the first column of the table. Play the recordings. Ss listen and write in the jobs. Don't check the answers at this point as Ss' notes from exercise 13b might help them identify the jobs.

b ▶ Play the recordings again. Ss take notes for the two remaining columns in the table.

c ▶ Ss check their answers in pairs. Get feedback for exercises 13a and 13b. Ss then discuss the questions in pairs. Finally, get feedback from the whole class.

Answers			
Speaker	Job	Activities	Abilities/skills
1 Jonathan	senior designer and buyer	design layouts for insides of books	You need to be creative, organised, able to control budgets, able to set schedules, methodical and able to work in a team.
2 Polly	teacher of English to foreign students	prepare lessons, do photocopying and marking	You need to be able to explain things clearly and logically, be very positive and encouraging and very organised.
3 Rachel	professional actress	setting up performances, doing three shows a day, six days a week	You have to have huge passion and drive for what you're doing as well as stamina. You also need to be fit and flexible.

Speaking

14a ▶ Read through the instructions and topics with the Ss. Give Ss time to make notes. Monitor and help where necessary.

b ▶ Put Ss in pairs to discuss their chosen jobs and answer the questions. Monitor and note down any errors. Get feedback from the whole class and discuss which of the jobs sound interesting. Write errors on the board and elicit the corrections. Finally, read out any language that Ss have used correctly and praise Ss for good examples.

9 Vocabulary | UK and US English

In this lesson, Ss look at some examples of the differences between UK and US English and practise using these varieties of English.

> **OPTIONAL WARMER**
>
> Draw two columns on the board. Write *UK* at the top of Column 1 and *US* at the top of Column 2. Write *tap* in Column 1 and *faucet* in Column 2. Elicit the meaning of these words and the fact that there are differences between UK and US vocabulary. Divide Ss into two groups. Each group notes down words they associate with one of the countries. Get feedback and write Ss' ideas on the board in the relevant column. Make sure these are removed from the board before Ss do exercise 2 below.

1a ▶ ⊙ 2.40 Focus Ss on the photos. In pairs, Ss discuss whether they know the US names for the items in the photos. Get feedback but don't confirm any answers. Play the recording for Ss to answer the question. Get feedback from the whole class.

Answers
car park (UK): In the US this is called a *parking lot*.
lift (UK): In the US this is called an *elevator*.
chips (UK): In US this is called *French fries*. *Chips* in the US means *crisps* in the UK.

b ▶ Play the recording again. Ss listen and answer the questions. Check the answers with the whole class.

Answers	
1	Americans tend to be more direct.
2	She didn't know that *given the sack* meant *be fired* (he had lost his job).

c ▶ Ss discuss the two questions in pairs. Then get feedback from the whole class.

2 ▶ Ss do the activity in pairs. Check the answers with the whole class.

Answers			
1	cell	9	resumé
2	check	10	round trip
3	fries	11	subway
4	mail	12	soccer
5	gas	13	movie
6	freeway	14	vacation
7	mall	15	restroom
8	apartment		

3a ▶ Ss do the activity in pairs. Let Ss compare their answers in pairs but don't get feedback at this point.

b ▶ ⊙ 2.41 Play the recording for Ss check their answers. Elicit the answers from the whole class.

Answers

1	resumé (US)	6	cell (phone) (US)
2	subway (US)	7	movie (US)
3	return ticket (UK)	8	bill (UK)
4	freeway (US)	9	restroom (US)
5	flat (UK)		

4a ▶ With books closed, ask Ss if they know of any differences between UK and US spelling. Get feedback and then focus Ss' attention on the table. Elicit more examples of words to add to the table.

b ▶ Ss do the activity in pairs. Check the answers with the whole class and write the US versions of the words on the board.

Answers

criticize	prioritize
flavor	summarized
humor	theater
meter	realized
neighbor	

Pronunciation | UK and US English

5 ▶ 🔊 2.42 Play the recording. Ss listen to the different pronunciations of the words and try to identify the differences. Get feedback from the whole class and refer Ss to the Pronunciation bank on page 164. Ss can then identify words which have similar differences in pronunciation.

9 Communication

In this lesson, Ss find out how to answer interview questions. Ss then interview each other, using the advice given.

1a ▶ Put Ss in pairs to discuss the questions. Get feedback from the whole class.

b ▶ Ss read the advice and discuss the questions in pairs. Get feedback from the whole class. Encourage Ss to give reasons for their answers.

c ▶ Ss read the text and compare it with their ideas from exercise 1b. Get feedback from the whole class.

Answers

1	good idea
2	good idea
3	not a good idea (dress smartly)
4	good idea
5	not a good idea (it's OK to think for a few seconds)
6	not always a good idea (give a positive reason)
7	good idea

2 ▶ Read through the questions with the Ss and check understanding. Ss then note down answers they would give to each question.

3a ▶ Put Ss in pairs (A and B) and read through the instructions with the Ss. Ss A turn to page 148 to read about questions 1–4. Ss B turn to page 150 to read about questions 5–8. Ss then compare the advice with the notes they made in exercise 2 and update their notes as necessary.

b ▶ In their pairs, Ss tell each other what they learned and help each other to improve their notes. Ss can then rehearse their questions and answers together.

c ▶ Now put Ss in different pairs. Ss interview each other, using the questions from exercise 2 and the advice from exercise 3a. The interviewers take notes during the interviews and then give feedback to their partners. Get feedback from various Ss to see how their interviews went.

OPTIONAL VARIATION

When Ss have given feedback, they should decide who gave the best interview. Identify four nominated Ss and tell them they are all trying to get the same job. Choose four other Ss to be the interviewers. These Ss conduct interviews with the nominated Ss. At the end of the interview, invite a different student from the class to ask the interviewees a new, extra question. When the interviews are finished, the class should decide who gets the job. They must give reasons for their choice. If your class is large, you can divide Ss into two groups for this stage.

Review and practice

1 ▶

Answers			
	2	do	
1 to work	3	do	4 to take
			5 to take

2 ▶

Answers
1. My boss didn't let me make personal phone calls.
2. I was also made to work weekends.
3. My boss didn't allow me to use the Internet.
4. But when I was sick she let me have as much time off as I needed.
5. And she allowed me to take my holiday when I wanted, too.

3 ▶

Answers
1. Jim said (that) he had just started at Manchester University.
2. Jim told me (that) he was studying Engineering.
3. Jim told me (that) he had made lots of new friends.
4. Jim told me (that) they had been to a fantastic concert the weekend before/last weekend.
5. Jim told me (that) they were going to the Lake District that weekend/the following weekend/the next weekend.
6. Jim said (that) he would call me tomorrow/the next day.
7. Jim said (that) he had been to a brilliant lecture that morning/this morning.
8. Jim told me (that) he lived in a flat with three other students.
9. Jim said (that) they were having a party that night.

4 ▶

Answers
1. She asked if I knew where the post office was.
2. He asked where he could change some money.
3. She asked if I had been here/there before.
4. He asked me what time the meeting had finished this morning/ that morning.
5. She asked if I would look after her plants (for her).
6. They asked if we had gone/been to the cinema last night/the night before.
7. She asked what time I/we had arrived.
8. He asked if I was meeting anyone here/there.

5 ▶

Answers		
1 had to	5	had to
2 couldn't	6	didn't have to
3 had to	7	could
4 weren't allowed	8	were allowed

6 ▶

Answers		
1 confused	5	annoying
2 delegate	6	methodical
3 tiring	7	formal qualifications
4 persuaded	8	relaxing

Writing bank

See page 161 in the Students' Book

1 ▶ Ss read the letter of application and answer the questions in pairs. Get feedback from the whole class.

Answers
1. She has a good degree in Italian, has visited Italy many times, has excellent communication skills and enjoys team work.

2a ▶ Ss read the letter again and underline the phrases which have the same meaning as sentences 1-5. Ss check their answers with a partner. Get feedback from the whole class.

Answers
1. I would like to apply for the job of Tour Guide.
2. I would be delighted to have the opportunity to live and work in the country.
3. I believe that I possess excellent communication skills.
4. Although I do not have any directly relevant experience, I understand that training would be given.
5. I enclose/attach my C.V. and look forward to hearing from you in the near future.

b ▶ Discuss this question with the whole class.

Answers
The phrases in the letter are more formal and would be more suitable for a job application.

3 ▶ Ss complete the How to... box with words from the letter in exercise 1.

Answers
Dear Sir/Madam,
I would like to apply for the job of ...
I attach my C.V. and look forward to hearing from you in the near future.
Yours faithfully,

4a ▶ Ss read the job advertisements and choose a job to apply for. Ss then make notes on the necessary qualifications, skills and experience.

b ▶ Ss write a formal email or letter of application for the job they chose, using their notes and phrases from the How to... box.

Overview

Lead-in	**Vocabulary:** Memory
10.1	**Can do:** Respond to a poem **Grammar:** *I wish/If only* **Reading:** *It was long ago* **Listening:** Childhood memory, Erma Bombeck
10.2	**Can do:** Briefly describe a famous person **Grammar:** Review of past tenses **Vocabulary:** Biographies **Speaking and Pronunciation:** Pronouncing numbers **How to...** say numbers **Reading:** The Making of ___ , Gianni Versace **Listening:** Some famous people
10.3	**Can do:** Understand cultural differences **Grammar:** Phrasal verbs **Speaking and Pronunciation:** Word stress in phrasal verbs **How to...** say goodbye (in person) **Reading:** We're letting you go **Listening:** Some goodbyes, Saying goodbye on the phone
Vocabulary	The senses
Communication	Talking about memories
Writing bank	Write a simple essay **How to...** write a simple essay
Extra resources	ActiveTeach and ActiveBook

CEFR Can do objectives
10.1 Respond to a poem
10.2 Briefly describe a famous person
10.3 Understand cultural differences
Communication Talking about memories
Writing bank Write a simple essay

CEFR Portfolio ideas
a) With your friends, create a video showing different ways of saying goodbye in different situations.
b) Write a short brochure for British and American visitors to your country, describing some of the cultural differences they might experience.
c) Write a simple essay on the topic 'Life is better today than it was a hundred years ago'. Use the How to... box on page 162 to help you.

Lead-in

Hyde Park is one of the largest parks in central London. The combined area of the park is larger than Monaco. It is also famous for being the home of Speaker's Corner, where anyone can stand up and speak about almost any topic.

Princess Diana (1961-1997) was the wife of Prince Charles and the mother of Prince William and Prince Harry. She and Prince Charles divorced in 1996. She was killed in a traffic accident. Her death created a media phenomenon unparalleled in the UK at the time.

OPTIONAL WARMER

Ask Ss: *What do countries do to remember events or people in their history?* Write up important feedback from the class on the board. Ask Ss: *What does your country remember? What are the most important events and people?* Ss discuss the questions in pairs. Then get feedback from the whole class.

1a ▶ Ss do the activity individually and then compare their answers in pairs. Even if they don't know the words or phrases, Ss may be able to work out answers from the grammatical structure of the sentence. Check the answers with the whole class. If Ss are having difficulty with the meaning of the words or phrases, encourage Ss to check in a dictionary before confirming the answers.

Answers	
1 memorial, to commemorate	4 homesick
	5 nostalgia
2 remember	6 in memory
3 remind us	7 memento

b ▶ Draw Ss' attention to the photos. Put Ss in pairs to discuss the photos and decide where they are or what they represent. Get feedback from the whole class. Ss then match the photos with sentences from exercise 1a. Let Ss compare their answers in pairs before getting feedback from the whole class.

Answers	
Main photo: 2	Middle photo: 3
Top photo: 6	Bottom photo: 1

2a ▶ 2.43 Ask Ss: *Who was Princess Diana? What do you know about her?* In pairs, Ss read the text and try to complete the summary. Play the recording. Ss check their answers in pairs. Then check the answers with the whole class.

Answers					
1	Park	3	died	5	modern
2	2004	4	fountain	6	children

b ▶ Play the recording again. Ss listen and answer the question. Check the answer with the whole class.

Answers
because she really liked children

c ▶ Put Ss in pairs to discuss the questions. Get feedback from the whole class, making sure Ss give reasons for their answers. Then decide as a class which person is most worthy of a memorial and what it would look like.

OPTIONAL VARIATION

In groups, Ss decide who they are going to build a memorial to and what the memorial will be/look like. They then design the memorial and present their ideas to the rest of the class. Ss vote for the best idea (they can't choose their own memorial).

10.1 Childhood memories

In this lesson, Ss read a poem and listen to people talking about childhood memories. Through this context, Ss learn how to use *I wish* and *If only* and learn about rhyming.

OPTIONAL WARMER

Tell Ss about one of your earliest childhood memories in detail. Encourage Ss to ask you follow-up questions about the memory. Ss then tell their partners about one of their earliest childhood memories. Again, encourage Ss to ask each other follow-up questions. Get feedback from the whole class and decide as a group who had the most vivid childhood memory.

Reading

1a ▶ Put Ss in pairs to describe the old woman in the picture and answer the question. Get feedback from the whole class.

b ▶ Ss read the poem and answer the questions. Let Ss compare their answers in pairs before getting feedback from the whole class. Make sure Ss give reasons for their answers to question 4.

Answers
1 an adult (probably an old person) who was three/a very young child at the time of the remembered event.
2 The old lady called her over and gave her a saucer of bilberries and cream.
3 These phrases involve the reader and make the poem more like a conversation.
4 Ss' own answers.

c ▶ Elicit from Ss the names of the five senses. Tell Ss that effective poetry encourages you to use your five senses. Ss then re-read the poem, noting down the things they can see, hear, smell, taste and feel. Let Ss compare their answers in pairs before getting feedback from the whole class. Go over any new vocabulary. Encourage the use of dictionaries.

Answers
See: a dusty road; a mountain; an old house; tree; an old woman in a red shawl; a grey cat on her knee, berries and cream
Hear: what the old woman said to her: 'Do you like bilberries and cream for tea?', the old woman humming, the cat purring
Smell: everything that used to be
Taste: berries
Feel: the sun, the heat on the road

2 ▶ Check understanding of *rhyme*. Ss read through the Lifelong learning box. Focus Ss on *ago* and *know* at the end of the first two stanzas in the poem and discuss how finding words which rhyme can help when remembering the pronunciation of difficult words. In pairs, Ss look for words which rhyme with *me* in the poem. Get feedback from the whole class.

Answers
tree, knee, three, tea, see, be

Listening and speaking

3a ▶ Ss make notes individually. Monitor and help Ss with any new vocabulary.

b ▶ Put Ss in pairs to discuss the memories they chose. Get feedback from various Ss by asking them to report what their partners said.

OPTIONAL VARIATION

Ss have to guess their partner's earliest memory. One student describes what they felt, tasted, smelt, heard and saw. Their partner can interrupt at any time and guess the memory. Get feedback from Ss and if Ss can't guess the memory, repeat the activity with the whole class.

4a ▶ 🔘 2.44 Give Ss time to read through the questions and then play the recording. Let Ss compare their answers in pairs before checking the answers with the whole class.

Answers
1 a farm
2 her cousins
3 four
4 terrified because her cousin told her there were monsters in the shed
5 the noise was probably cows

b ▶ In pairs, Ss try to do the activity from memory. Then play the recording again for Ss to check. Finally, check the answers with the whole class.

Answers
e, h, c, j, b, d, f, i, a, g

c ▶ Ss do the activity in pairs. Check the answers with the whole class. Elicit words or phrases which helped Ss find the answers.

Answers
a: e and h (these set the time and place)
b: c, j, b
c: d (or possibly b and d)
d: f, i, a, g

5a ▶ Ss read the text and decide who is telling the story. Ss compare their answers in pairs, giving reasons for their answers. Get feedback from the whole class.

Answers
Sarah's aunt

b ▶ Put Ss in pairs to retell the story through the eyes of Sarah's cousin. Ss should think about each of the senses: what the cousin could see, smell, hear, taste or feel. Ss write their story using the structure from exercise 4c.

Let Ss compare their stories with another pair. Then get feedback from the whole class and rebuild the story on the board.

OPTIONAL VARIATION

Divide the class into two teams and divide the board down the centre. Tell both teams that they are going to rewrite the story from the point of view of the cousin. Nominate one student from each team to be the writer. They have to stay at the board. Then give different people in each team one of the following roles: writing what they did, what they said, what they saw, what they heard, what they smelt, what they tasted and what they felt. Ss need to recreate the story in their team with each team member contributing their section. Monitor what is written on the board, underlining mistakes without correcting errors. The first team to produce a story including all five senses and all the relevant information in a coherent structure is the winner.

Listening

6a ▶ Read through the instructions with the Ss. Ss read the extract and identify the points she makes. Get feedback and write each point on the board. Ss then discuss the points in pairs, saying why they agree or disagree with them. Get feedback from various pairs.

b ▶ 🔘 2.45 Read through the instructions with the Ss. Play the recording. Ss complete the table with notes about things Claire and Matt would like to change about their lives (present and past). Check the answers with the whole class.

Answers

	Present	Past
Claire	watch less TV travel more	listened more to grandfather's stories eaten more healthily
Matt	listen more and talk less lose some weight	continued playing football

Grammar | *I wish/if only*

OPTIONAL GRAMMAR LEAD-IN

Write *lose some weight* on the board. Elicit who said this in the listening (Matt). On the board, write: *I wish I _____* . In pairs, Ss think of what Matt would say to complete the sentence. Write *could lose some weight* in the space. Ask Ss: *What tense is this?* Explain that we use *I wish* + Past Simple to express a present wish. Tell Ss to read through the notes on Reference page 145. Ask Ss: *What tense do we use with* wish *to talk about past wishes?* (Past Perfect) Draw Ss' attention to the fact that tenses shift back when using *wish*: for present wishes Past Simple, for past wishes Past Perfect. Tell Ss that this is similar to the way tenses are shifted back in reported speech which they studied in Unit 9.

7 ▶ Ss read through the Active grammar box and choose the correct options. Check the answers with the class. If you didn't do the warmer activity, refer Ss to the notes on Reference page 145 now. Answer any questions Ss may have.

Active grammar

We use *wish* + Past Simple to talk about imaginary things we would like in the <u>present</u>.

We use *wish* + Past Perfect to talk about imaginary things we would like in the <u>past</u>.

We use *wish* + *could* to talk about ability in the <u>present</u>.

---

8 ▶ Ss do the activity in pairs. Get feedback from the whole class. Accept alternative answers which make sense and are grammatically correct.

Suggested answers

1   I wish I was/were better at Maths.
2   I wish you would try harder not to be late.
3   I wish we hadn't gone to the museum.
4   I wish I could dance.
5   I wish you wouldn't leave your dirty plate on the table!
6   I wish I had more friends.
7   I wish I could quit smoking.

OPTIONAL EXTENSION

Ask Ss to rewrite the sentences from exercise 8 using *If only … .*

---

9 ▶ Ss write three sentences about wishes for their lives (past or present). Monitor and help where necessary. Ss then discuss their wishes in pairs. Monitor and note down any errors. Get feedback from various pairs and review any important errors.

OPTIONAL EXTENSION

On the board, write: *I missed the plane.* Ss think of the type of regrets that someone who had missed a plane might have. Write the following example on the board: *If only there hadn't been so much traffic… .* In pairs, Ss think of more sentences using *wish* and *If only*. Get feedback and write correct sentences on the board. Put Ss in pairs (A and B). Each student writes down a problem without showing it to their partner. Student A then makes sentences using *wish* and *If only* which somebody who had this problem might say. Student B listens and tries to guess the problem. When Student B has guessed correctly, repeat the activity with Student A guessing what Student B's problem is.

10.2 Memorable people

Marie Sklodowska Curie (1867–1934) was a Polish physicist and scientist, famous for her work on radioactivity. She was the first person to receive two Nobel Prizes and the first female professor at the University of Paris.

Tanni Grey-Thompson (1969–) is a Welsh athlete and TV presenter. She was born with spina bifada and has spent her whole life in wheelchair. This has not stopped her winning eleven Paralympic gold medals. She has held thirty world records and has won the London marathon six times.

Edison Arantes do Nascimento, or Pelé (1940–) is widely regarded as one of the greatest footballers of all time and was named player of the century in 1999. In 1,363 games, he scored 1,281 goals. In 92 games for Brazil, he scored 77 goals. He is the only footballer to have three World Cup winner medals. Since retirement, he has worked for many charities and international bodies.

Albert Einstein (1879–1955) was a German theoretical physicist who was responsible for discovering the theory of relativity. He won the Nobel Prize in 1921 and is known as the father of modern physics. He wrote more than 300 scientific papers and 150 non-scientific works. His name has become synonymous with the word 'genius'.

In this lesson, Ss listen to information about important people from the 20th century. Ss then read a text about the fashion designer Coco Chanel and through this context, review past tenses. Ss look at how different numbers are pronounced in English and practise saying these numbers.

OPTIONAL WARMER

In a monolingual class, put Ss in pairs to write a list of five famous people from their country. Ss then discuss why these people have been important in shaping their country. Get feedback by asking various pairs to report back to the class. In a multilingual class, Ss individually write a list of five important people from their country. Ss then work in pairs with a student from another country. Ss explain to each other how these people have helped shaped their country.

Listening

1a ▶ Focus Ss on the four photos. Put Ss in pairs to discuss the questions. Tell Ss to think about how the people helped to shape the twentieth century. Get feedback from the whole class and write Ss ideas on the board.

b ▶ ● 2.46 Play the recording. Ss listen and make notes about memorable things the four people did. Let Ss compare their notes in pairs before checking the answers with the whole class. Compare the answers with the predictions on the board.

Answers
1 Marie Curie was a brilliant scientist. She discovered radium with her husband and won the Nobel Prize twice.
2 Tanni Grey-Thompson won many Paralympic gold medals for wheelchair racing.
3 Pelé was one of the greatest footballers of all time.
4 Albert Einstein was a famous scientist who is best known for his theories of relativity.

c ▶ Give Ss time to read the texts. Then play the recording again. Let Ss compare their answers in pairs before checking the answers with the whole class.

Answers

1	1	medical school	3 1	a poor family
	2	son	2	seven
	3	marry	3	couldn't afford
	4	teaching	4 1	six or seven
	5	1895	2	successful
	6	1911	3	300
2	1	thirteen		
	2	1988		
	3	her back		
	4	gold medals		

Vocabulary | biographies

2 ▶ Ss do the activity in pairs. Play recording 2.46 again for Ss to check their answers. Then get feedback from the whole class.

Answers

1	d	3	a	5	b
2	c	4	e	6	f

3 ▶ Ss do the activity in pairs. Then check the answers with the whole class.

Answers
1 from an early age
2 is best known for
3 a difficult start in life
4 is widely considered to be
5 one of the greatest (footballers) of all time
6 against the odds

4a ▶ On the board, write the name of someone famous who succeeded against the odds. Encourage Ss to ask you questions about this person and why they succeeded against the odds. Ss then choose a different famous person and make notes using words and phrases from exercise 2.

b ▶ In small groups, Ss take turns to talk about the people they chose. Encourage the rest of the group to ask follow-up questions. Then get feedback from various Ss.

OPTIONAL VARIATION

In pairs, Ss ask each other twenty *Yes/No* questions to find out the identity of the famous person. Partners can only answer *Yes* or *No*. If Ss cannot guess the person after twenty questions, their partner reveals the answer. Ss then discuss why the famous person succeeded against the odds.

Reading and listening

5a ▶ Focus Ss on the photos. In pairs, Ss guess who the text is about and what type of life she might have had. Elicit ideas from the whole class. Tell Ss they are going to read an article to find out who the famous woman is. Ask Ss to underline any words or phrases they don't understand and say that you will deal with them later. Ss read paragraph 1. In pairs, Ss discuss the question at the end of the paragraph and choose the best answer: a, b or c. Ss then read the next paragraph, as directed (paragraph 5), and discuss the questions at the end. Ss continue until they have read the whole text.

b ▶ When Ss have decided who the famous person is they can write her name in the title. Check the Ss' answers. Go through any words or expressions Ss don't understand. Encourage Ss to answer each other's questions before asking you.

Answers
Coco Chanel

6a ▶ ● 2.47 Read through the instructions with the Ss. Play the recording. Ss write down the three facts which the speaker gets wrong. Check the answers with the whole class.

Answers
Her mother died, not her father.
In her first shop, she sold hats, not perfume.
She went to Switzerland, not Hollywood.

b ▶ Give Ss time to read through the numbers and dates in the box. In pairs, Ss retell the story of Coco Chanel's life using the numbers and dates as prompts. Monitor and take note of any errors Ss make with the numbers and dates. Keep a note of these errors for exercise 9a below. Ask various pairs to read out their stories for the class.

Grammar | review of past tenses

OPTIONAL GRAMMAR LEAD-IN

Think of a traditional story such as a fairy tale to tell the class. Before telling the story, tell Ss they are going to hear a story and ask them to notice the tenses used. When telling the story, include examples of the Past Simple, Past Continuous and Past Perfect. Ss note down examples of tenses used in the story and compare their ideas in pairs. Get feedback and write examples of the Past Simple, Past Continuous and Past Perfect on the board.

7a ▶ Ss do the activity in pairs. Get feedback from the whole class and write examples of the Past Simple, Past Continuous and Past Perfect on the board.

b ▶ Give Ss time to read through the Active grammar box and complete the rules. Check the answers with the whole class. Then refer Ss to Reference page 145. Give Ss time to read through the notes. Ask Ss: *What structure do we use for the main completed events in a narrative?* (Past Simple) *What structure do we use if we want to show that one action happened before another action?* (Past Perfect) *What structure do we use for an action in progress when the main events happened?* (Past Continuous)

> **Active grammar**
>
> Past Simple
> Past Perfect
> Past Continuous
> Past Continuous / Past Simple

8a ▶ Ss do the activity individually. Remind Ss that there is one passive form. Let Ss compare their answers in pairs before checking the answers with the whole class.

Answers			
1	was growing up	6	were
2	moved	7	brought out
3	opened	8	was walking
4	presented	9	was shot
5	had already designed	10	had become

b ▶ Ss find three things Gianni Versace had in common with Coco Chanel. Let Ss compare their answers in pairs before getting feedback from the whole class.

> **Answers**
> Both Coco Chanel and Gianni Versace opened shops.
> They then both started designing women's clothes.
> They both brought out perfumes.

Pronunciation | pronouncing numbers

9a ▶ Ss read the How to... box. Then refer Ss back to the numbers and dates from exercise 6b. Ss read through the numbers in pairs. Ask various Ss to read different numbers aloud.

b ▶ In pairs, Ss practise saying the numbers. Monitor and correct where necessary. Ask various Ss to say the numbers aloud. Refer Ss to the Pronunciation bank on page 164.

c ▶ ● 2.48 Play the recording for Ss to check the pronunciation. Then put Ss in pairs to answer the questions. Get feedback from the whole class.

> **Answers**
> We use *and* before the smallest part of a big number (one thousand <u>and</u> ten, ten million, six hundred <u>and</u> forty), and between whole numbers and fractions (three <u>and</u> a half, nine <u>and</u> three-quarters).
> We use *the* before dates (<u>the</u> fourth of June) and time periods (<u>the</u> fifth century, <u>the</u> nineteen seventies).

10 ▶ Put Ss in two groups (A and B). Ss A look at the sentences on page 151. Ss B look at the sentences on page 152. In their groups, Ss think of questions they can ask to find out the missing numbers. Monitor and check the questions Ss write. Then put Ss in pairs (A and B). Ss ask each other the questions they prepared and write in the missing numbers. Monitor and take note of any errors Ss make with numbers. Check the answers with the whole class. Finally, write any number errors on the board and practise saying the correct versions with the class.

Speaking

11a ▶ Write five numbers that are important to you on the board. Include dates, years, numbers, etc. In pairs, Ss discuss the numbers and decide why they might be important to you. Elicit ideas and confirm the answers. Individually, Ss then write down five numbers that are important to them.

b ▶ Ss work in pairs and swap their numbers. Ss ask each other questions to find out why each number is important. Encourage Ss to ask follow-up questions. Monitor and note down any errors. Ask various Ss to report what they found out about their partner. Then write any errors on the board and encourage Ss to self-correct.

10.3 Saying goodbye

There are many ways of saying goodbye in English, e.g.
goodbye, bye, see you later, see you, later, bye for now
and *catch you later*.

In this lesson, Ss read about how companies fire people
and how relationships break up. Through this context,
Ss look at the grammar of phrasal verbs and practise
using some phrasal verbs. Ss then listen to people saying
goodbye and practise different ways of saying goodbye.

OPTIONAL WARMER

Tell Ss to think of places where they could say goodbye to
someone. In pairs, Ss write a list of places and discuss who
they could say goodbye to in these places. Put Ss in different
pairs to tell each other about the places and people they have
written down. Ss then make a list of different ways to say
goodbye in English. Get feedback from the whole class.

Reading and speaking

1a ▶ Ss discuss the question in pairs and discuss
whether they have ever been in these situations
themselves. Get feedback from the whole class.

Suggested Answers
A   firing someone from a company
B   seeing someone off on a cruise
C   ending a relationship/splitting up with someone
D   sending off a footballer (giving a footballer a red card)
E   leaving a child at school/dropping a child off at school

b ▶ Ss discuss the question in pairs. Get feedback from
the whole class.

2a ▶ Put Ss in two groups (A and B). Ss A read the text
on page 140 and Ss B read the text on page 151. Ss answer
questions 1–5 for their article and check their answers with
another student from the same group. Check that each group
has the correct answers and help with any difficult vocabulary.

b ▶ Put Ss in pairs (A and B). Ss explain the articles to each
other using their answers from exercise 2a. Get feedback from
the whole class about questions 4 and 5 from exercise 2a.

Answers
1   Ss A's text is about saying goodbye to your staff. Ss B's
    text is about saying goodbye to a partner.
2   Companies used text messages, emails, post-it notes and
    Facebook. One company disabled an employee's security
    card. One actor sent his pregnant girlfriend a fax; another
    split up with his partner on live TV; someone else emailed
    his wedding guests and a king executed two of his wives.
3   There's no nice way to fire someone, but managers should
    show respect for the employee. In relationships, some
    people have always been insensitive when it's time to say
    goodbye.
4   Ss' own answers.
5   Both texts suggest you should show respect to others.

OPTIONAL EXTENSION

In pairs, Ss decide which way of firing people from the text
on page 140 is the worst and why. Get feedback from the
whole class and discuss Ss' ideas. Ss then decide which
way of splitting up with someone from the text on page 151
is the worst and why. Again, get feedback from the whole
class. In small groups, Ss then decide what would be the
best way to fire someone and what would be the best way
to split up with someone. Get feedback from each group.

3 ▶ Ask Ss what a phrasal verb is. Elicit that a phrasal
verb is a verb with one or two particles. Ss do the activity
in pairs. Get feedback from the whole class and write the
phrasal verbs on the board.

Answers
find out – discover
turning up – arriving
came back – returned
going on – happening
come up with – think of/invent
turned into – became
split up – finished a relationship
carry on – continue
get over – recover from
called off – cancelled
went through – experienced (something bad)
put up with – tolerate

Grammar | phrasal verbs

4 ▶ Give Ss a short time to read through the Active
grammar box. In pairs, Ss look back at the phrasal verbs
from the texts and match them with the phrasal verb
types (A–D). Ss compare their answers with another pair.
Then check the answers with the whole class. Refer Ss to
Reference page 145. Give Ss time to read the notes and ask
any questions they may have.

Active grammar

A: come back, go on, turn up, split up, carry on
B: call off, find out
C: turn into, get over, go through
D: come up with, put up with

5 ▶ Ss do the activity in pairs. Let Ss compare their
answers with another pair. Then check the answers with
the whole class and ask various Ss to read out the correct
sentences.

Answers

1 I split up with my girlfriend.
2 We didn't find out until later.
3 When are you coming back?
4 I couldn't carry on because I was tired.
5 She always turns up late.
6 Did they come up with any good ideas?
7 What is going on here?
8 The match was called off because of rain.
9 The company is going through a difficult period.
10 I can't put up with him anymore.
11 The water turned into ice.
12 It can take weeks to get over a serious illness.

6 ▶ Ss cover boxes A and B. Ss think of phrasal verbs that could complete sentences 1–8 and compare their ideas in pairs. Get feedback and write any correct possibilities on the board but don't confirm any answers. Ss then use the words from A and B to complete the sentences correctly. Remind Ss to change the verb form if necessary. Check the answers with the whole class and write the phrasal verbs on the board.

Answers

1	put up with	5	going on
2	turned into	6	went through
3	carry on	7	split up
4	turned up	8	come up with

Pronunciation | word stress in phrasal verbs

7a ▶ ● 2.49 Check that Ss remember how to mark stress. Tell Ss to look back at the phrasal verbs from exercise 6. Play the recording. Ss mark the stress in each phrasal verb and check their answers in pairs. Check the answers with the whole class.

Answers

The main stress is on the particle in all sentences except 2 and 6, where the stress is on the verb.

b ▶ Elicit which phrasal verbs from exercise 6 have the main stress on the verb. Then ask Ss to look back at the Active grammar box and match the verbs with a type (A–D). Check the answer with the whole class. Refer Ss to the Pronunciation bank on page 163 and answer any questions the Ss might have.

Answers

turn into and *go through* have the stress on the main verb.
They are both type C.

8 ▶ Put Ss in pairs. Ask Ss to individually look at the pictures and write a sentence about one picture using a phrasal verb. Ss then read out their sentences for their partner to guess the picture. If Ss need extra help, refer them to the phrasal verbs from exercise 6. Get feedback from the whole class.

Answers

A	split up	D	come back
B	put up with	E	find out
C	call off	F	come up with

OPTIONAL VARIATION

Before looking at the gapped sentences in exercise 6, focus Ss on the pictures in exercise 8. Write the following sentence on the board: *Today's concert was called off because of bad weather*. In pairs, Ss decide which of the pictures is being described. Ss then write five sentences to describe the other pictures. Ss read their sentences to their partners who decide which picture each sentence is describing. Ss then complete exercise 6 using the words from boxes A and B. Finally, Ss can compare the sentences they wrote about the pictures with the sentences in exercise 6.

Listening

9a ▶ ● 2.50 Read through the instructions and situations with the Ss. Play the recording and then check answers with the whole class.

Answers

1 a speaker at the end of a conference
2 a father and daughter before she goes away
3 two colleagues at the end of a day
4 friends at the end of a party

b ▶ In pairs, Ss read the questions and try to remember the answers. Then play the recording again for Ss to check their predictions. Check the answers with the whole class.

Answers

a	4	b	1	c	3	d	2

c ▶ Read through the How to... box with the Ss. Then play the recording for Ss to tick the phrases they hear. Check the answers with the whole class.

Answers

Right then, it's time I made a move.
Sorry, I've got to dash.
Thank you very much for coming.
Thank you and goodbye.
Thanks for everything. I really enjoyed it.
We'll see you in a couple of weeks.
Have a safe trip.
Take care.
See you.

10a ▶ Ss try to do the activity in pairs before they listen. Get feedback from the whole class but don't confirm any answers at this stage.

b ▶ ● 2.51 Play the recording for Ss to check their answers. Check the answers with the whole class. Then elicit the answers to the three questions.

Answers
A: Right, well I'd better be going. (1)
B: Yes, me too. I've got loads to do. (1)
A: Maybe see you next Wednesday then?
B: Yes, that sounds good. See you then. (2)
A: Have a good weekend. (2)
B: You too.
A: See you. (3)
B: Yeah, bye. (3)

c ▶ Discuss the question with the whole class.

11 ▶ Put Ss in pairs (A and B). Ss read the role cards and roleplay both situations using the words and phrases from the How… to box. Ss then swap roles and repeat the activity. Monitor and take note of any errors to discuss during feedback.

OPTIONAL VARIATION

Number all Ss A or B. Put Ss A into pairs with Ss B and do the first roleplay. Then move the Ss around so that each person is with a different partner and do the second situation. Then tell Ss A that they are now Bs and vice versa and move the Ss around twice more.

10 Vocabulary | the senses

In this lesson, Ss look at vocabulary related to the five senses.

1a ▶ Ss discuss the question in pairs. Monitor and help with vocabulary if necessary. Get feedback from various pairs.

Suggested Answers
A smell   D sound
B touch   E taste
C sight

b ▶ Ss decide what sense they associate with the words in the box. Draw five columns on the board and write a sense at the top of each one. Allow Ss to compare their ideas in pairs and then get feedback from the whole class. Write the words in the columns as Ss give you their answers. There are no correct or incorrect answers as it depends on how Ss feel about the words.

c ▶ Ss complete the phrases with their choice of words. Put Ss in groups to discuss their ideas. Again, there are no correct or incorrect answers.

d ▶ Put Ss in pairs to talk about which things from exercise 1b they like and dislike. Monitor and take note of errors. Then get feedback from the whole class. Finally, write the errors on the board and encourage Ss to self-correct.

2a ▶ Ss read through the table. Focus Ss on the word order: verb + adjective or verb + *like* + noun phrase. Ss cover column B of the table. In pairs, Ss think of responses to the sentences and questions in column A. Elicit ideas from various pairs. Ss then uncover column B and match sentences from A and B. Check the answers with the whole class.

Answers		3	g		6	b
1	d	4	f		7	h
2	e	5	a		8	c

b ▶ Ss cover column B and practise saying the dialogues in pairs.

c ▶ ● 2.52 Read through the instructions with the Ss. Play the recording. Ss listen and think about what has just happened in each case. Ss check their ideas in pairs and decide which sense is being used in each situation. Check the answers with the whole class.

Suggested Answers
1 A woman is cooking. She's just burned her hand! (touch)
2 He's eaten something disgusting. (taste)
3 Some birds have just started singing and the person wants to hear them. (sound)
4 She's just eaten something delicious. (taste)
5 She's just smelled something horrible. (smell)

3a ▶ Put Ss in pairs to discuss the differences in meaning. Check the answers with the whole class. If necessary, allow Ss to check in a dictionary.

Answers
1 see: to notice something using your eyes, deliberately or by chance, for a long or a short time
   look at: usually for a short time deliberately
   watch: for a long time deliberately, paying attention to what is happening (e.g. a TV programme)
2 listen to: deliberately / hear: probably by chance
3 touch: for one moment, usually with your hands; hold: for a long time, in your hands or arms

b ▶ Ss do the activity individually. Remind Ss to change the verb form if necessary. Check the answers with the whole class.

Answers
1	hold	5	looking at
2	seen	6	listen to
3	hear	7	watch
4	touch		

OPTIONAL EXTENSION

Ss write a sentence for each word using their own ideas and then tell their partner.

4a ▶ Read the instructions with the Ss. Ss then write their own versions individually. Help Ss with vocabulary where necessary and let them use dictionaries.

b ▶ Put Ss in groups of three or four. Ss take turns to read out their poems and get feedback from the rest of the group. Each group then chooses one poem from their group and makes any changes. Finally, each group presents their poem to the rest of the class.

10 Communication

In this lesson, Ss read instructions about how to play a memory game. Ss then use these instructions to play the game in even-numbered groups of two or more. To play the game, you will need counters for each group.

OPTIONAL WARMER

In pairs, Ss discuss any table games that they play or have played. Get feedback and ask Ss to explain how these games are played. In a monolingual class, ask Ss to tell you the rules of any typical table games played in their country. In a multilingual class, form small groups and ask Ss to explain to each other how typical table games from their countries are played.

1 ▶ Focus Ss on the topics on the game board. Ss read through the topics and check they understand them all. Make sure Ss realise that the letters and numbers in brackets refer to the units in which Ss studied the topic. Ss then read the instructions in the 'How to play' box. Check understanding by asking: *How do you play?* (by taking it in turns to choose a block) *How do you move round the board?* (by choosing blocks on the board that you want to collect) *What do you have to do when you choose a block?* (you have to talk about the topic in the block for one minute) *What happens if you cannot talk about the topic for one minute?* (you don't get the block) *How does Team A win?* (by winning a line of blocks from top to bottom) *How does Team B win?* (by winning a line of blocks from side to side)

OPTIONAL EXTENSION

Give Ss time to plan their strategy and revise language that they might need from the relevant units. This can therefore be a good revision task just before the final test/exam at the end of the year.

2 ▶ Put Ss in groups of equal numbers to play Memory Blockbusters. Divide each group in half to create a team A and a team B. As Ss are playing, monitor carefully to offer help where needed. Take note of errors that Ss make as well as any examples of good language and expressions that Ss use. When Ss have finished the game, get feedback from each group by asking Ss to report something they learned about the other Ss in the group. Finally, write any important errors on the board and invite Ss to come up and correct them on the board. Congratulate Ss on any good language and expressions they used in the class and praise them for their efforts throughout the course.

OPTIONAL EXTENSION

When Ss have finished the game, organise the class into new groups so that Ss aren't working with anyone from their original group. Ss choose one block that they haven't yet landed on and prepare a three-minute talk about the topic. Monitor and help where necessary. When Ss are ready, they give their talk to the rest of their group. Monitor carefully and take note of errors as well as use of correct or interesting language. When all the Ss have finished giving their talks, write up any errors on the board. In their groups, Ss decide how to correct the errors. Get feedback and ask Ss from each group to come up and write the correct forms on the board. Finally, write examples of correct or interesting language that Ss have used on the board and congratulate Ss on its use.

Review and practice

1 ▶

Answers

1	wasn't	5	could work
2	hadn't eaten	6	had shown
3	had gone	7	could play
4	had	8	were

2 ▶

Answers

1	didn't answer	6	went
2	were you doing	7	had stopped
3	was listening	8	didn't you go
4	didn't hear	9	had got back/got back
5	Did you have	10	was visiting

3 ▶

Answers

1 She had changed a lot.
2 I had never read it before.
3 At 6:30 a.m. he was swimming.
4 He was sleeping in his room at midnight.
5 I had lost my passport.
6 She was looking for a job.

4 ▶

Answers

1	split up	5	called off
2	turned up	6	carry on
3	going on	7	find out
4	put up with	8	came up with

5 ▶

Answers

1	against the odds	4	from an early age
2	is widely considered to be	5	best known for
3	of all time	6	remembered

Writing bank

See page 162 in the Students' Book

1a ▶ Ss discuss the statement in pairs, deciding whether they agree or disagree and why. Get feedback from the whole class.

b ▶ Ss read the essay and find out if the writer agrees or disagrees with their opinion and why. Ss check their answers in pairs.

> **Answers**
> The writer does not think that fashion is a waste of money.

2a ▶ Ss read the text again and underline the sentences with the main idea in each paragraph. Let Ss check their answers in pairs before getting feedback from the whole class.

> **Answers**
> Some people believe that fashion is a waste of money.
> In the first place, I think that most people would agree that designers are wonderfully creative and that fashion can even be an art form.
> Secondly, it is well known that people have been interested in fashion for hundreds of years, perhaps even longer.
> Finally, fashion can be good for the economy.
> To conclude, I do not believe that fashion can be said to be a waste of money when there are so many clear benefits.

b ▶ Check that Ss understand what a *supporting idea* is. Ss do the activity individually and check their answers in pairs. Check the answers with the whole class.

> **Answers**
> However, I would like to argue that there are many positive aspects to fashion.
> Designers such as Chanel or Versace are still famous long after their deaths for their beautiful designs.
> It is natural for people to want to dress up and look their best.
> Italy's fashion industry, for example, is worth more than 60 billion euros a year.

3 ▶ Ss read the How to... box and tick the phrases used in the essay.

> **Answers**
> Some people believe that ... However, I would like to argue that ...
> In the first place, ...
> Secondly, ...
> Finally, ...
> To conclude, ...

4a ▶ Ss discuss the statement in pairs and decide why they agree or disagree

b ▶ Ss do the activity in pairs. Get feedback from the whole class and ask Ss to give reasons/examples for their answers.

c ▶ Elicit other opinions from the class to agree or disagree with the statement from exercise 4a. Draw a table on the board with two column headings: Agree and Disagree. Add the Ss' opinions to the relevant column.

d ▶ Ss choose three ideas from exercises 4b or 4c which support their opinion from exercise 4a. Ss write a supporting idea and/or example for each one.

5 ▶ Ss write an essay explaining their opinion, using their notes from exercise 4d and phrases from the How to... box.

Audioscripts

Track 1.2

Dialogue 1

M = Man, W = Woman

M: What activities and hobbies are you good at?

W: I'm quite good at juggling ... .

M: Are you? How did you learn to do that?

W: Well, I started off just throwing and catching one ball, then two and now I can juggle with five balls at once.

M: Can you juggle with plates?

W: No! I don't think I could do that!

Dialogue 2

M = Man, W = Woman

W: What clubs do you belong to?

M: I don't belong to any, but my daughter is a member of an astronomy club.

W: Is she? Can she tell you what will happen in the future, then?

M: No, astronomy, not astrology! She studies the stars and planets.

W: Oh, whoops. I always get those two mixed up ... Does she have a telescope then?

M: Yes, it was expensive, I can tell you ... .

Dialogue 3

W = Woman, T = Teenager

W: What types of exercise are you keen on?

T: I'm keen on snowkiting.

W: Really? What's that?

T: It's like snowboarding, you know, going down a mountain on a board, but you have a kite attached too, so you go even faster.

W: I haven't even been skiing! Isn't it terrifying?

T: Yes, it is. That's the whole point!

W: Do you do it regularly?

T: No, I don't. About once a year.

Dialogue 4

M = Man, W = Woman

W: What cultures are you interested in?

M: I'm really interested in Chinese culture.

W: Have you been there?

M: Yes, I have. I went there on holiday a few years ago and just found it fascinating. I'm trying to learn Mandarin now, oh, and I've started t'ai chi classes as well.

W: Have you? Isn't that a kind of martial art?

M: Well, yes, but it doesn't involve any fighting. It's a series of slow movements, almost like a slow dance. It's really relaxing.

Dialogue 5

M = Man, W = Woman

M: What do you spend too much time on?

W: Oh, that's easy! Sudoku.

M: What's that?

W: Sudoku? It's a kind of number puzzle invented in Japan. You have to complete a grid so that all the lines and boxes contain all of the numbers from one to nine.

M: I haven't tried that.

Track 1.5

Right, well let me tell you a little bit about Rob. Um he's my best friend, um, which many people find difficult to believe. Um, many people don't have, er a best friend who is eighteen years older than them, so I suppose this is quite an unusual friendship. Um, we met, er, about three years ago. We were working in the same school and, um at first I found Rob to be quite an eccentric character, um, with lots of gestures and animations um but he – he also seemed a lot younger than he actually was, which is what I liked about him. ... Um he's also – he's a very sincere, er funny, kind um person as well, which is also what I like about him, too. Um, we share the same

interests as well. We like the same books, we enjoy the same films and we have the same sort of sense of humour. Er, the only real difference between us is that he – he loves cricket, but I absolutely hate it. Um, but we're still very good friends.

Track 1.8

Speaker 1:

My father has been a big influence on me. I really respect him. Um ... partly because of what he does – we do the same job – but I think also his character.

We're quite similar in many ways. Um ... he's sort of very calm. The only time he got angry was once, about twenty years ago when I was fifteen. I came home at five in the morning and I didn't call to say I'd be late. We had a big argument and didn't speak to each other for a week. But apart from that, I've never seen him lose his temper and he has always been very kind to me.

Speaker 2:

So, I want to speak about Romina. She was my best friend for about twelve years. Before meeting her most of my friends were boys and I didn't have many good girlfriends. We met at university and began studying together and going out in the evenings together, and we developed this method of studying before exams. We basically spent the whole night drinking coffee and testing each other. It was terrible for our health but good for our friendship. Unfortunately, we're not in touch any more. We fell out over money while we were on holiday last year, and we haven't seen each other since then. I miss her.

Speaker 3:

I work in a supermarket and I've been there for about two years. When I started, I got on really well with all my colleagues. They were all really nice, except one. This one girl – I think her name was Sarah – she was always unfriendly to me. I don't know why. Then I found out that she was saying bad things about me. She said I was lazy and a bad worker, that kind of thing. I really saw red and we had a huge row. I still don't know what it was really about though ... Anyway, Sarah stopped working at the supermarket about a year ago. I don't know what she's doing now.

Track 1.9

Online dating is becoming the twenty-first century way to find a partner. In the UK last year more than seven million people used a dating website. Far from being unusual, it now seems that everyone's using the Internet as a way to meet people. There are special websites for readers of particular newspapers, for animal lovers, for classical music fans and one which allows only beautiful people to join! For many people though, the idea of having to write a profile, a description of themselves, is very off-putting. Canlintroduceyou.com has a clever way to get round that problem. Rather than writing your own profile, a friend describes you, which makes the whole process much less embarrassing. It seems that there really is a dating website to suit everyone.

Track 1.10

B = Ben, S = Sue, E = Ekaterina

B: Do you prefer watching foreign films with subtitles, or dubbing, Sue?

S: Um, well, I lived in Spain for a while and most of their films and their cinemas

actually have dubbing, you know, when they have different actors doing the voices, so I used to try and go to cinemas where there were original version films because I prefer to read the subtitles than – than listen to actors' voices pretending to be different actors. I just hate watching a film with a famous actor, like, say Al Pacino, and hear a different voice coming out. He has such a distinctive voice. It's really odd.

B: And what do you think, Ekaterina?

E: I agree actually, because I think that subtitles allow you to hear the original actors' voices and all their emotions and so I think it's more kind of realistic I'd say, yeah.

B: But you lose so much of the meaning because you can't put all of those spoken words onto a short subtitle.

E: And sometimes the translations are really poor, so that you miss the whole point of what they're trying to say.

S: Well, that's true, but that can happen with dubbing as well, can't it? If the translation isn't good quality.

B: Well, I just think it's really hard to watch the film and read the subtitles at the same time. And it's particularly hard for children, isn't it?

E: Yes, that's why in my country children's films are usually dubbed.

S: That makes sense. And anyway, for cartoons it wouldn't really matter, would it?

B: No.

E: But you know, we have another way of translating foreign films. Sometimes, especially on TV, we have one person translating all the voices, it's called the lektor.

B: One voice for the characters?

S: Isn't that confusing? How do you know when it changes from a female character to a male character for example?

E: Well, if it's done professionally, it's fine. I don't know, I guess it's what you're used to. But a lot of people like it and, of course, it's pretty cheap to translate films in this way.

S: Can you still hear the original film underneath?

E: Yes, usually you can, but at a lower volume. So it's actually quite good if you do speak some of the language the film is in ... .

Track 1.11

1 Going to the cinema is too expensive these days.

2 Films are becoming too violent.

3 The use of computerised special effects has made films more exciting.

4 Big film stars deserve to earn millions of dollars.

5 Watching films in English is a great way to learn.

Track 1.12

P = Presenter, Ju = Julian, A = Anna, C = Chris, Jo = Joe

P: And in today's programme we hear from our panel of testers. This week they've been trying out some of the hottest new eco-gadgets. What did they think of the products, and are they actually any better for the environment? Julian, what was your gadget?

Ju: Mine was the weird-looking thing with the propeller and the glove. It's actually a device you can wear while riding a bicycle that makes you go fast – much faster in fact! The glove controls the speed, and you can do up to 130 km an hour. I can't say I tried going that fast myself, but it was certainly a lot faster and easier than cycling normally. It's powered by petrol, which is really what I didn't like about it. Basically, it's made a completely eco-friendly means of transport, a bike, use fuel. That said, it does apparently use a lot less petrol than needed by a car, so I guess it could be a better choice.

P: And Anna, what did you take home?

A: I took home the two cardboard boxes. They're actually speakers for plugging into your MP3 player. I wasn't expecting much, to be honest, but I was pleasantly surprised. The sound they produced was actually very clear. They're cheap, but to be honest, I still don't think they look very good.

P: Chris, how did you get on with your gadget?

C: Well, mine looks like a soft toy, and it's a kind of octopus shape. In fact, it's a webcam – you know, a kind of camera for seeing and talking to people over the Internet. It worked really well and it looked a lot nicer than a plastic one … .

P: But is it more eco-friendly?

C: Yes, I think so; most of the material used to make it has been recycled. Of course, it doesn't exactly look professional if you wanted to use it at work.

P: And, finally, Joe, what was your gadget?

Jo: It was a rather clever kind of radio. It's quite small and square and it has a handle which you can wind up to get energy to make the radio work, or you can use the solar panel on the top. It was easy to wind up, and I got about twenty minutes of playtime out of winding it up for one minute. The solar panel was less successful – but perhaps that's because it just isn't sunny enough in this country … .

Track 1.16

R = Rachel, E = Eben

R: Do you believe everything you read in the news normally?

E: No, not really. Um, I read lots of different papers and I find that they all report the same story differently. The interesting trick they play is that each newspaper seems to tell a different part of the story, so they withhold the information.

R: Yeah they seem to decide differently as to what they think is going to be worthy of a story for somebody to read and they do reflect on it completely differently sometimes. It's difficult to know what's important and what's not.

E: Yes, and as I said, it's strange that – it seems that sometimes they will hold back information so that the story sounds worse than it actually is and it almost comes across as if the newspaper wants you to get angry.

R: Or sometimes they'll express something that's supposed to be so exciting, and you're not quite sure whether you really agree with it being that exciting, or that interesting, as it actually is … .

E: Which is – yes, I suppose that raises the other point, writing news is a business, it's an industry. They have to come up with stories every day, all day, and so they have to almost write a little bit like fiction as a, you know, to make it exciting.

R: Well yeah, and they have to – they have to sell newspapers, they have to make money. So sometimes you think that that's the only reason that they may be writing a story.

Track 1.18

It's a horror film, set in Spain. It's about a woman who buys the house where she used to live as a child. Her son starts to see the ghosts of children in the house and then he suddenly disappears. The main characters are the woman and her husband. There is also a rather spooky old woman.

Track 1.19

The house that the woman, Laura, buys, used to be an orphanage and the ghosts are of children who lived there. When Simón, her son disappears, the police think that he may have been taken by the spooky old woman, Benigna, who, it turns out used to work at the orphanage. However, Laura becomes more and more sure that he has been taken by the ghosts. In the end Laura finds Simón, but I won't spoil the ending by telling you how!

Track 1.20

1 The Dos Santos family

I = Interviewer, M = Miriam, C = Carlos

I: So how do you feel about the house swap?

M: Oh, I can't wait. I can hardly believe we're spending more than one month in London. We've never been there before.

I: I'm sure you'll love it.

M: Yes, I'm sure we will.

I: What are you going to do while you're there, Carlos?

C: We're going to see all the sights and the museums … .

M: And I'm going to do lots and lots of shopping.

I: Great. There are some wonderful shops in London. I'll give you the address of a great shoe shop.

M: I'm going to spend lots of money, and buy beautiful clothes and souvenirs for my family … .

C: And we're visiting some friends in Oxford on 3rd June.

M: I think they'll have nice shops there too and of course … .

2 The Armitage family

I = Interviewer, J = Jeremy, S = Sarah

I: So, are you ready for Spain?

J: Yes, I think so. We've always wanted to visit Spain. It has such a rich culture. I want the girls to experience that while they are young, even though they're not very keen. We're going to see the cathedrals …

S: And we love Spanish food, so we're going to try all the local dishes, particularly the seafood. Of course the girls will probably want to go to MacDonalds …

J: Yes, but we won't go to McDonald's. Forget it!

S: Oh, and we're also going to go to the beach.

J: Yes, we're looking forward to that. I really hope this'll be the holiday of a lifetime for us all.

Track 1.21

Miriam Dos Santos

I = Interviewer, M = Miriam

I: Hi Miriam. So how was London?

M: Well London was fantastic, but the house was a disaster.

I: Oh dear. Why was that?

M: First of all, it was in the middle of nowhere. It was a long way from the centre, and very difficult to find. We got completely lost looking for it. In the end we had to ask a taxi driver to take us there, which was very expensive. And when we went inside, my goodness, it

was so old, and dark. I don't think they had changed anything in that house for thirty years. It was like something out of a film. Nothing worked properly. Even the heating didn't work, so there was no hot water, and the shower didn't work either. Anyway, I was really disappointed, and so we're going to complain to the company. We'll ask them about the central heating and why the information on the website was wrong and we'll also ask them … .

Jeremy Armitage

I = Interviewer, J = Jeremy

I: How was Spain?

J: I have to be honest with you. It wasn't good.

I: Oh dear. Why was that?

J: Well, the main problem was the flat. It was too small. The girls had to stay in the single room together, but it was more like a cupboard than a room. It was tiny! And the other rooms weren't much bigger! And it was so hot, and there was no fan, so we had big arguments. Also, the mosquitoes were terrible, so it was very difficult to sleep at night. And downstairs there was a bar, which played loud music until four in the morning. I think the only reason the area was quiet during the day is because everyone was sleeping after being awake all night!

Anyway, the girls refused to do the things I wanted to do. All they wanted to do was try and get a suntan. They don't care about culture, and didn't want to eat the delicious food. They just wanted chips! At the end of the month, I was so pleased to get home. I am never going to do a home swap again!

Track 1.22

R = Representative, M = Miriam

R: Hello, yourhome-myhome. How can I help you?

M: Hello, my name is Miriam dos Santos. I recently did a house swap with one of the properties on your website and I'm afraid I wasn't at all happy with the experience.

R: Oh, I'm sorry to hear that. Can you just give me some details? What was the reference number of the house?

M: 742778.

R: OK, I'm just getting the details … Yes, right, what was the problem exactly?

M: Well, I don't like to complain but there really were a lot of problems. For starters, we couldn't find the place. It was in the middle of nowhere. The information on the website said that it would be easy to get into the city centre, but in fact it took over two hours to get there … .

R: Well, of course, it does depend on the time of day. Rush hour can be a problem.

M: No, I'm sorry, but it was just a long way from the centre. And when we got there the house was in a terrible mess. There were dirty dishes and cups everywhere; the bathroom was disgusting and far too small.

R: Oh dear, yes, there was supposed to be a cleaner coming in before you arrived but she was ill, so it didn't happen. We must apologise about that.

M: Oh, well, that wasn't the only problem, actually. There weren't any clean sheets or towels, so we had to go out and buy some more and the central heating wasn't working, so the house was freezing and there was no hot water.

R: Ah, actually, the heating was working but it was switched off. You needed to switch it on.

Audioscripts

M: Well, in that case, why didn't the man I spoke to at your office explain that at the time? I'm sorry, but it just isn't good enough.

R: No, I do apologise for the inconvenience.

M: Well, actually, I'd like you to give me a full refund of the fee we paid to yourhome-myhome.

R: Well, it isn't company policy to give a refund. Perhaps we could give you a goodwill payment of, say, £100 to pay for the sheets and towels you had to buy? How would that be?

M: Well, I think you should give me a refund, but I suppose that's something.

R: And I do apologise again … .

Track 1.25

I loved living in Japan. I lived there for two years, um, and I had a really great time. I went – I lived in Kyoto, which is a really, really beautiful city, it's got, um, it's got amazing – lots of old architecture, um it's very beautiful and it's a very lively bustling city. There's lots to do there, um it's got really good um restaurants with traditional Japanese food and it's got restaurants with um food from all over the world as well.

And it's got great shops and very good night life and it's – the thing I liked about Japan is, although it's very crowded and bustling and you've got lots of people on the streets and lots of bikes um you can sort of step off the streets and go into the er the older traditional temples, um, and when you go in those areas its – it's really quiet and calm and it's – it's nice, it's very peaceful in those places. Um, the only thing I suppose that was a disadvantage in – in – in Kyoto was the –the heat. In the summer it gets very hot, there's a lot of humidity, um, so actually it's quite a relief to go into some of the more modern shopping areas so you can have the, er, the air-conditioning on, which is – which is really nice because actually in my apartment in Kyoto I didn't have any air-conditioning so it was – it was very uncomfortable in the summer and sleeping at night was a real problem.

So yeah, sometimes at weekends to escape I used to just walk around, um, the shopping areas and go in the shops so I could enjoy the air-conditioning, which was really nice as well. The people were very, very friendly um in Kyoto and that was one thing I liked, even not speaking the language very well and not knowing the area very well you could go out and feel that you were quite in good hands really because the Japanese people would always look after you.

Track 1.26

T = Tracy, S = Stig

T: I don't think there's any doubt that the way we live now we have – we have to change somehow, um, you know. We're gonna end up with – with no water, with no heating, with – with nothing if we don't change the way that we all live, so I think the point that he's making about um homes being smaller um so that we can afford to heat them and to have water for them and, you know, different furniture and things like that is a really great idea.

S: I'm not sure I agree with that. I think rich people will always be able to buy big houses. It'll only be the poor people perhaps who get smaller and smaller houses as we run out of space.

T: You think – you think rich people won't give up their swimming pools for anything?

S: Well, not necessarily their swimming pools, but there'll always be rich footballers who can afford to buy massive houses. I don't think that's gonna change.

T: I think maybe, maybe, having lived in Hong Kong and places that don't have as much space is that you realise suddenly how little space you really do need and that, you know, things like table tops being used as computer screens as well, um, isn't so out of the realms of possibility.

S: No, I think that's – that's true, I mean countries that don't have much space certainly will need to think about how they use that space and might – might need to build smaller and smaller homes but I think the people who have the money for the homes will definitely continue to buy massive houses.

T: Yeah, that's true. I mean I can't imagine that, um, anyone will ever give up their cars. I can't see a future where there's definitely fewer cars or definitely, er, fewer people moving around like that. I can't ever imagine that happening, can you?

S: No, I can't really. I think people will just have to develop new fuels, for example hydrogen's being used to run cars. Er, you've got an increase in the number of electric cars and I think governments will just have to develop, you know, filling stations for electricity instead of petrol.

T: Yeah, these things don't tend to happen unless you're kind of forced into them. You know, if you're given the choice between a flashy car or an electric car, you're never going to choose the – the cheap option. You're always gonna go for the – for the nice one. …

S: Yeah, this idea about fish tanks that – that will provide fish to eat and produce fresh vegetables … I can't see this happening at all. I mean people will keep fish as pets but I can't see them growing quickly enough to keep in your kitchen and then have for dinner.

T: It's hard to imagine a load of tropical fish in your kitchen that you then – your kids pick out and eat.

S: Yeah, I agree.

T: Um but they, I mean they are things that are around already, like um fridges that you can send messages to from your mobile phone to um … .

S: Can you?

T: Yeah, that you can tell them what you want them to – to order from online supermarkets and things like that, you know, it knows when you're running low on things.

S: Cool.

T: Um, I haven't heard of it being able to tell you when it's about to go out of date but sounds like a good idea to me.

S: Yeah I think, you know, the thing about robots being er more common in the future: I think that's probably right. I mean, you know, they already have the little vacuum cleaners that run round your living room cleaning it for you. So I think they'll be developed further.

T: It seems hard to imagine but I don't think any of us anticipated what kind of things we'd already all have in our homes, you know, having a computer in every home was unimaginable at one point. So – so you never know where we're gonna end up.

S: No, you don't.

Track 1.28

Speaker 1:

I live in the suburbs of the city. I'd say my lifestyle was very busy and stressful. I wear a suit every day. I work sixty hours a week and it takes me more than an hour to commute into the centre to get to work. I hate it! So I need a change, and I'd like to move to the country. I hope to become completely self-sufficient, grow my own food and have some chickens. I'm going to take a course in farming at the local college and I'll probably get some bees as well. I love honey! I might even get rid of the television, do some reading in the evenings instead, but I'll probably keep my computer.

Speaker 2:

I'm from a very small town. It's the most boring place you can imagine. It's for people who want a quiet life. There's one school, one post office and only a few shops and that's all. I guess it's quite healthy, no pollution or anything, but it's also very dull. So, I want to experience city life. My dream is to live right in the middle of a big city where there's loads going on. So, what am I going to do there? I'm going to find a job, of course, because I know the city is expensive. In my free time, I'll definitely go clubbing a lot to try and meet people and make friends. I imagine there'll be people from lots of different countries and cultures. I could also do a course, learn another language … .

Track 1.29

Frank Abagnale, a good-looking English boy, pretended to be first a pilot, then a doctor and then a lawyer. For five years he travelled the world for free, stayed in expensive hotels and had relationships with beautiful women. Furthermore, by the age of twenty-one he had tricked and cheated his way to $250 million. In the golden age of James Bond, Abagnale really was an international man of mystery. He was wanted by the FBI and Interpol (International Police) in twenty-six cities. Abagnale's charm was his most important tool. He dressed well and everybody believed everything he said. Leonardo DiCaprio, who plays Frank Abagnale in the film *Catch me if you can* said, 'Frank Abagnale is one of the greatest actors who has walked the Earth.' Abagnale was a lonely child. When his German mother divorced his father, Abagnale had to choose which parent to live with. Instead, he ran away from home and began his life as an international trickster. He got a Pan Am pilot's uniform by saying that his was stolen and that he had an urgent flight. This allowed him to stay in any hotel he wanted: Pan Am always paid the bill. What's more, he even pretended to be a footballer and played for a professional team for a year.

He broke the law constantly but he never went to prison until he was finally caught in the USA. Despite his crimes, Abagnale never had any enemies.

These days Abagnale doesn't need to trick anybody: he is a successful consultant. He advises companies on how to cheat their customers, and he also lectures at the FBI Academy. He wrote his autobiography in the 1970s and sold the film rights for $250,000.

Track 1.30

A: OK, so which of these do you think is the most dishonest thing to do?

B: Right, well, I think it would have to be copying work from the Internet, don't you?

A: Mmm, I guess so. What about copying a CD from a friend? I do that a lot, don't you?

B: Er, yes, I suppose I shouldn't really, should I? What about taking stationery home from work?

A: I think that depends what it is. I don't think the odd pen is a problem, is it?

B: No, but you haven't taken anything bigger, have you?

A: No, of course not! I do know someone who took a whole box of pens though. That's a bit different, isn't it?

B: Definitely. Now, have you ever lied about your age on an Internet dating site?

A: If I had, I wouldn't tell you, would I? I think that's pretty dishonest, actually, but people do it all the time, don't they?

B: Yes, and not just about their age ... .

A: Hmm. What about switching price labels in a shop? I wouldn't do that, would you?

B: No, definitely not. That's just stealing, plain and simple. And I wouldn't buy something, wear it and then return it either.

A: No, neither would I. So, which is worst? I think switching price labels, actually.

B: Yes, and then, maybe ... .

Track 1.32

1 Right, well, I think it would have to be copying work from the Internet, don't you?

2 I guess so. What about copying a CD from a friend? I do that a lot, don't you?

3 I don't think the odd pen is a problem, is it?

4 No, but you haven't taken anything bigger, have you?

5 That's a bit different, isn't it?

6 If I had, I wouldn't tell you, would I?

7 I think that's pretty dishonest, actually, but people do it all the time, don't they?

Track 1.33

Thank you for coming. It's good to see so many young entrepreneurs here. Today I'm going to talk about how to get rich. The American writer Scott Fitzgerald once said, 'Let me tell you about the rich. They are very different from you and me'. He's right. The super-rich have a number of personal qualities that make them different. But they aren't all good qualities. Here are some ideas for you entrepreneurs who want to get rich.

Track 1.34

Here are some ideas for you entrepreneurs who want to get rich. The first thing is, you sometimes have to be a bit mean. You shouldn't be too generous. John Paul Getty, one of the richest men in history, put payphones in the bedrooms of his house so that his friends couldn't make free phone calls. Number two: you should start early. Really rich people know they want to be rich even when they are children. Matthew Freud sold mice to his school friends. He said he would be a millionaire by the time he was twenty-five years old. He was right. Number three: don't be too extravagant. You mustn't waste your money on stupid things. Bill Gates doesn't wear a suit. He doesn't care about looking good because he doesn't have to look good. If you spend all your money on expensive holidays and presents, you will probably never be rich. Number four: be confident. You must believe in yourself. Everyone has great ideas but 99.9 percent of us never do anything about them. Anita Roddick, the boss of Body Shop, said 'It's all about having a good idea and having the confidence to sell it to the public.' Number five: you have to work hard. Work long hours. This is the most important thing. No one ever got rich by sleeping half the day. Rupert Murdoch goes to five o'clock meetings. That's 5.00 in the morning. Bernie Ecclestone, the Formula One billionaire, went to his office at 6.00 in the morning. Every day. Even when he reached the age of seventy. Number six: think big. Be ambitious. You

shouldn't think about the limits of your business. Sell yourself to the world, not only your home town. Of course there are lots of other ... .

Track 1.36

P = Presenter, M = Maria

P: In the old days, before TV remote controls were invented, when the adverts came on TV, you had to actually stand up, go over to the telly and turn down the volume or turn the TV off to avoid seeing them. Nowadays, not only can we switch the sound off instantly, but we also often record programmes and just skip the adverts. Similarly, with the Internet, most people now choose to turn pop-up windows, those annoying little adverts that appear on your webpage, off, so we never even see them.
But advertisers have a new weapon in the fight to get our attention – behavioural advertising. Here with us today to talk about it, is Maria Schulz, author of a new book on advertising in the Internet age. Maria, hi, can I start by asking you, what exactly is behavioural advertising?

M: Hi. Well, behavioural advertising is basically advertising which sends adverts to specific people based on what they are actually interested in.

P: Sorry, I'm not with you. How do they know what people are interested in?

M: By monitoring their web habits, or the websites that they visit. So, if you have recently visited a site to find out about flights to Paris, you may be sent advertisements for hotels in Paris and so on.

P: Are you saying that advertisers will be watching which Internet sites we visit? I have to say that makes me feel pretty uncomfortable. I really don't like the idea that a company has that kind of information about me.

M: Well, they have the information, but they don't actually know who you are – they won't have an address or a name or anything. But you're not alone in feeling uncomfortable about this. In a recent poll, 95 percent of people asked were against the idea.

P: I'm not surprised. It's a terrible idea.

M: But would you rather have adverts which you have no interest in at all?

P: I'd rather not have any adverts, I suppose.

M: Even if that meant you could no longer watch, say, a TV programme you've missed for free? In the same survey, 60 percent of people asked said that they would rather have adverts than pay to watch TV programmes online.

P: I suppose that's a good point ... .

Track 1.37

J = Jonathon, P = Polly

J: What do you think of a hundred and forty million dollars being spent for a single painting?

P: Oh you mean the Jackson Pollock painting? Um, I don't think it's that much of a waste of money there's only, um, one of those paintings so it's a, it's a piece of history and if you get to own that then that's quite cool, wouldn't – wouldn't you like to have that hanging on your wall?

J: I would for the – for the worth of it that's true, and it's attractive to look at, but I just feel for instance a Picasso is, you can see the skill in the paint work but I just feel it's a – it's a dribble that a child could produce.

P: Oh really?

J: Mmm, oh well.

P: Yeah. Well, um, compared to say spending money on sending a man to the moon, it's not as worthwhile as – not as worthwhile as that, I think sending a – a man to the moon and spending two point two billion dollars on it would be a ... .

J: Yes I can see, I can see that that has got some meaning for man and with the problems we have on this planet such as starvation and shortages of water and mounting debt we have to look at alternative ways of housing all the people, so I can see the justification of that compared to spending so much for a single painting. From that point of view it's worth it.

P: Oh OK. Um, well sticking with science, what about the Hadron Collider?

J: Ah yes, well with that one I think there's, it's looking like the world's biggest waste of money don't you agree, because there's, ah ...

P: Mmm, I do agree there yeah.

J: ... there's still, there's still big questions and there's been so much go wrong with it and it's such a, four to six billion is such a vast amount and – is it four to six billion?

P: Ah, four point six billion.

J: Ah, it's such a – a vast amount of money and no – and what would we do if we did find out how the Earth actually came into being?

P: Yeah I think there's too much risk that it's, um, not going to work at all.

J: Mmm. What have you, um – have you ever tasted a – an expensive sandwich made with Wagyu ... Wagyu beef?

P: Um, no I think that's crazy, um, I think that five pounds for a sandwich is too much and eighty-five dollars is, um, just ridiculous the ... .

J: Yeah.

P: ... the relationship between the taste and the cost can't, ah ... .

J: Mmm. Did you realise that every day they fly it from Chile to Heathrow at five thirty in the morning, what an expense to the carbon footprint?

P: Oh yeah that's a waste of money and of, um, and of carbon.

J: And it's also full of fat apparently it's, ur, I can't see how people would want to spend that amount of money and it's just like caviar, it's just a food for the rich and there's so many people going short of food it just seems almost unjustifiable. I don't know how people could pay that amount.

P: Yeah, I think it's crazy.

J: Mmm.

Track 1.39

J = Jon, M = Maddy, S = Sara

J: So what do you think about that one?

M: I'm not sure if I like it or not. It makes me feel really sad. I do like the way the artist has done so much with just a few colours though. It reminds me of an old sepia photograph. Do you think they're homeless?

S: I'm not sure, but I agree it's a bit depressing. I really like this one. The colours are really vivid, aren't they? The way the different women are sitting at different angles. It's really striking. Oh, and I like the way you can see how hot the sun is.

J: This is my favourite one. It's just so unusual...

M: Really? I think it's horrible, really quite disturbing. It looks as if someone has been covered in dead fish! Eurgh. This one is more my kind of thing.

Audioscripts

S: Yes, I like that one, too. It tells a story. Why is she looking out of the window? Is she just bored, or is there something really interesting going on out there? It's really intriguing, isn't it?

Track 1.40

Mike:

I've been taking classes in origami for three months. Basically, you learn how to make beautiful objects using paper. It's an ancient Japanese art and I really love it. It's very creative because you actually make very beautiful things, birds, animals … and you can keep them forever. I've given some away as birthday presents and people love them!

Tom:

Well, my hobby is cooking. I think it's actually quite creative because I've made up lots of my own recipes. It isn't really creative if you just follow a recipe book. People say I'm a good cook. I've been trying to open my own restaurant for ages but I don't have the money yet. But it's something I'll definitely do in the future.

Ruth:

I think you have to be creative to look after children. It's important to really let them develop their own ideas and imagination. I've been playing with my three children this morning and the room is a complete mess because we've been pretending it's a zoo. But letting them be creative is much more important than being tidy!

Track 1.42

I = Interviewer, H = Hannah

I: Hannah, did it surprise you how you spend your free time?

H: Yeah, I didn't expect to see these results at all. Um … I'm a film-maker so I think it's normal to spend a lot of time watching films at the cinema and on DVD, but a lot of other things surprised me.

I: For example?

H: For example, I spend eight percent of my free time shopping. Well, I can't stand shopping. It drives me mad.

I: Really?

H: Yeah, and the housework – I don't mind doing the housework, but it's not very interesting and I'd prefer to do less of that kind of thing. Also, I noticed that I spend fifteen percent of my time watching TV and only ten percent reading, which surprises me because I enjoy reading and I always look forward to starting a new book.

I: You don't like TV so much?

H: Well, most TV is like junk food for the brain and I should watch less. Other things … um … I love cooking, and I try to cook a proper meal at least four nights a week. And I often invite friends over to have dinner so it doesn't surprise me that I spend seven percent of my time cooking and eating.

I: Is there anything you'd really like to change?

H: Um … I never manage to do much exercise. I'd really like to go running every day just for half an hour but I never seem to find the time. So that's one thing I'd like to change.

Track 1.44

I = Interviewer, J = Julia

I: So, can you tell me a bit about some typical Argentinian dishes?

J: Well, the first thing to say is that everyone eats quite a lot of meat. They love grilled meat on the *asado*, or barbecue. The meat is sometimes marinated first – they put it in a sauce overnight to soak up the flavour before it's cooked. A popular marinade is *chimichurri*, which is made with garlic, oil and herbs. Another favourite type of food is *empanadas*. These are a kind of little pie, baked in the oven and stuffed with different fillings – meat, again, cheese and vegetables. These can be served hot or cold.

I: And what about dessert?

J: The most famous sweet has to be *dulce de leche*. It's made by boiling milk and sugar together. It's usually served with cake or biscuits.

Track 1.45

Last summer I went to a wonderful restaurant in Bruges in Belgium – it was for my boyfriend's birthday and we decided to go to Bruges for the weekend. We went to a lovely restaurant in the centre of Bruges which used to be a cathedral so the inside of the building was very, very old. It was summertime so we could sit outside, and the atmosphere was – was very peaceful and relaxing.
It was quite, um, a nice evening so we sat outside and enjoyed the sunshine. The restaurant's quite expensive, but we decided to treat ourselves and I had vegetarian lasagne and my boyfriend had steak. The restaurant serves quite a lot of different types of food but it's famous for, um, fish and meat. Probably the worst thing about the restaurant is the service, the service is quite slow, but it didn't matter, we still had a nice time.

Track 1.46

1 It's a type of sport which you do in the sea. You need a board and big waves. It can be dangerous, but it's really exciting.

2 It's a kind of meal you get in Indian restaurants. It's hot and spicy and usually has meat in it. You eat it with rice.

3 It's the stuff you find under the grass. It's brown. You see it when it rains.

4 It's something you use for cleaning the house. It's a machine that picks up dust and small pieces of dirt.

5 They're usually made of wood. They're a useful thing to have in the house, because you can put your books on them.

Track 1.47

A computer screen is rectangular. An egg is oval. A plate is round. A floppy disk is square. An elephant is heavy. A mouse is light. The Grand Canyon is enormous. Buckingham Palace is huge. An ant is tiny. The main road is wide. The back streets are narrow. Soap is smooth. A beard is rough. Toffee is sticky. Ice cream is soft. A stone is hard.

Track 1.49

I'm going to tell you about capoeira. Capoeira is a kind of martial art, which is also like a dance. It originated in Brazil, where it was started by the African slaves. The story goes that the slaves were forbidden from fighting, so they developed a kind of fighting which, to the slave owners, just looked like a dance. The music is very important as the songs are sung while a game is being played to tell the story of capoeira and the slaves' struggle. The most important instrument is the *berimbau*, a kind of guitar with just one string.
You need to be very fit and strong, particularly your arms, as you often have to use your hands to balance. Every movement needs to be done perfectly, so you should have good control of your body. Everyone sits around in a circle, singing and playing music, and two people fight in the centre. To fight the other person you kick with your feet, but … er … nowadays, there's no contact. As soon as you see the other person's hand or foot coming towards you, you have to move away quickly. You must be careful the other person doesn't kick you. If the other person kicks you, then you lose.
People who play capoeira are called *capoeiristas*. Capoeiristas usually wear white clothes. If the white costume is still clean at the end of the game, that shows how skilful you are because it means you haven't been kicked or knocked to the floor.
Afterwards, you can … er … relax and talk about the fight. And … er … we often spend the evening together, listening to music. I've been doing capoeira for three years. I've improved a lot since I first started, and now I wear a green belt. In the future, I would like to become a trainer, called a Master, and teach other people about this beautiful sport.

Track 2.1

Helen:

This is a photo that I took um in Thailand on the island of Ko Samui. Um, I took it about lunchtime. It was a very, very hot day and it was monsoon season, so sometimes it was very, very hot and clear and then sometimes it would just suddenly rain. But at this time it was – it was very hot.
In the photo there's a big fishing boat, which was just on the beach and then behind the – the boat you can see the sea and some islands. It was a very peaceful day and very quiet and we had a bit of breakfast on the beach and after that we sat on the beach reading books and not doing very much, so it was a very relaxing and a very nice day.

Matthew:

This photo was taken last summer while I was on holiday with my wife. Um we were in Kent and this is a – a photo of a place called Scotney Castle. We'd been walking around in the countryside and we suddenly stumbled upon this place and it was so beautiful.
So in the photograph you can see in the foreground a castle reflected in a lake. Um I took the photo and then for the rest of the day I had to do um other things because it suddenly started pouring with rain.
Um but it was so lovely just to have found such a beautiful place, um just – just by exploring the countryside.

Tracy:

This is a photo of the centre of Hong Kong Island. It's kind of a long er road that that – that travels kind of the whole length of the island and um I'm actually on a tram looking down at um all the people, much like the one in the centre of the photo. Um, in the foreground you can see all the people crossing the road there.
… Um, it's a really, really busy part of the road, a really busy junction, um and then on the left-hand side you can see all the shops and um there's a little market just down the – the side road there. Um, it was taken in November so the weather was really, really nice, um not too hot but um not getting really cold yet, so it was beautiful for taking photos.
… We had a really amazing day, um we spent a lot of time walking around that day and just hopping on and off the tram to try and find nice places to visit and it was a – a really lovely trip.

Track 2.2

Dialogue 1

M = Mark, W = Woman

M: I'd like two tickets from Melbourne to Adelaide, please, leaving tomorrow morning.

W: Standard class or premium?

M: Standard, please.

W: That's a hundred and eighty dollars, please.

M: Thank you. Could you tell me what time the train gets into Adelaide?

W: 17.45. But we are expecting some delays to the service. You need to listen to the announcements.

M: Oh! Thanks.

Dialogue 2

K = Kate, M = Man

K: Excuse me. How do we get to the National Railway Museum?

M: Um … right. The quickest thing to do is to take the Outer Harbor train to Port Adelaide Station.

K: Is it far?

M: No, the station you need is just a short walk from here, and then it takes about ten minutes.

K: OK. Thank you.

M: But the museum is closed at the moment.

K: Oh! Thank you anyway.

Dialogue 3

M = Mark, W = Woman

M: Excuse me. Is there a post office near here?

W: Yes, there's one just down the road. Just go straight on and it's on your left.

M: Thank you.

W: But it's closed now. You need to go before 5 o'clock.

M: Oh no! Thank you.

Dialogue 4

M = Mark, W = Woman

M: Excuse me. Does this bus go to Werribee Park?

W: No, this one's for the airport. You need the shuttlebus. Look, it's just over there.

M: OK, thanks.

W: But you need to buy a ticket in advance.

M: Oh, OK … Thanks for your help.

Dialogue 5

K = Kate, M = Man

K: Two student tickets, please.

M: Have you got a student card?

K: Yes. One moment. Oh. I can't find it. I think I've left it at the hotel.

M: Then I'm afraid you'll have to pay the full price. That'll be forty-two dollars please.

K: Forty-two dollars! OK. Thanks.

Track 2.5

P = Presenter, J = Joanne

P: And with us in the studio today we have Joanne Bright, author of a new book about women travellers in the eighteenth and nineteenth centuries. Joanne, it can't have been easy to travel the world then, especially as a woman. These women must have been terribly brave and adventurous.

J: Well, some of them certainly were, but we mustn't forget that probably most women travellers didn't actually choose to make their journeys in the first place. Their husbands decided to go abroad, or were sent abroad, and the women followed. That was certainly the case with Lady Mary Wortley Montagu, whose husband was sent as ambassador to Istanbul in Turkey, in 1716.

P: Didn't she want to go?

J: Well, we don't know for sure, but she certainly seemed to enjoy herself when she got there! She wrote a series of letters back to her friends and family, which were published after her death. The unusual thing about Lady Mary is how open she was to the new culture. In fact, in many ways, she decided that it was much better than her own. She commented on how polite the Turkish ladies were about her European dress, pointing out that English ladies would probably have laughed at someone dressed as differently as she was. In fact, she started wearing Turkish dress herself. And she noticed the Turkish women protecting their children against the disease of small pox by using inoculation, where a small dose of the disease was given to prevent them catching the disease badly later. Lady Mary had recently caught smallpox herself and her face was very badly damaged as a result, so she very much wanted to protect her children from it. She had her son inoculated in Turkey, the first English person to be protected in this way, and, when she returned home to England, she helped to persuade the English doctors to develop a similar technique.

P: Goodness, she really achieved something through her visit then … .

Track 2.7

K = Kate, H = Heather, E = Ekaterina

K: OK. So we need to plan this day in London. I think because there's gonna be so much to do, it would be good to get it planned before we get there.

H: Yeah, there's a lot of choice, isn't there?

E: Yeah, sure.

H: What do you guys want to do?

K: Well I like the idea of the show in the evening. Um … .

H Oh yeah, it says here that um *Les Mis* is playing, um oh yeah, but tickets are forty pounds. Are you guys OK with paying forty pounds for the show?

K: I'm happy with that.

E: It sounds quite expensive but probably it's worth it.

H: Yeah, I think so.

E: It's one of the most famous ones in London. So … .

H: Cool. OK, let's do that then. What about the daytime?

K: Um I quite like the sound of the London Walks. They're quite cheap and it's not gonna take up all day. Yeah, you guys OK with that, too?

E: Yeah, I think so.

H: Yeah, we'd probably see quite a bit going around … walking.

K: Yeah. Yeah, I think we should.

H: Alright, cool. Oh, oh, oh, can we go to Camden Market, too? I heard it's really good there.

K: Yeah, I heard that, too.

H: There's loads to see and, you know, you can eat good food and …

E: … visit different shops and …

H: Yeah.

E: … buy something.

K: Absolutely.

E: … artistic.

H: Oh but what if it rains? Hang on a minute.

K: Mmm, that's true.

E: We have a couple of museums here so we can probably pick one.

H: Which one were you looking at?

E: Um, how about the British Museum?

H: Oh and it's free.

E: Yeah, wow.

K: I like the sound of that.

H: Yeah, me too. Looks like we've um chosen a few things.

K: Yeah, and I think we can hopefully dodge the rain.

H: Alright, as long as we're there on time for the show then we'll be OK with the day.

K: OK.

H: I look forward to it.

Track 2.8

Natalie:

When I was a child I used to do music exams and for every music exam I had to learn a piece of music. Now I used to play the drums. I started when I was five and I did, er, seven different music exams, seven grades, and for every exam I had to learn a piece of music. … At the beginning it was only ten bars or something but it was really hard and I used to practise them over and over again and I used to drive my parents crazy because um obviously I was playing the drums at home. At the beginning I used to play just on books and so it was quite quiet. But then when I was seven I got my first drum kit and I, um, played constantly and the same pieces over and over again. That was one thing that I had to learn by heart.

Track 2.9

Phil:

About a year and a half ago I took an interest in the language Yiddish, which is the language that my family spoke when they came to this country about a hundred years ago. Um, it's quite a – a beautiful language, or I think so anyway, and it's about a thousand years old. Although I knew a few words of Yiddish from my family and from TV shows, you hear them on American TV shows all the time, um I didn't realise it was related to German and er I was amazed how quickly I started picking it up.

… I did German at school you see. I'm now at about GCSE level, having found myself er, a weekly class, and um, I did a week intensive course last summer and er it's opened up a whole new culture, as well as a language, including sort of poetry and music and the way that my ancestors lived, and so hopefully I'm going to attend the summer course again this year and, er, impress them with how much I've learnt since last year.

Track 2.10

Rachel:

Um, an occasion where I had a really steep learning curve was when I um got the job to go and work in a kids' camp in America and I really didn't know what to expect and when I got there it completely surprised me.

… I was just thrown into everything, my whole day was taken up either looking after children or running a class or taking them to and from somewhere and I had no time to myself, and I think it was the closest thing ever to being a parent, where you were just – your – your time is just completely consumed by lots of other people and I had no time to myself at all really.

Track 2.11

Sean:

For my eighteenth birthday my parents asked me what I wanted as a present and I can't remember why I asked for a parachute jump. And so, about a month later, I took a one-day crash course in parachuting and it took place at a local airfield and there must have been about seven or eight other students there and there was already a great atmosphere. Everyone was really excited to be there. And in the morning we looked at how parachutes work, how to put them on properly and how to do a safety check and also how to steer the parachute back to the airfield. And then after lunch we covered what to do if the parachute didn't open properly and how to use the emergency chute and we spent – spent a lot of time on how to land safely. ... And of course at the end of the day we went up in the aeroplane to do the jump and I remember really trembling and I don't really know why, whether I was scared or just very, very cold. Doing the jump was fantastic, I mean really thrilling. It really made you feel alive. Um but it was all over too soon, although I'm not sure I'd want to do it again.

Track 2.12
Yvette:
Um, the time I was most thrown in at the deep end um was when I took a job in Indonesia, um, about six years ago. Um it was the first time that I'd been to Asia so um firstly there was the culture shock of living in a – a completely different country, with lots of different customs. Um, secondly, I took a job, er, where I was managing four teachers, so I had a lot of responsibility; um, I had to work very hard.
... Um, er on top of managing the teachers I had to teach classes and organise exams as well so I was working quite long hours. It was – it was a great experience, even though it was hard work. Um, I met some fantastic people, I learnt a very small amount of the language, um, but I had a really good time.

Track 2.13
A: Hey, do you remember Mr Halsworth, you know, the History teacher?
B: Oh yeah, I think so. Yes. He was that short man, with those terrible glasses. Oof, he was really boring, wasn't he? ... And we were always so naughty in his classes. We'd throw paper at him and one time some of the boys actually climbed out of the window while his back was turned ... !
A: Poor man. He used to shout so much he'd go bright red in the face ... .
B: What about Miss Matthews – the Music teacher? Do you remember her? Oh, she was lovely. She used to play us Mozart, and teach us songs from Africa. I think she used to live in Zimbabwe. I really liked her lessons: they were so relaxing and enjoyable. And she was inspiring. I wasn't particularly musical, but she got me listening to music.
A: Yes, she was lovely. And so patient. Not like Mrs Sharp, eh? You remember, the Physics teacher? She was frightening! I didn't use to like her lessons at all. She used to make me sit at the front of the class, right under her nose, and ask me all the most difficult questions. And if you failed a test, or forgot to do your homework, she would punish you. Oh, and, what about, do you remember Mr Ford, the Religious Studies teacher?
B: Oh yes. He was great!
A: He was so clever, wasn't he? He used to teach us all about different religions of the world, like Rastafarianism, and he was also interested in astronomy, so we'd learn about the stars, too. He was very knowledgeable. Wasted on us, really ... .
B: Yes, and he never lost his temper, not even when we used to ... .

Track 2.16
P = Presenter, B = Brenda
P: In the late 1960s a university was set up in France, which now has more than 3,000 branches worldwide and 200,000 students in the UK alone. But you can't get a degree at this university; in fact it has never set a single exam. Brenda Johns is here to talk to us today about this university;

the university of the third age, or U3A for short. Brenda, what does 'third age' mean?
B: Well, the first age is childhood, the second age, your working life, and the third age is after retirement. Our members are usually over fifty-five and not working full time.
P: And why no exams?
B: Well, it's a university in the very widest sense, a learning organisation for people who want to learn and share their knowledge. Some of the branches are very academic, with courses in subjects like Philosophy, Mandarin Chinese or Latin; others are more relaxed, with groups learning to paint or do yoga. But none of them have any formal assessment. Every U3A has a study group coordinator who finds out what people want to learn and brings them together. Anyone can suggest starting a course in any subject and if enough other people like the idea, the course goes ahead.
P: Obviously, the idea is pretty popular. What's the attraction, do you think, of studying when you're retired? Surely that's the time to take things easy?
B: A lot of people feel that it keeps their brains active, and, for some people, it's the first time they've had a chance to spend some time on what really interests them. And it's very much a social thing, too. When you retire you suddenly find yourself spending a lot of time at home on your own.
P: I had no idea it was so popular worldwide.
B: Oh yes, there are branches all over the world, all doing things in their own way. Last year members of the Cape Town branch, in South Africa, went on a twenty-one-day study tour of Central Europe and the Prague branch then made a return visit a couple of months later. In Valencia, Spain, they do things slightly differently from here in the UK: there the U3A students go to lectures and seminars alongside the regular university students. Oh, and in Montreal, Canada, the U3Aers spend some of their time doing community work, such as teaching English to speakers of other languages.
P: And can't you study online now?
B: Yes, the Virtual U3A was launched in 2009 for distance learning. It's great if people can't get to local meetings for whatever reason. Some of the courses are free, or there's a small charge if there's a tutor to mark work and so on ... .

Track 2.17
P = Polly, E = Eben
P: And so Eben, at what age do you think um someone is old?
E: That's an interesting question, isn't it, because thirty or fifty years ago I think, when you were in your fifties or sixties you were considered old, and these days, that's when your second life starts and I don't think you're old until you hit seventies or eighties and maybe it also depends on your physical health, how healthy are you.
P: Yeah, and your mind as well.
E: Yes and I think a lot of people are younger these days; they're closer to their kids for example. There isn't much of a generation gap. So do you know any very active old people then?
P: Um, yes, one in particular: er my friend's granddad, um he's about seventy-five and he lives, er, on the coast and when he comes to visit my friend um it's an eighty-mile journey but he still comes

on his bike, even though he's, um, he's seventy-five, and I just think that's amazing that someone who's seventy-five can, er, cycle that really long journey.
E: I suppose that proves the point. Seventy-five is old under any definition but if you're physically fit, you act young.
P: He is so fit, he's always going out on his bike and doing all these really long – really long journeys. Um, so the people in the text, are you inspired by – by any of them?
E: Actually by most of them. It's incredible to think that you could be past fifty and start a new career and succeed at it. I was particularly impressed by Mary Wesley, who started writing, who – when she was in her seventies because I think her husband had died and the text says she was almost destitute so she had to make a living and she'd had a very interesting life by anybody's standards, she starts writing about it.
... She turns out to be a brilliant writer, makes a huge success, writes another ten books before she turns ninety and is now admired and well-known across the country.
P: Oh that is impressive. Yeah, yeah.
E: So what do you reckon you'll be doing when you're old, whatever that means?
P: Well um I would like to be a – a grandma with lots of grandchildren, so I'd like to see myself looking after my large brood of er, er of grandchildren and being a – a cool grandma.
E: So you won't be writing novels or climbing mountains or doing outrageous things. You'll be a grandma.
P: I hope so. Er, well, if I don't have enough grandchildren I'll have to find something else, but the grandchildren would be ideal, yeah.
E: Sounds good.

Track 2.20
I = Interviewer, J = Jake
I: Would you mind telling me a bit about your abilities? Is there something unusual that you can do?
J: Oh, er, I don't know really. Er, Oh, I can knit, actually. That isn't something that boys tend to do, but my granny taught me.
I: That could be useful! And can you give me an example of something that you can do now that you couldn't do ten years ago?
J: Lots of things, I expect. Well, I can drive. When I was a student I didn't use to have a car so it wasn't really worth learning, but I passed my test last year, after I graduated. Oh, and I can cook now.
I: So why did you learn to do that?
J: Well, when I moved away from home I kind of had to learn!
I: Right, now, would you mind telling me about something you could do when you were a child that you can't now.
J: Oh, yes, that's easy. I used to be able to sing really nicely, but then my voice broke and now my singing voice is pretty awful.
I: That's a shame. Right, finally, could you tell me about something difficult you managed to do recently?
J: Yes, I managed to climb the three peaks. That's where you climb the three biggest mountains in Britain all on the same day. It was pretty hard work, I can tell you!
I: I bet it was. I'd love to hear a bit more about that ... .

Track 2.21
S = Stig, C = Carol
S: So tell me about the time you changed your mind.

C: Well, when I first got married I thought I was going to change my last name, because my husband's name was much easier to spell and much easier to pronounce, but then, because we were living in China, it was very complicated to change my passport and all of my details so I decided against it.

But now that we're in the UK I'm thinking that I might actually change it anyhow. How about you, have you ever had an experience like that?

S: Er ah, a few years ago actually, when I was er living in Japan, I – I got a new job and because the apartment I was living in was tied to my old job, I had to move as well, so I changed city, changed job, changed apartment and it was almost like I took over someone else's life because not only did I take this woman's job, I took her apartment, I took her furniture, I was almost kind of expecting to have her friends as well, but that – it didn't work like that.

But anyway, I moved into this new apartment and I didn't really like it actually, it was dark and cold and it was near a main road so when the – the lorries used to go by I'd actually wake up from my whole apartment shaking from the lorries going by so ... Fortunately I only lived there a year and then I moved again, into a much nicer place.

C: That's good.

Track 2.22

Emma:

Well, I live in Madrid, er, I've been here for about nine years and I really love living in – in a big city, um it's really vibrant, it has lots of things going on, um I go out quite a lot with my friends, um well I think the nightlife here is quite famous and we, er, we always have a good time. Um, there are just a few things that maybe I'd like to change.

Um it's quite a noisy city, um lots of traffic, er, cars making noise, horns honking etc, and also there always seems to be a lot of congestion um building work going on, um lots of construction, er, roads being blocked and things like that.

Um and in the summer, as well, it can be really polluted, so there's lots of congestion problems. But generally I'm really happy here and er, I think it's quite um a good city to live in, good experience, and if you like um city life I'd really recommend Madrid.

Kirsten:

Well I love Edinburgh. It's a beautiful city, it's historical, it's interesting, it's one of the most pleasant places I've ever lived. There's not very much I'd change about it. I suppose I'd like to change the weather because it's terribly cold, but there's not much I can do about that.

Other things I'd like to change perhaps, there's a lot of congestion at the moment. Er, the city council decided to build a tram system, which will probably be really good one day er and is certainly environmentally friendly, but it's taking years to build and meanwhile there's a lot of traffic jams and people complain an awful lot about it, which isn't very pleasant.

Um, there are a lot of very beautiful buildings in the centre of Edinburgh, but if you go to the outskirts there are a lot of quite ugly tower blocks, which kind of gives you a feeling of two cities. So it would be nicer perhaps if more money was spent on making the outskirts of the city as beautiful as the centre. But apart from that, I love Edinburgh and I don't think I'd want to live anywhere else.

Track 2.25

W = Woman, M = Man

W: The biggest change? I think it's probably been medical progress. The situation has really improved. Luckily, doctors and surgeons can cure so many diseases now that were just impossible when I was younger.

M: Well, that's certainly true.

W: Life-saving cures and operations have become more and more common. In the future, disease probably won't be such a big problem, because we'll discover cures for most of the really bad diseases.

M: I don't know about that. There are still no cures for some of the most common diseases, like flu. And in developing countries, there isn't enough money to pay for some of the cures, so the situation hasn't changed.

W: Yes, you have a point there, but ... .

M: No, I think that the biggest change has been the change in our awareness of the environment. Unfortunately, although we're more aware, the situation is getting worse and worse.

W: Well, that's your opinion.

M: And the number of cars on the roads is growing quickly, so not surprisingly the amount of pollution just grows and grows. And it's starting to affect the climate. We're seeing more extreme weather and more natural disasters ... .

W: Oh, come on. I think you're over-reacting a bit ... .

Track 2.26

Roger:

I stopped work a year ago, when we discovered Jack, our three-year-old son, had a kidney problem. Before that, I just worked all the time. All I thought about was making money for my family. But when we discovered Jack was seriously ill, it changed our world completely. I decided to give up my job, so that I could spend time with him. Now I pick up the children from school every day, and we walk home through the park. It's been great to be with Jack, and now he has had an operation, which hopefully will mean that his life will go back to normal. As for me? Well, I won't be able to go back to my old job, so maybe I'll change career and start my own business. But for me it was the right decision. If I'd stayed at work, I wouldn't have spent time with Jack when he really needed me.

Tunde:

My family wanted me to work in the family business, like my brothers did, but I was never interested in that. I had always dreamed of going to study in another country, to study Art. So when I finished school, I applied, and I was offered a place at the university in Paris. It was a big decision to come here, leaving my family and friends, and ... er ... coming to this country. Everything is so different here and I don't even speak the language, but it has worked out very well. I met my fiancée, Nancy, here, and we are planning to get married when I finish my degree. So I'm happy I came here. If I hadn't come to France, I wouldn't have met Nancy!

Sarah:

My boyfriend was working nights as a lorry driver. We weren't very happy because we didn't really see each other. Then we went on holiday to Italy, and while we were there, we saw this old olive farm for sale. It needed lots of work doing to it, but it was beautiful, and we just fell in love with the house the moment we saw it. We came back to England, sold our house, left our jobs, and said goodbye to our friends. Two months later, we drove down to Italy to start our new life growing olives to make olive oil. It was very hard for the first year and we nearly changed our minds. We didn't have much money, and we knew nothing about farming olives or how to run our own business. But now things are much better, and we enjoy working together. I am glad we didn't have a change of heart. If we'd gone back to England, we wouldn't have been happy.

Track 2.29

A

Yes, definitely. I work on a cruise ship and when we have stopovers we get to see a bit of the country. Just for a day or two, but it's enough to get a taste of what it's like. I've been all over the world ... to some really interesting places ... South America, the Caribbean and so on. You get to meet some interesting people too. I was talking to a passenger recently who turned out to be a doctor, some sort of famous doctor, who'd treated some really important people. So, yes, my job can be very interesting.

B

I joined the gym about three months ago and it's made a real difference to my life. It was difficult at first ... you know there were times when I just wanted to go home and watch TV ... but it quickly became part of my daily routine. I feel so much better now. I've got so much more energy ... and I've made a lots of new friends too.

C

My wife and I are going to open a restaurant near where we live. It'll be an Italian restaurant as she's from Italy. We're a bit worried about it, of course, but it's something we've always wanted to do and it's now or never. Um ... at the moment, we're doing all the financial calculations, but I'm planning to leave my job next month. It'll be a major change for both of us but we're really looking forward to it.

D

Well, I don't want to stay in my present job for too long, that's for sure. And I certainly don't want to settle down at the moment either. I'm always looking for new experiences ... new places to go ... new people to meet ... so yes, I think it's true to say that I like change!

E

I think it depends really. Some people need a routine. Babies, older people ... perhaps. They like to do everything in the same way, in the same order. I don't know. I think life is probably a bit boring if you always do that, but it depends. My granddad had a very strict routine. He always ate at the same time and went to bed at the same time, and it worked for him, but it's not for everybody, is it?

Track 2.30

I = Interviewer, W = Woman

I: When you **apply for** a job, do you normally **send a CV**? Do you need to include **references**?

W: It's usually better to fill in an application form, that way you can really show how your experience and qualifications really fit this job. And I don't usually give references until they ask me for them, but I know who I can ask to give me a good reference.

I: How do you hear about **job vacancies** in your profession?

W: In the newspapers or specialist magazines.

Audioscripts

I: Are you employed or **self–employed**?
W: Employed, I work for a big manufacturing firm.
I: Do you do **a nine to five job**, then?
W: Pretty much. There isn't much flexibility.
I: Would you like to **work flexitime**?
W: It would be useful, so I could drop the children off at school, for example.
I: How often do you **work overtime**?
W: I sometimes do overtime in the evenings or at weekends.
I: Would you like to be **self-employed or work freelance**?
W: Yes, I'd love to be my own boss or at least be able to choose who I work for and when.
I: How often do you expect to **get a pay rise** in your job? Is it easy to **get promoted**?
W: I usually get a small pay rise every year as prices go up. I've been in the same job for ten years though, so it obviously isn't that easy to get promoted!
I: And what are the **perks** of your job?
W: There are a few perks, like a company car and the occasional nice meal out with clients.

Track 2.31

C = Carol, V = Verity, J = James

C: People who work sitting down get paid more than people who work standing up. What do you think about that?
V: I think it's probably true. If I think about teachers, construction workers, nurses, they all work standing up and they don't tend to get paid, at least in the UK, that much.
J: No, certainly not as much as people who work in finance, people who work in the city, who are sitting or are – people who generally work in, er, the financial sector who work in front of computers I think get paid more, don't they?
V: Possibly. Um, how about the next one, the longer the title, the less important the job?
J: I was sent an article recently which was related to this, which said that as companies are, um, not raising people's wages er very much at the moment, they're trying to boost their employees' morale by giving them um interesting job titles, longer job titles, er which makes them sound more important.
V: Oh gosh. That seems quite cynical to me. Um it's just a way of paying people less, isn't it? There are different ways of making people feel important I suppose. What do you think Carol?
C: Um, I think it's um it's all very relative, I suppose. Um, you've got lots of people with long titles who do have, you know, um an important job. You know, we've got the Work Flow and Research Manager here at our place and that's quite an important job, but then again um you know, 'President' …
V: … is quite short …
C: … is quite short and that's obviously a very important job.
… What about the next one? Most work places have too many rules. Employees aren't children and the office isn't a junior school. What do you think?
J: I think some places have many rules. I don't think people create rules just for the sake of creating rules though. I think larger places in particular, rules are built up, learning from things that have happened in the past, um, and it's the easy way for management to go to create lots of rules I think. Er um …

V: I agree with you, but the trouble is, if one, person abuses the rules, for example, they look at something on the Internet that they shouldn't be looking at and then the management uses this to punish almost the rest of the workforce who are completely innocent, I don't think that's fair.
C: Let's look at the next one. Most managers spend their time making it difficult for workers to work. I think that – that could be true, um, in some cases. Um you know, and again, kind of going back to the last one, with kind of having too many rules for their employees and – and by having too many rules, not actually being able to do the job that they need to do. Dunno.
V: I suppose often the person who does the job knows, you know, knows it best and should perhaps be in more control of what they do than their line manager, in a way. It seems to make more sense.
J: Mmm, I'm not sure that managers spend time making it difficult for people though. I think they've got better things to do than make it difficult for people usually.

Track 2.32

Good afternoon everybody. Today I'd like to tell you about our idea for a new business. We want to open a restaurant that serves food from all over the world. Our main idea is that the chefs cook food from fifty or sixty countries. The most important thing for us is that the food is great. We'll allow the chefs to choose the dishes and the menu will be very big, with something for everybody. We'll employ three chefs and six waiters. We won't make the waiters wear a uniform, and they will have one special perk: we'll let them eat free at our restaurant. To sum up, our restaurant will be small and friendly but with a great international menu. The name of the restaurant is World Food! Thank you for listening. Are there are any questions?

Track 2.33

A1 = Audience 1, A2 = Audience 2,
A3 = Audience 3, S = Speaker

A1: Thank you, that was very interesting. What I'd like to know is will the food be fresh? If so, how can you have such a big menu?
S: Well, I'm not really sure … I suppose we will need to have some pre-prepared food.
A2: I like the idea of letting the chefs choose the menu. How will you choose the chefs?
S: That's a very interesting question … . Er, I'm not really sure.
A3: Could you tell me a bit more about the name of the restaurant? How did you choose it?
S: I'll have to get back to you on that one. It was my wife's idea you see.

Track 2.35

1
An *autocratic* style of leadership? Well, that's when the manager makes their decision on their own, without asking their staff. They just tell the staff to do whatever it is that they have decided. Personally, I find that style of management a bit annoying, but it's OK if it's a question of keeping people safe.

2
A *democratic* style of management is when everyone has an opportunity to contribute ideas or say what they think, and then the manager makes the final decision. I like working this way; I find I'm much more motivated than when I'm being told what do.

Having said that, it can sometimes mean that it takes a long time for decisions to get made.
3
A *laissez faire* style of management … well, laissez faire is French, it means 'leave alone', so this is what happens when the manager leaves the workers alone to make their own decisions. If workers have to make a lot of decisions every day, this style works well because they can't keep ringing the boss to ask what to do. But it obviously won't work if the workers haven't had enough training.

Track 2.36

I = Interviewer, W = Mr Wilkins

I: Can I start off by asking you, er, Mr Wilkins, why do you want this job?
W: Well, I have just graduated from the University of Brighton, with a degree in Business with Marketing, so obviously it's an area I'm very interested in.
I: Do you have any work experience in this area?
W: Well, not yet, but I'm very keen to get some.
I: OK. Well, are you good at communicating with people?
W: Oh yes, I think that's a real strength of mine. When I was at university I ran a tennis club, so I had to be able to manage meetings, send out emails and so on. It was good management experience really.
I: And what is your biggest weakness?
W: Oh, er, well I guess I do work too hard sometimes … .

I = Interviewer, S = Miss Southall

I: Miss Southall, why do you want this job?
S: Well, I think it fits very well with my skills and experience. I've worked in marketing for a couple of years now and I think I'm ready to move on to a more challenging job.
I: What skills do you have that are relevant to this job?
S: Well, I'm very organised and I can work very well on my own.
I: Do you work well with others?
S: Oh yes, but if I'm honest, I do prefer working on my own. I just get more done.
I: And what qualifications do you have?
S: I've got a degree in English and Art. It isn't directly relevant to marketing, I know, but I like to think I'm pretty creative.

Track 2.37

N = Nicky, J = Jonathan

N: Jonathan, tell me about your job.
J: Well my job title is Senior Designer and Buyer at a book publisher's, so what it really means is that I design the layouts for the insides of a book mostly.
N: What abilities would you say you need to have for this job?
J: Well apart from the creative abilities you do need to be organised and be able to control budgets and set schedules and keep to them really well so there is a – what I like about it there is a bit of er, being methodical as well as, um, having to be creative so it's a mixture of the two abilities really.
N: And you have to work as a member of a team as well, don't you?
J: Yes, that's – that's very important because you – you might be working on a project for six months or two years together so you have to support each – each other and cooperate um and just create some harmony within the team. So that's – that's true.

Track 2.38

N = Nicky, P = Polly
N: Polly, tell me about your previous job.

P: Um, I used to be a teacher. Teaching English to um foreign students.

N: Yeah. And what abilities, would you say, a teacher has to have?

P: Um, you have to be, er, able to explain things very clearly and, er, logically and er, if someone doesn't understand the first time, to think of a different way of explaining it and to, er, always be very positive and try and encourage students, even if they're not doing er, even if they're not doing very well.

Um, and you have to be very, er, organised to make sure you're never late for class and that you have your marking done when you said you will and that you've prepared all your lessons and your photocopying in advance. You're not photocopying about ten seconds before the class is about to start, which does sometimes happen.

N: Thank you very much.

P: OK.

Track 2.39

N = Nicky, R = Rachel

N: Tell me about your previous job.

R: Um, I was a professional actress and um, one of my first jobs was playing Peter Pan in a travelling pantomime, just the three of us.

N: Fascinating. Was it hard work?

R: It was incredibly hard work because we were doing three shows a day, six days a week, um, and we were travelling to and from those performances, setting up the performances and actually then performing as well.

N: And what qualifications did you have to have to become an actress in the first place?

R: Um, I didn't actually have any formal qualifications but I had a huge theatrical background, um, I'd done a lot of amateur work growing up and then to actually get the job though I did, um, audition for an agent and then he got me this first job when he took me on, so … .

N: Wonderful. And what skills would you say an actress or an actor has to have?

R: Huge passion and drive for what you're doing. I don't think you could do it without the passion and wanting to perform and act for people. You also need a lot of stamina, um, for the amount of performances that you're doing and you need to keep your training up um and just yeah, just keep very fit.

And you also need to be really flexible. Um, your performances, you know, you could be performing at any kind of venue, um, your shows might need to adapt to your audiences, so yeah, you need to be willing to be flexible all the time.

Track 2.40

Well, when I came to work in the UK, I thought it would be quite easy. After all, we speak the same language, don't we? Well, kind of … but there are a lot of differences in vocabulary. For example a car park is what we call a parking lot. And I got quite confused when I was given directions to my office because I didn't know what a lift was – it's an elevator in the US. Then at lunchtime the confusion continued. In the US we use the word 'chips' for the thin slices of fried potato which come in a packet. So I was very surprised when I asked for chips with my sandwich and they gave me French fries! Apparently I should have asked for 'crisps'. But it isn't just different vocabulary though; it's also the way we talk. Americans are much

more direct, I think. When a Brit says 'We have a bit of a problem,' they don't actually mean it's a small problem at all. And when you ask them how they are, Brits will often say 'fine thanks', when really they're not OK at all! The worst misunderstanding though was when I didn't understand what had happened when they told me a colleague had been given the sack. I thought it was some kind of game, but he'd actually been fired, he'd lost his job!

Track 2.43

N = Nicky, S = Sean

N: So I hear you've been to the Diana Memorial?

S: That's right. It's in, um, Hyde Park in London actually.

N: Oh yeah.

S: And um I think it was opened in 2004, which was what, seven years after Diana died.

N: Oh yes, yes …

S: And um, I didn't realise it was actually a fountain, um, a fountain in an enormous ring shape and um, the water sort of flows from the top of the ring and flows very gently around the ring until it collects in this pool at the bottom. And it's really sort of a really modern untraditional fountain, I guess for a really modern, untraditional princess.

N: Yeah, that's a nice way of putting it. Were there lots of people there on the day that you went?

S: Loads of people, yeah, lots of families with young children sort of having a picnic and I think Diana would have really liked that, you know, she was – really liked children.

N: Um, yeah I agree.

S: Um.

Track 2.44

I have a very vivid memory of being a child and visiting a farm with my cousins. I was probably four at the time. There was a dark doorway up some steps into some sheds and I really wanted to go up there and I went to the doorway and it was very dark. You couldn't see anything.

And there was a very, very strong smell coming from the sheds and I could hear scuffling, hear noises at the end of the sheds. And my cousin told me there were monsters there. It was a very, very strong memory. I was terrified and I remembered it for many years. Later I realised they were probably cows at the end of the shed and they were completely harmless.

But for a long time I thought there were monsters there.

Track 2.45

M = Matt, C = Claire

M: So, what did you think about the column?

C: Well, I think there's a lot of truth in it, actually. I mean, I wish I had listened more to my grandfather's stories, too. I just always felt too busy.

M: Yeah, I agree that we should probably listen more and talk less. I wish I was better at listening really.

C: And I think she's right about spending less time watching television and more actually getting out there and living. I'd like to travel a lot more than I do.

M: Yeah, I'm always talking about going to Australia, but there never seems to be a good time.

C: In fact, the only one I don't agree with. I don't wish I'd eaten more ice cream and

less cottage cheese. I actually wish I'd eaten more healthily. I think it's important to look after yourself.

M: Well, I guess, but I think she means that life's too short not to treat yourself from time to time, and I'd agree with that. I wish I could lose some weight though, if I'm honest. I shouldn't have given up playing football.

C: Yes, exercise is important too, isn't it?

Track 2.46

1

Marie Sklodowska Curie was a brilliant scientist. She had a difficult start in life, however, as her family had lost all their money. Marie had to work as a governess to support her sister through medical school. She fell in love with Kazimierz Zorawski, the son of her employer, but he was not allowed to marry her because she was penniless. She moved to Paris where she studied physics, mathematics and chemistry, supporting herself by teaching in the evenings. In 1895 she married Pierre Curie and together they discovered radium. She won the Nobel prize in 1903 and 1911.

2

Baroness Tanni Grey Thompson was born with a disability and had to use a wheelchair from an early age. Her teachers remember her as a very determined little girl, who wanted to try lots of different sports. She first tried wheelchair-racing aged thirteen, and two years later won a national event. In 1988 she won her first Paralympic medal, but soon afterwards she had to stop racing because she needed surgery on her back. But four years later she entered the Paralympics again and this time she won four gold medals. She went on to win a further seven gold medals over her racing career.

3

In 1940, Edson Arantes do Nascimento, better known as Pelé, was born into a poor family in Minas Gerais, Brazil. He had his first job aged seven, as a shoe-shine boy, cleaning shoes for a few coins. Pelé used to play football in the streets, but he was so poor that he couldn't afford a proper ball and used to play with a grapefruit or an old sock stuffed with newspaper. Against the odds, Pelé went on to become one of the greatest footballers of all time.

4

Albert Einstein is widely considered to be a genius. However, his education did not start off so well. He didn't learn to speak fluently until six or seven and one of his teachers wrote on his school report, 'He will never amount to anything', meaning that he would never be successful. How wrong he was! Einstein is best known for his theories of relativity, but he published more than 300 other scientific works.

Track 2.47

Coco Chanel was born in France in 1883. Her father died when she was a child and her mother sent the children away to grow up with relatives. When she was a young woman Chanel met two rich men who helped her to start her business. She opened her first shop in 1913, where she sold perfume. Soon afterwards she opened a shop in Paris and began designing clothes. Her clothes and perfume business did very well until 1939, when she left France to go and live in Hollywood. In 1953 she returned to France. She dressed many famous film stars and she was still working when she died in 1971.

Audioscripts

She is considered one of the most influential designers of the twentieth century.

Track 2.50

1

So, thank you very much for coming, everybody. I hope you found the talks interesting and useful. If you want any more information, you can find it on our website. The address is in the programme, so do send us an email. Thank you and goodbye.

2

F = Father, D = Daughter

F: OK, you've got everything? Passport, ticket, money?
D: Yeah, I think so. Let me just … .
F: Have you got the address where you're staying?
D: Yes.
F: Your mobile?
D: Yeah, it's right here.
F: So you'll give us a call when you arrive?
D: Yeah, it'll probably be late this evening.
F: OK, have a safe trip.
D: Thanks, Dad.
F: And we'll see you in a couple of weeks.
D: Two weeks. OK, bye.
F: Bye, darling.

3

M = Man, W = Woman

M: Right then, it's time I made a move.
W: Are you off?
M: Yes, sorry, I've got to dash.
W: Oh, OK. Have a nice weekend then.
M: You too.
W: Bye.
M: Bye.

4

M = Man, W = Woman

M: Thanks for everything. I really enjoyed it.
W: You're welcome. It's been great to catch up.
M: Yes, it's been a great evening.
W: Maybe see you next weekend. There's a party at Joe's.
M: Oh OK, yeah, sounds good. Alright then, thanks. See you.
W: Take care.

Track 2.51

A: Right, well I'd better be going.
B: Yes, me too, I've got loads to do.
A: Maybe see you next Wednesday then?
B: Yes, that sounds good. See you then.
A: Have a good weekend.
B: You too.
A: See you.
B: Yeah, bye.

Track 2.52

1 Ouch!
2 Yuck!
3 Shh!
4 Mmm!
5 Phoo!

ActiveBook and ActiveTeach contents

The ActiveBook component features the Students' Book pages in digital format and includes integrated audio and video as well as interactive exercises for students to do in class or at home. The ActiveTeach component will help you get the most out of the course with its range of interactive whiteboard software tools and extra resources.

ActiveBook

Students' Book pages and interactive activities

Audio bank (Class CD material)

Video clips

Interactive video activities

Phonetic chart and dictionary

Video clips to play on DVD player

ActiveTeach

Students' Book pages and interactive activities

Interactive whiteboard tools with save functionality

Audio bank (Class CD material)

Video clips

Interactive video activities

Phonetic chart and dictionary

Extra resources for the teacher:
- class photocopiables
- video photocopiables
- printable audio and video scripts
- editable tests

Video clips to play on DVD player

Pearson Education Limited
Edinburgh Gate
Harlow
Essex CM20 2JE
England
and Associated Companies throughout the world.

www.pearsonelt.com

© Pearson Education Limited 2011

The rights of Will Moreton and Grant Kempton to be identified as
authors of this Work have been asserted in accordance with the
Copyright, Designs and Patents Act 1988.

First published 2011
Fourth impression 2013

ISBN:
**New Total English Intermediate Teacher's Book and Teacher's
Resource Disc Pack**
978-1-4082-6727-1

Set in Meta Plus Book-Roman
Printed in Malaysia (CTP-VVP)